FAR

from

HOME

FAR
from
HOME

AN ALASKAN SENATOR FACES THE EXTREME
CLIMATE OF WASHINGTON, D.C.

LISA MURKOWSKI

WITH CHARLES WOHLFORTH

FORUM
BOOKS

Forum Books

An imprint of the Penguin Random House Christian Publishing
Group, a division of Penguin Random House LLC

1745 Broadway, New York, NY 10019

forumconservativebooks.com

penguinrandomhouse.com

FORUM BOOKS and colophon are trademarks of Penguin Random House LLC.

LIBRARY OF CONGRESS CATALOGING-IN-PUBLICATION DATA
Names: Murkowski, Lisa, 1957– author. | Wohlforth, Charles, 1963– author
Title: Far from home / Senator Lisa Murkowski with Charles Wohlforth.
Description: First edition. | New York: Forum Books, [2025] |
Identifiers: LCCN 2024061110 (print) | LCCN 2024061111 (ebook) |
ISBN 9780593728666 (hardback) | ISBN 9780593728673 (ebook)
Subjects: LCSH: Murkowski, Lisa, 1957– | Women legislators—United
States—Biography. | United States. Congress. Senate—Biography. |
Legislators—United States—Biography. | Women
politicians—Alaska—Biography. | Politicians—Alaska—Biography. |
United States—Politics and government—21st century. | Alaska—Politics
and government—21st century. | Anchorage (Alaska)—Biography. |
LCGFT: Autobiographies
Classification: LCC E901.1.M87 A3 2025 (print) | LCC E901.1.M87 (ebook) |
DDC 328.73/092 [B]—dc23/eng/20250221
LC record available at https://lccn.loc.gov/2024061110
LC ebook record available at https://lccn.loc.gov/2024061111

Printed in the United States of America on acid-free paper

2 4 6 8 9 7 5 3 1

1st Printing

First Edition

Book design by Caroline Cunningham
Title page photo: mgfotos.com/Adobe Stock

The authorized representative in the EU for product safety and compliance is Penguin
Random House Ireland, Morrison Chambers, 32 Nassau Street, Dublin D02 YH68,
Ireland, https://eu-contact.penguin.ie.

For details on special quantity discounts for bulk purchases, contact
specialmarketscms@penguinrandomhouse.com.

Dedicated to my family, with gratitude for their love and support.

And to Alaska. Always.

CONTENTS

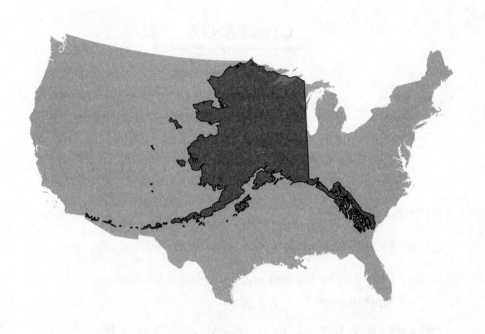

INTRODUCTION

M Y TRAVEL DAY STARTED on Capitol Hill, by car to Reagan National Airport, a flight to Seattle and another to Anchorage, eleven hours in all, and then another Alaska Airlines jet, far beyond the road system to the Yup'ik community of Bethel, on the banks of the Kuskokwim River in Southwest Alaska. Then we took off again, this time aboard a single-prop Cessna, another hour over the river delta, half of it freshwater lakes and half green marshy wetlands, to the gravel airstrip at Newtok, an Alaska Native village of a few hundred. The airstrip was the only linear thing in that landscape of curving waterways. When the engine stopped, I felt the sudden quiet soak into me, with the calm of that vast, life-filled space. I felt like I had come home.

The distance I had traveled was great, more than four thousand miles across four time zones, but it was nothing compared to the cultural distance from my workplace in the Senate to the riverbank in Newtok. Unless they visited, my Senate colleagues couldn't conceive of a place such as this, five hundred miles from the nearest road connection. Here, Washington obsessions evaporated—people were concerned with survival, not political images or partisan strategy. They hunted, fished, and gathered berries to feed their families. I looked forward to the hugs and sincere conversations.

The needs were very basic. The village itself was washing away. The warming climate had thawed permanently frozen ground, called permafrost, turning the land to mush, with buildings sagging on sinking foundations. The Ninglick River was rapidly eating away at the community, foot by foot. At the same time, families in Newtok lived, as they always had, without running water or flush toilets. We met for an hour in the community hall to discuss both of these problems.

I had worked to bring sewer and water systems to other villages, essential for a community's health, but we couldn't install utilities here, where the entire village needed to move before it eroded away. On the wall of the community hall, village leaders displayed a copy of the bill I had passed through Congress years earlier, authorizing a land exchange for a new site, nine miles upriver at a place called Mertarvik (meaning "getting water from the spring" in the Yup'ik language). But relocating the village would cost more than $100 million, far beyond the means of people who lived a subsistence lifestyle, largely outside the cash economy. I had come on this day, now more than ten years later, to check on our progress. We would go see the new barge landing at Mertarvik that had been built as part of a military training exercise.

But first, I had to use the toilet. The community hall had no facilities, so one of the leaders took me to the home of the mayor's mother. We entered a run-down plywood house with two rooms, similar to many rural Alaska homes, with one room for sleeping and the other for everything else. An older woman and her daughter sat at the kitchen table beading. Across from them, in the kitchen area, stood a five-gallon plastic bucket, similar to those sold at Home Depot, with a toilet seat on top. This was the so-called honey bucket. The ladies chatted with me cheerfully as I sat down and as I reached for the toilet paper, which was resting next to me on the stovetop. Families would dump honey buckets such as this one in a sewage lagoon near the school, at the edge of the village. I thought they deserved better: decent housing, safe drinking water, and sanitation—the essentials other Americans have taken for granted for a century. It was my job to help address those needs.

My political philosophy is simple: I work for these people. I work for the women beading at that kitchen table in Newtok and for the many Alaskans with basic, practical needs, to help them survive in our wonderful, often harsh, and largely undeveloped state. I work for deckhands netting our sustainable harvests of fish, for tour guides greeting visitors stepping off cruise ships, for airmen defending us at Alaska's strategic northern bases, and for teachers and road crews, whose salaries depend in large part on oil industry revenue flowing through our state government—and, of course, I work for many others who directly and indirectly depend on federal decisions, as Alaskans do more than any other state. The federal government owns more than half of Alaska, and our resource-based economy rises or falls on federal policy changes.

The United States has a trust responsibility to the Native people of Newtok, and the challenge of saving this millennia-old tribal community can be solved only with funding on a federal scale. The work is hard. We are still helping that one village, and we have dozens more threatened by climate change or lacking water and sewer systems.

My hope is to show readers the complexity of this wild and unique state and the self-reliant people who inspire me. I was born in the small coastal town of Ketchikan, where my parents were both raised, and I grew up in communities across the state. There could be no better place to grow up, playing in the woods and on the beaches. Knowing that, my husband, Verne, and I raised our own children where the Alaska outdoors defined us. Others have recognized this connection in me. Of the many honors I have received over the years, the most precious was being adopted into the Tlingit

Deisheetaan clan and gifted the name Aan Shaawátk'l, meaning "Lady of the Land." I'm an Alaskan at heart. This will always be my home in every sense. It anchors my roots and holds my future.

What a contrast to the Senate and my other life, in Washington, D.C.! Over twenty-three years there, I've watched as the practical needs of Americans increasingly took second place to partisan fights and political point-scoring. Both parties have been at fault, and I have often found myself in between them. I cast a deciding vote against a Republican priority in 2017 to save the Affordable Care Act from repeal, because no alternative plan had been advanced to take care of Alaskans. I passed a landmark bipartisan energy bill in 2020 that made a down payment on addressing climate change, and in 2023 I won a go-ahead for the Willow oil field in Alaska's Arctic—because we need the energy and jobs. I never sought the role that came to me, so often in the middle, standing up to the extremes—including against President Trump, who tried to defeat my reelection—but I didn't shy away from it when that was my job.

I have one overriding purpose in the Senate: to get things done for Alaskans. I believe in public service, good government, and solving problems. I am a Republican because I believe in personal responsibility, limited government, and individual liberty, but my party comes after my country, and Alaska is always first in my heart. I believe in working with everyone, compromising for the benefit of all, and sharing the credit. I think that is what most Americans want. Most are like me: they want their leaders to cooperate for the good of all rather than engage in partisan rancor or culture war. Perhaps that makes me a moderate, but I don't care for labels, and I don't think problem-solving occupies a particular spot on the political spectrum. Most of us treasure democracy, whether we stand at the left, right, or center. We understand that participating in democracy means accepting the legitimacy of those who disagree and respecting the institutions that allow us to make decisions together. Many of us fear we are losing our democracy because those on the extremes have forgotten these virtues.

I want to offer hope. The traditional tools of American democracy do still function. I wrote this book to tell the story of one consensus-building senator—grounded in her home, aware of who she serves, and honoring the process—who produced results and won elections. The chapters ahead explain how this happened. I began as president of my sons' elementary school PTA. That satisfying community leadership encouraged me toward state elected office before I found myself suddenly catapulted to the national stage and challenged by overwhelming responsibilities. My story took a major, positive turn in 2010, after I lost a primary election and voters themselves convinced me that my service was still important, and why. A diverse coalition of Alaskans returned me to the Senate in a write-in campaign, with a mandate to vote my conscience and keep their practical needs foremost, not my party. With their confidence, I became a newly self-directed and more successful senator.

Alaskans' voices still guide me every day. Independent Alaskans became the largest part of my electoral coalition, and they supported me in thinking for myself, even if they sometimes disagreed with the result. I took that to heart, and followed my own judgment on votes, many times contrary to party leadership. For example, as the Senate process of confirming presidential appointments degenerated, with party-line votes for or against nominees based purely on politics, I chose to prioritize qualifications rather than party. In one of my toughest stands, I was the only Republican to oppose the confirmation of Brett Kavanaugh to the U.S. Supreme Court. I got heat for these choices, but I believed I was helping the system work as the founders intended. At times, my independence also yielded political benefits, although that had not been my goal. Senators began working for my vote, knowing they couldn't take it for granted. The White House realized nominees had to be qualified to gain my support.

The system works if we use it. We don't need an overhaul with drastic reforms (although I will touch on election changes in Alaska that empowered the center and could help elsewhere). The more discouraging message is that being a pro-institution problem solver is hard, and not many of us remain in the Senate. We have passed a lot of good laws, because our swing votes controlled the balance of power, but our team of roughly a dozen senators spread across both parties has been shrinking. Intense pressure weighed on bipartisan lawmakers such as Joe Manchin, Kyrsten Sinema, and Mitt Romney. The parties demand conformity, and their loudest voices are also their most extreme and uncompromising. As holdouts for bipartisanship, those of us building consensus brought abuse on ourselves. Now all three of these smart, honorable, productive colleagues have retired from the Senate.

The solution is to keep electing people who want to solve problems. We can do this only one senator—and one voter—at a time. The partisanship and division in our country has come with a loss of community and a weakening in many of the local organizations that connect us. We no longer spend enough time talking to people with different points of view. I'm an example of someone who started out in public service, in our highly diverse neighborhood in Anchorage, learning about families unlike my own while we worked together to improve our children's lives. We build up American democracy from that community level. It is up to each of us to get involved.

And that brings me to one more reason for this book: We need stories so we can see the possibilities. We need to be able to imagine ourselves in our leaders' roles. Washington, D.C., should be visible from Newtok and from every community in our country. This is why I've chosen to be open about my feelings and my failures as well as my successes. I have no exceptional talent. One reason I legislate with partners is that others have great ideas I would never think of. I know how to bring people together and get things done, but I'm no better than anyone else.

My hope is that when you learn my story, my struggles, and my fears, you will realize that you can do this, too. We need you. Only good people can get our government back on track. We need regular people who care about their communities and are willing to do the work, follow the rules, and think for themselves. We have plenty of ideologues and party-oriented political warriors in Congress. We need more Little League coaches and soccer moms. If I can do it, so can you. In fact, it's your responsibility.

FAR *from* HOME

CHAPTER 1

Becoming a Reluctant Senator

ON MY FORTIETH BIRTHDAY, with a brand-new mountain bike in my living room, life was just about perfect. My husband, Verne, who had engineered the gift, was a great partner and dad. Our high-energy young sons, Nic and Matt, kept us going all the time, along with our two black Labradors. This new bike would help take us on more Alaskan adventures. I wanted nothing more. We lived in a modest house in Anchorage's mixed-income neighborhood of Government Hill. Verne owned and operated Alaska Pasta, making ravioli and other fresh pasta for restaurants by himself and with one employee. I practiced law from a home office on my own part-time schedule. We had the income we needed and the time to enjoy our sons' childhoods. Our family was constantly outdoors, fishing for salmon and playing soccer in the summer, hunting ducks in the fall, and skiing all winter. That new bike, which I still ride a quarter century later, excited me as if I were a little girl getting my first set of wheels, with the loving world opening ever wider for me.

At roughly midlife, I had not even the slightest inkling of ever becoming a U.S. senator. I didn't desire any career in politics. Many of my Senate colleagues dreamed of power from a young age, as they relate in their memoirs. Those dreams never occurred to me as a kid, and by the time I was forty, such a dream would have seemed utterly extraneous to this comfortable life. Adding political office to my résumé would add nothing to my happiness, and could take away time with the family. Besides, there was no reason for me to put myself forward as a leader. I am not a special person. Many others could do those jobs.

But I did understand the rewards of public service. I had learned that as the president of the Government Hill Elementary School Parent-Teacher Association, a position that helped launch me as a leader.

Verne had first seen the promise of the Government Hill neighborhood when we were house hunting, before Nic was born. The dated house had been for sale for most of a year. Inside, it was a crazy maze of little rooms. The neighborhood, one of Anchorage's oldest, squeezed between a railroad yard and an Air Force base, was among Alaska's poorest, according to the census, with small middle-class homes and duplexes, and with the largest low-income complex in the city. My parents tried to talk us out of buying the house. So did our real estate agent. But the house was sunny, we could afford it, and Verne believed he could remodel it into something special. And he did.

When the time came, I had doubts about sending our boys to the nearby elementary school, in a cramped, old former military building. Government Hill Elementary received Title I funding under federal regulations supporting schools stressed by poverty. In addition to serving the neighborhood kids, the school offered a dual language immersion program, where the student body was half native Spanish speakers and half English speakers, with morning instruction in English and the afternoon only in Spanish. Many of the children came from the low-income housing complex, often with parents who were recent immigrants, while others came from around the city for the Spanish. I worried that Nic and Matt would fall behind academically in this educational experiment, but I wanted to encourage the language skills the boys had acquired from their Colombian caregivers. Verne needed no persuasion, because he had grown up speaking Spanish in Latin America, where his father, an American businessman, had managed factories making Arrow shirts.

At Government Hill, the boys gave me an education in how people of different races, ethnicities, and backgrounds can learn together and be true friends. I had grown up differently, in Alaska towns where I knew only White or Alaska Native people, and I had perceptions I wasn't aware of. Matt confided that he worried about his Hispanic friend Victor, who had trouble understanding the classwork in the morning, when the teacher spoke English. But then Matt recognized that he had the same trouble in the afternoon, when the lessons were in Spanish. So Matt could be "the smart one" in the morning and Victor could in the afternoon, as they helped each other learn. When Nic came home from first grade excited about his new girlfriend, Angela, I couldn't picture who she was, although I knew all the kids in the class. Nic described her by her clothes, her pink backpack, and her pigtails. Finally, I realized he was talking about an African American girl, a detail he thought too insignificant to mention, and that I had never considered.

Academically, the school worked better than I ever could have hoped. Besides learning all the basics, the boys gained a fluency in Spanish that gave them the confidence of being experts, far beyond what I had learned in high school language classes, with their focus on conjugating verbs. At the dinner table, they babbled away in Spanish with their father, craftily supposing I couldn't understand their boy jokes. I got the gist, but I couldn't respond.

We were all equal at our school, but not in the world, and that mattered because Government Hill Elementary had major needs. I was a lawyer with a well-known name—my father, Frank Murkowski, was a U.S. senator—but my main qualification for the moms who recruited me to follow them as the leader of the PTA was that I showed up. In fact, no one else wanted the responsibility.

Our worn-out school, crammed with 45 percent more students than it was designed to hold, needed a major expansion and remodel. I had no idea how to address that.

We organized a group of about eight parents to meet at a brewpub in downtown Anchorage, and we began to devise a plan to make our case, splitting up the tasks. We contributed as a team, gathering facts, trading contacts, calling elected officials, attending school board meetings. We all worked hard as parents trying to do something for kids, bringing attention to our funky, diverse little community school. It was extra effort for all of us, as working parents, but it felt good because we knew we were doing something positive for everyone. And we succeeded. After a vigorous campaign and lots of phone calls, we won. Our project was included in a bond package, received approval from voters, and the remodel took place. Some of the poorest kids in town got one of the nicest schools. And I benefited greatly, myself, as the effort had a foundational influence on me.

I believe that practical, solution-based politics are the true heart of our democracy. That's why I think this simple story is important to tell. There was nothing exceptional about what we did. We were just fulfilling our duty as citizens to our families and our community. Our group included Democrats and Republicans, working parents and stay-at-home dads. It was not about politics or notoriety. We got together and accomplished something big for our kids that would improve many lives. And it felt great.

This kind of work is as old as America. As early as 1835, Alexis de Tocqueville described how Americans govern themselves with voluntary associations, from those he mentioned, which distributed books or started hospitals, to our Government Hill PTA and our group gathering at the brewpub. These are the volunteers, at many levels, who create a social consensus that gives the government real legitimacy. The system works best, as it did for most of our history, when citizens enter into it with goodwill, prepared to see everyone as a potential ally with a legitimate point of view. The dirty and ugly part of politics cannot be denied, but that is not what makes America work. Our country is built on communities.

As Alaska grew up from statehood, in 1959, it was a prodigy of this kind of participatory democracy. I was one year old at statehood, and my generation of Alaskans could sing our state song, "Alaska's Flag"; we knew that fourteen-year-old Benny Benson had designed the flag and that educator Marie Drake had written the song. Most of us could tell the story of the Alaska Constitutional Convention drafting our model founding document. In its declaration of rights, our Alaska Constitution dedicates us to life, liberty, the pursuit of happiness, the rewards of industry, and to equality and equal protection under the law. It also asserts, "All persons have corresponding obligations to the people and to the State." Those words anchored the statehood generation, which wrote and adopted them, and they taught us well those values, especially the obligations of citizenship. I learned them as deeply as any catechism.

As Tocqueville noted, local associations not only solve local problems, they are also schools of democracy for leaders headed for higher levels of government. We build a certain kind of people in these settings. Ordinary citizens learn to grapple with issues collectively and to develop common cause. Today we call those skills social capital. They include both the ability to work with others collaboratively and the sense of community and belonging that gives us the hope to engage.

Certainly, I had many formative influences before the Government Hill PTA, and many more lessons in leadership were in my future. Those stories will fill this book. My purpose in writing is to show what I learned along the way. I want to revive your hope that it is possible for our democracy to function again as a forum for Americans of goodwill to collectively solve our problems and protect our liberties. And, moreover, that doing so does not require extraordinary efforts by special people. On the contrary, it calls for the everyday dedication of ordinary people with shared values. Maybe there is such a thing as a born leader, but I suspect most people are like me—hardworking and sincere but essentially unexceptional, and unsure that we have anything important to contribute. We do. In fact, we are the critical ingredient to cure American democracy.

I'm just one woman doing her best to represent the people of Alaska while listening to my conscience—one example out of millions—but the only one I know well enough to write about. The solution to our country's ills will come with the involvement of many others, people rising up from PTAs, neighborhood groups, churches, and tribal councils, who follow the path of service that our founders intended, and develop their volunteerism into leadership.

————

In the autumn of 1970, when I was attending Romig Junior High in Anchorage, all hands in our large Catholic family worked in the basement of our house on St. Elias Drive, stuffing thousands of envelopes with my father's campaign materials and sorting them into zip code piles on the Ping-Pong table, chairs, shelves, and any flat surface. He lost that race for Congress—to the relief of us kids, as we didn't want to leave Alaska. He returned to his career in banking and didn't run for the Senate until 1980, so as kids we didn't have to worry much about politics. But my parents always remained civically active. My five siblings and I grew up under the expectation that everyone should give to the community by getting involved. I had a couple of minor political jobs as a young person, but not because I was drawn to politics—they were just jobs. As adults, my sisters and I started a club for Republican professional women that put on an annual food festival at a notorious bar, with all the proceeds donated to charity, not the party or its candidates.

Alaska's sparse population lives in isolated communities divided by continental distances. Politics involves small numbers of people who know each other well. Around the time I turned forty, I volunteered to chair my legislative district party committee—essentially a committee of one. A year later, our longtime State House representative retired, and the job of recruiting a replacement fell to me. During that cycle most of the city's legislative elections would be uncontested, and I soon learned why, as I tried to persuade the few active Republicans I knew in the district that they should run for the seat. It was almost a free ride to our state capital in Juneau, as our Republican-heavy district, mostly contained in the military base, was unlikely to attract a Democratic candidate. Yet no one was interested. It was like finding a new president for the PTA.

Some of the folks I called suggested I should do it myself. I didn't even consider the idea. The same reasons that made it unappealing for others influenced me, too. The Alaska Legislature meets in Juneau from January to May every year, without road access and six hundred miles from Anchorage by air. The annual salary at that time was $24,000. Why would I want to make that sacrifice, being away from my boys for so much of the school year? I didn't even mention the suggestion to Verne, who I assumed would feel the same way. Verne always backs me up, but he gives me space to make my decisions. His quiet, competent presence supports my confidence. One evening when I was helping him make dinner, he asked how the search was going, and I told him the only name coming up was mine. He asked, "Why don't you run?" Feeling indispensable, I told him I couldn't leave the family, but he calmly asserted that he could handle it—as I honestly knew he could.

My sisters expressed more concern about my family. We rarely hear such worries about fathers going into politics, but I understood their feelings, having been brought up at my parents' traditional dinner table. My own family was different. Alone among the four sisters, I kept the name Murkowski after marriage, not as a statement but because it made sense for us, with my established legal career. Verne and the boys all encouraged me to run. Nic was seven and Matt five years old at the time. Nic said, "You probably won't like being a legislator, but you should try it because you should try everything once." It was sound advice we had given him about eating his dinner. My friends from the school urged me on, as well. We were well on the way to winning our remodel-and-expansion project. And Verne insisted, again, that he could take care of home while I was away. A skilled chef, he had always handled the kitchen and the shopping for our family, and his schedule at the pasta shop allowed him to be home with the boys after school. Although he refused to sort the colors when loading the washing machine, he certainly could do every domestic task I could do, and more.

With family and friends' urging, I decided to try it and see what kind of good I could do. Early on the morning of Monday, June 1, 1998, Verne, the boys, and I went to the Alaska Division of Elections office, where I paid a $100 filing fee and signed the papers to be a State House candidate. Despite weak opposition, I knocked on every accessible door in my district, with no app to tell me who was a super voter or which were Republican households, just me introducing myself to the voters.

I won the August primary over a single opponent, with a total of 830 votes, the most I would ever receive on a contested ballot for the legislature, but also a measure of just how small this election contest was. No Democrat had filed, so I was unopposed in the general election. In January, I began commuting to Juneau on Monday mornings, flying back on Thursday nights or Friday mornings to fill the weekends, as much as I could, with being a good mom. To keep me from worrying, Verne worked hard during the week to make sure everything was perfect when I arrived home, with all the laundry washed and folded, unaware that doing so made me feel expendable and forgotten—the family wasn't supposed to get along so easily without me. My guilt about missing school events accumulated. Some of that I never did forgive myself for. I still keep a picture of Matt flipping on the switch for the Christmas-tree-shaped lights on the huge telecom tower near the school on Government Hill, an annual tradition in which the school principal draws the name of one lucky student from the whole student body. I wasn't there for Matt's big moment. The photo reminds me of my sadness over missing so many special days, but when I told Matt why I keep it, he didn't even remember my absence. He and Nic always assured me they were fine—as I have finally come to accept, now that they are happy, successful adults.

The dirty side of politics touched me before I was even sworn in as a member of the State House. I received a call from Bill Allen, the CEO of the oil field services company Veco, and one of the most powerful men in Alaska at the time. I knew his oil patch drawl, as everyone did. I had been to his annual pig roast fundraiser, with a whole pig cooking on a spit in his backyard, as had every Republican candidate who had raised campaign dollars in the state. He even controlled a daily half page in the state's largest newspaper, an opinion section called "Voice of the Times," which was the state's most influential conservative media outlet—despite the paper's revelations of his illegal campaign contributions dating back to the 1980s.

Allen had called to say he "needed" Representative Pete Kott to be elected Speaker of the House, apparently expecting that I would vote as asked because he had contributed money to my campaign. I was stunned and felt filthy. Did people think I would be receptive to such a call? I ended the conversation quickly and swore to myself to never tell anyone it had happened. But when I got to Juneau, talking late with my freshman colleague Andrew Halcro in his office— I had nowhere to go after work but a tiny apartment—he related getting the same gross call, and we shared our mutual disgust. We both voted for Brian Porter, who won the Speaker's chair. Bill Allen didn't abandon his sleazy practices, although he never gave me any more contributions while I was in the legislature, and I had no dealings with him. Over the years to come, his corruption and the fallout from it would devastate Alaska and indirectly change the course of many lives, including my own.

For the most part, however, I enjoyed being a legislator, and I found I was pretty good at it. I've always done my homework, and I had plenty of time alone during the week to read every bill that came to my committees—something that is practically impossible in the U.S. Senate. The Labor and Commerce Committee appealed to me, and in my second term I became chair, because we dealt with hard, substantive issues that affected people's lives, like workers' compensation and retirement issues. I'm a nerd. I like working with colleagues and stakeholders to pass complex bills that solve problems.

But even in those gentler times, partisanship and party discipline sometimes interfered. I never played a team sport growing up, and I was unprepared to think of my party as a team dedicated to beating the other side. This style of partisanship demanded that legislators set aside our own judgment to act in unison and called for us to exercise all the perquisites of power. I learned this on the first day of the session, when I fell in love with a charming old-fashioned couch in my tiny legislative office. Representative Beth Kerttula, a freshman Democrat from Juneau, recognized the couch when she dropped by to introduce herself, as she fondly remembered it sitting in her father's office during the more than thirty years he served in the legislature. Each of us insisted that the other should take the couch. When I shared my dilemma with one of the male leaders in my caucus, he dismissed my concern. "You want the couch?" he said. "It is your couch. You're in the majority. She's in the minority. When she's in the majority, she can have the couch."

That answer didn't sit well with me. The next morning, I made a proposal to Beth: I would take the couch this session, and she could have it next session, and we would trade it back and forth each year after that. It was my first legislative compromise.

I discussed my loose party loyalty in another late-night conversation in the capitol (they were many). I sat on a bench outside my office with Ethan Berkowitz, who at that time was the outspoken House minority leader for the Democrats. I had supported a Democratic amendment that day—I no longer recall the issue—and Berkowitz asked how I'd been brave enough to break with my caucus. I assured him that this was not a matter of courage. Courage isn't needed to do what you believe, unless doing so risks consequences you cannot accept. And that wasn't the case. I said, "Look, what's the worst that can happen? If I am not reelected, it's not the end of the world. I've got a husband and two sons at home who love me. And I can go back to a job that was very satisfying. I don't need to be a legislator to be happy."

I had political freedom. The reasons why I decided to serve gave me different motivations from some of my colleagues. I don't understand the drive that places the prestige of public office above so many of the other good things in life. My drive came from a feeling of responsibility and membership, as an Alaskan, in the cause of making our state better, something I really believed in and cared about. I never felt a strong desire to take credit for accomplishments or to defeat opponents—later, in the Senate, that would drive my staff crazy—and I don't believe that's something special about me. I think it comes from the community tradition that brought me to politics.

Arliss Sturgulewski embodied that tradition. She was a trailblazer for women leaders in Alaska, coming up from the League of Women Voters in the 1950s, with its nonpartisan mission of good government. She earned her living (and raised her son, Roe, my brother-in-law) after her husband died in a small plane crash, and went on to a long career in politics. She had retired by the time I joined the legislature, but she still held a place of immense esteem among Alaskans. With her bright, slightly conspiratorial smile and warm, deep voice, she periodically held court in the back room at Jens Hansen's restaurant in Anchorage's Midtown. Every couple of months about two dozen women would gather for dinner, all highly accomplished, and we would share, in unstructured conversation, what we were working on and where we thought the state was going, with the problem-solving attitude that Arliss had taught so many of us. Jens, I later learned, called this group "The Smart Women in the Back Room." Being younger, I was thrilled to be included. I felt empowered by those women, able to talk freely, to feel supported as well as challenged, and to leave with a new sense of energy and fresh ideas.

In my first two years in Juneau, my political personality had developed and become clear to me and to others. There weren't many tough votes—yet—but there was plenty of work to do. I realized I could make practical things happen, such as establishing a college savings plan for the state, and I found the process rewarding. I wasn't ideological, and I certainly wasn't an obedient Republican, but people knew who I was and where I stood. Firmly in the middle. I even got teased for that. One Christmas, my sister Carol gave me a T-shirt that said on the front, "Knee-Jerk Moderate."

———

Although my mother, Nancy, never held office, she may have been a bigger influence on my development as a leader than my political father. In 1966, when Dad was only thirty-three, he became Alaska commissioner of economic development, and he ran for Congress just four years later. He had a successful banking career in various Alaska towns, with leadership positions on the side in the local chambers of commerce or Elks Clubs. Mom raised the six children, baked cupcakes for school, hosted Dad's business dinners, and played piano at Mass, without ever seeming frazzled or tired. Dad led with decisiveness and a strong voice and always stuck to his guns (even sometimes when backing down would have been the smarter move). Mom made his success possible. She is one of the smartest people I know, but she doesn't worry about showing off her talents or pushing her ideas. Instead, she manages feelings and personalities, gets everyone cooperating, and births solutions like a midwife.

I do have a notable streak of my dad's personality, which may be one reason we sometimes butt heads over politics. When I get my teeth into something, I don't let go (again, sometimes when letting go would be the smarter move). One of my favorite stories along these lines involves my determination to get a horse soon after our family moved to Fairbanks, when I was about fourteen years old. Our family had lived in various places up to that point, but mostly in Southeast Alaska, with its steep mountains, mossy rainforests, and ocean waterways instead of highways—and no horses. Somehow, horses were my thing, with horse figurines of every kind filling my side of the bedroom I shared with my older sister, Carol (to her annoyance). I read every horse book and used every birthday wish, when blowing out my candles, to ask the universe for a horse of my own. Perhaps my wish was answered. In Fairbanks, we moved into a rambling house on the Chena River that had once been a log cabin on a dairy farm, with a barn, a pasture, and several retired railroad boxcars for storing hay. Now I had to get my horse.

Our sensible parents wouldn't consider it, so I went to work on my siblings, lobbying them to raise $125 to buy a horse I had found in the classified ads. They didn't want a horse, but I persuaded them to pool our birthday money and babysitting earnings, and we painted a long fence in the pasture to earn more. We dumped our combined wealth on the dining room table, just short of what we needed, and promised our parents we would haul hay in fall and shovel the manure in spring (in frigid Fairbanks, where winter temperatures commonly fall to forty degrees below zero, manure freezes like rock). Lady, a huge (almost eighteen hands) white former packhorse, came home ridden by her former owner, because none of us knew how to ride. The veterinarian recognized her immediately. He said she was the oldest horse in the Tanana Valley. Indeed, Lady was not beautiful or fast, and her teeth were worn, but she was my best friend. Lady came before any boyfriend. I loved her, and during my four years of high school, I cared for her every day. I learned responsibility from Lady.

Family surrounded and defined us. On Saturdays we all worked together, weeding the garden, cleaning out the boxcar, or doing projects Dad would make up to occupy us, like picking up seedpods that had fallen from the cottonwood trees. Sunday mornings were for Mass, and we usually stayed together that afternoon, too, with a family activity such as boating down the river for a summer picnic on a sandbar, or cross-country skiing through the hoarfrost-decorated birch trees in winter. Family dinners were mandatory. Every evening when Dad got home, we'd all sit around the table—in the summer, outside under the warm, dry midnight sun—and he would lead a discussion, seeking our opinions on the issues of the day, often going around the table in age order to make sure each of us spoke. He would quiz each of us about what we would do when we grew up, suggesting to the boys that they would be bankers, like him, and to the girls that we could be teachers or nurses, like his mother or aunt (for both genders, it went without saying that we would go to college). That didn't bother me at the time. This was the world we lived in, with its gender roles. I decided I would be a teacher.

At school, being a teacher seemed like a reasonable goal. I never worried my parents and I got respectable grades, but I was never an outstanding student. In another setting, I might have been lost in the crowd, but we attended the tiny Monroe Catholic High School, with only twenty-seven students in my graduating class, and every-one had to take turns as a leader because there were simply too few of us to go around. I was involved in student government, I was a cheerleader, and I was head of the yearbook—not because I was particularly talented but because I was needed and willing to try. I was an untalented actor and had no interest in drama, yet I was cast in a play about the Holocaust, set in a concentration camp, a pro-duction that I think must have been one of the worst ever presented on a stage. As much as the audience suffered, however, these high school experiences taught me that I could put myself forward, be a contributor, and that my leadership had value. Important lessons for any citizen in a democracy.

Two more incidents stand out in my mind as I think about the development of my political personality. Both reflect the obstinacy I inherited from my father and the family motto, "If there's a harder way, we'll find it."

As a sophomore at Willamette University, the small liberal arts school in Salem, Oregon, that my mother had also attended, I reached the midterm in my required economics class without showing any interest in or aptitude for the subject. College so far had been for having fun and making friends, attending to classwork as necessary, and rarely thinking about why I was there or what I was trying to accomplish, with the vague notion of "teacher" hanging somewhere out in my future. At a midterm meeting, my economics professor, Russ Beaton, said I should drop the class and take it again later, because I was on track to fail. From his perspective, it was reasonable advice, but I was indignant that he had doubted my ability. I threw myself into economics with everything I had. More important, I began to think about why I was at Willamette. Why had I taken such a safe path, following my mother and majoring in education? What was I missing by avoiding any risks?

I passed economics (although with only a C), and I signed up to study for a semester at the International College of Commerce in Kawagoe, Japan. I was determined to push myself beyond my comfort zone. I had studied high school French for four years but didn't speak a word of Japanese. That great adventure showed me the benefits of taking a chance on myself. I transferred to Georgetown University and changed my major to economics. I like to say I did it to spite Professor Beaton, but I think I had come to realize that if I wanted to do something substantial, I needed to push myself and not just settle for what was acceptable. Reach for the gold ring, as my dad would say.

The other story I tell on myself about my personality involves my repeated, humiliating failure to pass the Alaska bar exam, and how I dealt with it. Before going to law school at Willamette, I had been afraid I wouldn't measure up—I was accepted from the waiting list the last day before classes started—but it turned out everyone felt intimidated, and with hard work I seemed to grasp as well as anyone a new way of using my mind. No longer would it be enough to spit out memorized knowledge; law students learned to think and approach problems analytically. I enjoyed it. The law challenged me, and I loved learning about it for the sake of learning. After three years of classwork, summer work, and student loans, I graduated and took the Alaska bar exam. I passed the written portion without difficulty, but the multiple-choice section got me. The law firm that had hired me kindly kept me on board to try again in six months. But when I failed again, I knew I had to resign. I got a job as a clerk of the state district court in Anchorage and took the test again in six months. Again, I failed.

After each exam, the list of new lawyers would be posted publicly on the door of the courthouse, and each time my name was absent the humiliation and shame cut deeper, with the sense that I had wasted three years, the time and money, and the educational effort, and that I had let down my family and my employer. Maybe I really didn't have what it took to be a lawyer. My friend Jamilia George, who worked with me at the court in Anchorage, gave up after her third try (not unusual, since Alaska had one of the toughest exams in the nation). I stubbornly tried again, but failed on the fourth attempt. I got that news just before a post-Christmas family vacation in Puerto Rico. Although I had recently gotten engaged to Verne, the news about the exam hung over our gathering as if someone had died. My parents and siblings gave me space, never mentioning what was in the air. But near the end of the trip, as I sat next to the pool, my father sat down beside me.

Without looking at him, I said, "I'm done."

We both knew what I was referring to.

In his matter-of-fact way, he didn't try to console me, or even accept my decision.

He simply said, "You know we don't quit. We start something, we don't quit."

I fumed. I felt he was being unreasonable and insensitive. Soon, however, his comment got under my skin, and I knew I couldn't give up. But I also had to try something different. I convinced Jamilia to join me, and we superstitiously changed everything we had done in preparing for and taking the test: where we studied, how we studied, the city where we took the exam. We even published a novena to Saint Jude, patron saint of the impossible. Most important, I needed a new approach to answering the multiple-choice section of the exam. We flew to Portland, Oregon, for a bar exam preparation course specifically focused on strategy for these questions. To do well, a test taker had to quickly pick the least wrong choice, but in my studies I wanted to work until I got exactly the right answer. The new strategy worked. I learned to settle on the closest answer and move on. Jamilia and I both passed, on her fourth try and on my fifth, after two and a half years of taking the exam.

The experience taught me determination. I have proudly told the story many times, with the moral that failure is less important than how you handle it. After I passed, I contacted the bar review program in Portland and asked them to bring their three-day class to Anchorage, to help others. They declined but allowed me to offer it myself, using videotapes from the course and proctoring the tests, and I did so through five more test cycles, meeting students on weekend mornings in a dim, cold conference room at the Holiday Inn in downtown Anchorage, the least expensive space I could find. I also offered one-on-one tutoring, but with a prerequisite. I worked only with students who had already failed the Alaska bar at least once. Because only those students could understand the anxiety of facing that test after the shame of a failure. Most knew the law but were confronting their first taste of defeat. They needed to learn the mental game.

In comparison, making unpopular political decisions has been relatively easy. I began dealing with them in my second term in the legislature, in 2001, when some of us realized we needed to address a severe budget deficit without causing deep harm to public education or other spending that supported Alaskans and the economy. Alaska's main source of revenue for public services had crashed in 1998, when the price of oil dropped below $10 a barrel, and we had already cut the budget deeply. We needed new revenues to maintain our economic competitiveness and quality of life. But the public had paid no broad-based taxes in almost twenty years, when oil revenue surpluses first arrived, and most Republicans in the legislature considered taxation ideologically off-limits and as politically dangerous as the proverbial third rail. They preferred to continue cutting the budget, as they had done through the 1990s, covering expenditures by taking from the state's dwindling savings, with deficits in eight out of ten years. That no longer made sense.

Quiet conversations about addressing the problem began in my office, at night. When we got serious, we moved the meetings away from the capitol for greater secrecy, to a legislator's home. That's how risky it was to talk about solutions such as taxes, especially on the Republican side. We approached our leadership, but they would not consider working on a fiscal plan. Eventually, we gathered a core group of newer, moderate House Republicans—avoiding the old guard Republican committee chairs—and teamed up with some minority Democrats. Toward the end of the 2001 session, we announced the formation of the bipartisan Fiscal Policy Caucus. In the fall we would gather and write a fiscal plan to eliminate the structural deficit, including in it a small income tax and various other taxes, use of earnings from the Alaska Permanent Fund, and an alcohol tax increase. We would hit every interest group, hoping fairness would win us supporters. I was learning how to legislate with a bipartisan "gang," as I would do in the Senate two decades later.

At first, I didn't realize just how much political peril we were facing. The media called our plan historic. An editor dubbed me the "Moxie Moderate." The Democratic governor, Tony Knowles, shocked me with a shout-out in his State of the State address, noting that, within the plan, I had taken the lead on the alcohol tax. Speaker Porter, a former Anchorage police chief, had been convinced by social advocates that a slightly higher tax could provide money to address the damage of alcohol abuse, which is one of Alaska's worst problems. Porter asked me to lead on it.

Porter had recruited me in the way penguins seem to push one of their own into the ocean to check for leopard seals before the others jump. The alcohol industry had been among the most powerful lobbies in the capitol since before Alaska became a state. It employed the top lobbyists and helped fund most members' campaigns, especially Republicans. But the time was right, I was relentless in my advocacy, and I seemed to be winning. On one Friday in March, I was in a committee meeting when I got a tip that a member of the House Finance Committee had advanced an amendment to cripple my bill—an amendment written by the lobbyist for Anheuser-Busch. I walked out of my meeting and burst into House Finance, interrupting their meeting by declaring (rhetorically), "I'm going to kill somebody!" Everyone could hear my conversation with the House member who had put in the killer amendment. His colleague leaned over and said, "Careful. You don't want Lisa mad at you." The member went into the audience to talk to the lobbyist for permission to drop the amendment. The next day, the incident was on the front page of the Anchorage paper.

The backlash against the fiscal plan came as we were gaining momentum at the end of the 2002 session. An Anchorage financier, Bob Gillam, began running a series of nearly full-page ads attacking six of the legislators supporting taxes—five Democrats and me, the lone Republican. We struggled through the final days, rolling over powerful committee chairs to get our proposals to the floor, and passed the plan with a coalition of our moderate Republicans and almost all the Democrats. The plan died in the Senate, but my alcohol tax became law.

I had infuriated the alcohol industry, the well-heeled fiscal conservatives in my party, and some of my Republican legislative colleagues. On the second-to-last day of the session, just after the victory on the alcohol tax, conservative party leaders suddenly pushed a bill to the floor that would severely limit Medicaid funding for abortions by redefining what was medically necessary. The Alaska Supreme Court had already decided the issue the previous year, and I felt this was a messaging bill, certain to be vetoed, intended to smoke out those who supported abortion rights. It was directed partly at me. Legislative reapportionment had very intentionally redrawn my district to put me up against Eldon Mulder, the co-chair of the House Finance Committee, a powerful member of the Republican inner circle who aligned against our fiscal solutions. Mulder would surely vote for the abortion restriction. My friends and allies urged me to do the same. Why fall into this trap? Since the bill would be vetoed anyway, I was told, going along would be a free vote. The more I heard that argument, the angrier I got. An issue so important to so many women should not be a political football. I was adamant that I would not vote for a bill I didn't believe in. There was no such thing as a free vote.

When the time came, I not only voted against the bill, I also gave the most impassioned speech of my legislative career, gaining wide media coverage.

"I may have a very short-lived political future here," I said. "But you know, I've got great kids, and a great husband, and I'm going to have a good heart, and I'm going to stand up for the Constitution, and I'm going to stand up for the women of the state of Alaska, and I'm going to vote no."

Recorded phone messages of praise and condemnation flooded my answering machines. The message from my father, a consistent abortion opponent, was neither. He simply advised, "You know, on some issues it's best that you just vote and not say anything at all."

That was my last significant State House speech. But not for the reason I expected.

————

We began to see the political price of trying to solve Alaska's fiscal crisis with the filing deadline for reelection. That election of 2002 would be the first held under a new law passed by the legislature, which required each party to have its own primary ballot, with voters barred from crossing over to vote for candidates from other parties. Although the Republican Party was the largest in Alaska, it still had only 25 percent of voters as registered members—half the number registered without party affiliation. The new voting system had been designed by Republican insiders to get rid of moderates by narrowing the electorate to a smaller group of true believers. Those who dared support taxes or abortion rights were high on their list of targets.

The Fiscal Policy Caucus ceased to exist. Several of its Republican leaders decided not to run for reelection or faced tough primary opponents from the right. I expected to be in that category, with Eldon Mulder against me, and I seriously considered dropping out. But a lot of people liked what I had been doing, and I had accumulated a substantial campaign account. I didn't see why I couldn't run just as hard as he could, despite his greater power and seniority in the legislature. I knew Eldon well, as my sister Mary had introduced him to Alaska. We took a walk on a beach in Juneau. I told him I had decided to run and I hoped the race wouldn't affect our friendship. To my surprise, after thinking about it for a few days, he decided not to run, and later became a successful lobbyist. It looked like my reelection would be easy, with no Democrat declared and only one Republican opponent in the primary, an unknown political newcomer named Nancy Dahlstrom.

My low-key race gave me the opportunity to help friends with their campaigns and to try to stop Bill Allen from selecting the next Speaker of the House. Allen's influence in Juneau had become outrageous and grossly blatant, as in the past session he had quickly drummed up and influenced major legislation, including a bill, which failed, to build a private prison in which his company would be a partner. Now Allen was raising money for individual legislators on the condition that they would organize the House under the speakership of Pete Kott, who had carried his private-prison bill. I entered the race for Speaker to offer an alternative. But I also had critics. My father had decided to run for governor after his years in the U.S. Senate, creating the possibility that I would be Speaker while he was governor, an arrangement that Kott's supporters said would give our family too much power. In the media, I batted the point aside, but I privately knew that it was not unreasonable.

With Eldon's retirement, Bill Allen and the other special interest groups lost their candidate. My opponent, Dahlstrom, received enough money from Bob Gillam, the alcohol industry, and Alaska Right to Life to send out postcards and air radio ads, but I raised nine times more. I wasn't worried. I knocked on doors and sent my own mailers, but I ignored Dahlstrom and her frequent appearances on conservative talk radio, where the hosts bashed me for my stands on taxes and abortion and for losing support from the National Rifle Association, and called me a Republican in name only, or RINO. I chose not to engage on talk radio because these rants sounded to me like empty, bombastic rhetoric. Nor did I take seriously the rumblings I picked up from others' polling that Dahlstrom was becoming a threat—I didn't think it was important to poll, as a favored incumbent in such a small district. I didn't even spend all my campaign funds, figuring I could roll the money over to future reelection campaigns when I might need it more.

On primary election night, in August, family and friends came to our home in Government Hill for beer and watching the returns come in, a fun and casual gathering, as we had done before. But this one was different. As the first round of votes was reported, the room fell silent. Dahlstrom was winning. I felt simply incredulous and assumed we were seeing only results from some anomalous precincts. Still, with each additional increment of votes counted, her lead held. I remained behind in the count late into the evening, after the guests had quietly departed. I was stunned that I had been so wrong in my assumptions. With a tiny turnout of voters in the closed primary, special interest money and talk radio had been enough to power a complete unknown whose message was simply criticism of me. A total of only 915 votes were cast in our race, between both candidates. When the final precinct came in, from the Air Force base, I pulled ahead, but by only 23 votes (57 when the absentee ballots were counted, days later). I knew who to credit for my win. I told the newspaper, "My airmen, I love them."

This story is important because it was a lesson to me and many others. Our group in the legislature had stepped forward to solve a real problem for our state, working across party lines and against our leadership, daring to vote for new revenues that experts agreed were necessary for the health of the economy and for the future. People like Bill Allen, Bob Gillam, and members of the alcohol industry didn't want to pay those taxes, and they succeeded in removing many of our voices from the legislature, including nearly beating me. Their lesson was one of fear. Legislators afraid of voting for a fiscal solution would freeze the status quo for more than twenty years, beyond the time when the negative consequences of starving education and other state services had become obvious. Political courage is much easier before you have seen the consequences.

I felt some of that fear, too. Although I had said I was comfortable with being sent home by voters, and I'd meant it, I hadn't anticipated how awful that would feel. I found out on that primary election night in August 2002, when I thought I had lost. How had I missed the mood of a district I thought I knew so well? The money remaining in my campaign account was an embarrassing reminder of my overconfidence. As candidates, we carry responsibility for all those who support us and believe in what we stand for. For those hours, I believed I had let everyone down. I felt the uncertainty of losing my political footing. In all honesty, that unpleasant sense of doubt stuck with me, and may have made me more cautious in the years to come.

On top of the fear instilled in legislators by that election, there was the knowledge that, for all our efforts, Bill Allen and his allies had won. The fiscal plan was dead, not to be resurrected. That fall, Pete Kott became Speaker of the House. I would be chosen as majority leader.

My father, Frank, cruised through the primary and toward the general election for governor. Although I had worked hard on his previous campaigns, I didn't get seriously involved in this one, focusing instead on my role as a legislative leader helping my colleagues get reelected (I had no opponent in the general). In November, he easily defeated Democratic lieutenant governor Fran Ulmer. In doing so, he took on responsibility for the state fiscal problem, and it would dominate his term, as he also fought the politically precarious cause of crafting a long-term fiscal plan.

After the election, the political world obsessed on a single question: Who would Frank Murkowski choose to be Alaska's next U.S. senator? A generational shift was coming, after twenty-two years when the Alaska congressional delegation had consisted of the same three men: Senator Ted Stevens, Representative Don Young, and my father. Under rules passed by the legislature, he was able to hold the Senate seat until he was sworn in as governor, in December, and name his own replacement to fill out the final two years of the Senate term.

I didn't pay much attention to gossip about the appointment. I was busy, fully immersed in my family and organizing the House. But in political circles, my father's choice became a parlor game, with names floating up and down, while his closest advisers added ideas and self-nominations to a long list for consideration. Everyone knew the basic criteria: the appointee would have to be a Republican of proven ability who was relatively young and willing to stay in the Senate for a long career, building the seniority that would give our young state clout. Politicians campaigned to gather supporters who would influence my father. Among the most vigorous campaigners was our friend Mead Treadwell, and I did support him.

Ten days after the general election, to manage the speculation, my father released a list of twenty-six candidates. Some were serious, but many were obviously on the list for other reasons—such as the elderly retired Catholic archbishop of Anchorage, Francis Hurley. My name was on the list, as was that of Senator Ted Stevens's son Ben Stevens, who was becoming majority leader in the Alaska

State Senate. I considered myself to be in the same category as Archbishop Hurley, as one of the unrealistic choices added to the list just for show. A week later, my father interviewed fewer than half of those listed; that group of the most realistic candidates included Mead Treadwell, former Wasilla mayor Sarah Palin, a former Anchorage mayor, and several former legislators—and did not include me.

But one evening that November he brought up the topic. My parents were at our house in Government Hill for dinner, and my dad and I were standing together in the kitchen. He mentioned that the list contained a lot of names, including mine, and asked what I thought of that. I didn't take the question very seriously. He then asked who I would pick, and I said, "Mead."

He misheard me—he thought I had said, "Me." His response was "Well, yeah, a lot of people have said that you would be really good."

"No, no, no, Dad, I didn't say 'me,'" I corrected him. "I said 'Mead.'"

He responded that Mead was on the list and they had talked. But then he pressed again, asking if I would at least consider the position. I refused. I thought it was a crazy idea. It would be a scandal for him, setting him up for charges of nepotism—which would be accurate—and those charges would reflect on me, too. Besides, my future in the legislature was bright, I enjoyed what I was doing, and life was good at home. He pressed me again to think about it. I said my answer was no. But finally, I agreed to consider it, while assuming that when I talked to Verne later that night, he would agree with me, and that would be the end of the topic.

I was wrong. Verne didn't see the political danger of the appointment in the same way I did. He simply said I would be good at the job. I had not thought about that. But I remained adamantly opposed to the idea.

Over the years, I haven't told this story often. One reason is my sense that people don't believe me when I say I didn't want an appointment to the U.S. Senate. For anyone who hasn't seen the life of a senator close up, it is probably hard to understand. But I had seen the price my father paid. I knew that it was a tough job with immense responsibility and very little time for anything else. I knew that power could be a burden and that the trappings of prestige could be unfulfilling. And I knew that anyone who accepted the job was signing up for the long term—at least eight years, and perhaps a lifetime—as Alaska would need to have a senator with seniority.

My dad loves living in Alaska, but for twenty-two years he had been trapped in Washington doing a job that never stops. When he was first elected, in 1980, I had just finished college at Georgetown, which had included one summer session—I knew the miserable heat of a Washington summer and wanted nothing to do with it. My mother felt the same way. Although my parents are devoted to each other, they spent the summer apart, every summer, for two decades, as she lived in Fairbanks and he stayed in Washington.

Not long after I graduated from college, I saw the cost of that separation. It was a brilliant summer weekend in 1981, at their home on the Chena River, and the whole family was on hand, out on the river, at the picnic table in the evening, and enjoying all the fun that vibrant town has to offer under the sweet midnight sun. My father flew in, and then, just as quickly, he was gone. It was the first time I had seen what I call an Alaska flip-turn weekend— he had flown four thousand miles, across five time zones (since reduced to four), from D.C. to Alaska, and then headed back, traveling for at least fourteen hours each way, to spend about thirty-six hours on the ground. I couldn't imagine how he could do it, and he was doing this more than once a month. As for longer vacations and visits, they were unpredictable. When my sister Carol got married, she tried to schedule the ceremony at the only time the Senate would be certain to give our father time off to be there, during the April recess—but she had to negotiate with the church to hold a wedding during Holy Week.

In 2002, when my father asked me to consider that life for myself, I was only five years beyond my perfect fortieth birthday. My life still seemed close to perfect, even with the adjustment to legislative weekdays a third of the year. Why would I want to give that up? I didn't want to, and having my name on the list annoyed me rather than presenting any kind of temptation.

That Thanksgiving weekend, about two dozen members of our family joined a cruise down Mexico's west coast to Acapulco, celebrating Dad's victory. The rough, gloomy weather left us plenty of time to talk. I had shut the door on the Senate appointment, and the subject hadn't come up again between me and my father. But my parents must have reached an agreement. Instead of my father broaching the subject, I got my mother's less direct approach. I heard from my siblings, with comments like "I know this may be hard, but have you thought through the pros and cons?" I finally called a stop to it. I said, "I'm on vacation, too." It was too much like that trip to Puerto Rico, fifteen years earlier, when I had failed the bar and everyone tiptoed around me.

Finally, my father approached me when I was standing by the rail on an outside deck. He said, "Your mom and I have talked this through, and I have interviewed everyone on the list that could take over the seat. And I keep coming back to you. And I think you need to consider it."

I said, "Well, what happens if I don't want to?"

What he said next felt very unfair at the time, just as when he had used my sense of duty to keep me from quitting the bar exam. He simply made a statement: "You love the state as much as I do, and if you really care, you'll step up to the responsibility."

Again, I agreed to consider it. And, again, he left me alone. He flew straight to Juneau from the vacation to be sworn in as governor. Now he had one month, by law, to make an appointment to the Senate. Weeks passed without an announcement. His words kept turning over in my mind. The sense of obligation he had planted continued to grow, as I thought about the service to Alaska I could do as a senator. The personal concerns that were holding me back seemed comparatively petty, and perhaps selfish, in an objective sense. After all, members of the military make greater sacrifices for our country. And, in all honesty, I believed I did have something to contribute. I may have been a B student, and leadership was something I had learned rather than being born with, but I had proved myself as a legislator and I believed I could do a good job as a senator. Knowing that fact made the responsibility real. I had learned early on that leadership is a duty. This decision wasn't only about me.

The sun had finished setting in Anchorage by midafternoon on Wednesday, December 18, nearly the shortest day of the year. After school let out, I took the boys for haircuts so they would look good for our Christmas pictures. They were in the chairs at a Supercuts in a Midtown strip mall when my father called. I backed into a storage closet to talk to him. He asked, "Did you get the package?"

The day before, I had received a FedEx package that contained no note—nothing but a pair of funky homemade socks, knitted in the gold-and-blue design of the Alaska flag. A questionable Christmas present without wrapping or a card? Apparently, I now learned, Dad had sent them. But why? He told a story—he thought I would remember, but I did not—of when he had worn these ugly socks, a gift from a constituent, at our duck camp on Healy Lake, not long after he'd entered the Senate. I had teased him, saying, "I wish I was a senator, so somebody would give me socks like that." Dad, a bit of a pack rat, had kept the socks and remembered my comment all this time. Now he had sent them to me.

"I want you to take the seat," he said.

I was shocked. Three weeks had passed since we had discussed the appointment, and I had assumed, with a sense of relief, that he had moved on to someone else. I said, "I can't hear you, I'm in the barbershop." I suppose I was stalling. I left the closet and sought even more privacy outside.

The parking lot was cold, dark, and icy, and traffic roared through the multilane intersection of the Seward Highway and Fireweed Lane. Dad was calling from D.C., planning to fly to Anchorage the next day. He said he had thought it through. He knew I could handle the job and that I would carry on the values that had guided him during his two decades in the Senate. He had decided I was the right person.

I accepted.

The shape of the rest of my life would change in a matter of hours. My father said I should begin earning Senate seniority before other entering freshmen, and he wanted to make the announcement before Christmas week. That meant the day after tomorrow. The family entered panic mode. We scurried to plan a morning press conference for Friday, followed by a swearing-in ceremony at midday. Friends came over to help me pick out what to wear, but after one look in my closet—I am notoriously frugal about clothes—they gave up and my friend Jamilia brought over a selection of her classic outfits for me to try on. I was up past two in the morning working on my speech, reading it over the phone to my sister Carol, the family wordsmith, who told me which words to cut out.

At nine A.M. on Friday, we were at the governor's office in Anchorage, ready for the press conference, which would be carried live by various TV outlets. I would be accompanied by family, key legislators, and friends who had been with us since PTA days in Government Hill. Jamilia decided that my clothes still weren't acceptable and put her St. John knit jacket on me, still warm from her body. We stepped into the conference room. A crowd of about seventy people waited to see who would walk in beside the governor. Bright TV lights exposed us and blinded our eyes. At that moment, the media and the world learned of my father's extraordinary choice.

He spoke first and then introduced me, and I delivered my speech. Then he left the room and I took questions. Certainly, there was surprise, as the event was a historic first, and a wildly questionable one, of a father appointing his daughter to a U.S. Senate seat, but the reporters were respectful and even kind—I had good relationships with them, having worked with most during my time in the legislature. Indeed, the coverage was far better than I had expected—all but for the "Voice of the Times" newspaper section run by Bill Allen and Veco. The *Anchorage Daily News* summarized the political reaction in its leading story by declaring, "Not everyone was happy with the selection, including Democrats and Republicans alike who complained of nepotism. Some conservative interest groups, particularly Alaska Right to Life, say they are happy with the politics of the father but not the daughter. But others of wide-ranging political views hailed the choice, saying that Lisa Murkowski has proven to be a smart, talented and moderate leader who will reach out to all Alaskans." Ethan Berkowitz, the fiery Democratic minority leader in the State House, said, "Lisa is a friend of mine and I wish her well. This is one of the few times in my life that I will say no more than that."

The day got more complicated, not simpler. Verne found the freezer had stopped working at Alaska Pasta and two hundred pounds of ravioli were in danger of thawing. He set out on a frantic quest to buy a new industrial freezer on the last workday before Christmas. Our friend Branch Haymans, from our Government Hill school days, called every restaurant in town, looking for a room for our luncheon of thirty guests, and was also dispatched at the last minute to get proper clothes for Verne to wear at the swearing-in. Verne gamely dressed in a corner of the gubernatorial offices. Federal judge Andrew Kleinfeld, who had flown from Fairbanks to swear me in, asked who was on the program of speakers and who would hold the Bible. We didn't have a program or a respectable Bible. We quickly recruited speakers, and I called Holy Family Cathedral, a few blocks away. Archbishop Roger Schwietz had just returned from the airport and agreed to bless us and bring a Bible along. By noon, everything had miraculously fallen together, and the event looked as if it had been planned. Branch had found a place for the lunch, too. Later that afternoon, back at the house, our guests toasted with champagne, while I did hours of television interviews and Verne installed his new freezer. In the evening we ordered in Chinese food while the boys lit the yard with sparklers.

At lunch, Judge Kleinfeld had asked if I knew where the word "senate" comes from—I did not—and informed me that it derives from the Latin word *senex*, for "old man," which became *senatus*, or "council of old men." Was I ready to join a council of old men? I laughed. I thought so.

That very same day, Majority Leader Trent Lott abruptly stepped down, leaving the U.S. Senate without a leader. The Republican conference negotiated who would succeed him. The media asked who I was supporting. The whirlwind I had stepped into showed no signs of abating. I would have to meet as part of the conference by telephone on Monday to vote for the new leader. I already had a Senate office, my father's, where the staff now answered the phone with my name. There was no time to absorb the speed and intensity of these changes and the responsibility suddenly placed on me.

In fact, I had no idea how difficult a course I had chosen.

CHAPTER 2

The Distant and Dangerous
Climate of Washington

MY SUDDEN IMMERSION IN the nation's capital felt crazy. I got lost in Senate procedure, which uses different rules from those of the Alaska Legislature. I got lost in the buildings, with their maze of underground passages. The ornate, gilded ceilings distracted me with their beauty; after gazing up while I walked, I would realize I wasn't sure where I was. I'll never forget coming out of the Senate Chamber on one of my first days, my head tipped back, looking at my surroundings, and hearing a friendly "Hey, Lisa, how's it going?" from behind me. It was Hillary Clinton. A few weeks earlier, I'd been supervising my boys' haircuts at Supercuts, and now the former first lady was addressing me as if we were friends. It was like an out-of-body experience. I thought, "What am I doing here?"

The job never seemed impossible to me—at least, I always believed I could do it if I worked hard enough—but the responsibility I had assumed often felt overwhelming. Alaska's voters had picked my father to represent them, and now he had chosen me to finish his term, gambling his own political reputation on me by transferring his duty to me. I often felt uncertain. I knew I didn't deserve to be there in the same way as other senators who had won their seats in an election. Yet I had to show the confidence and determination of leadership, because I could succeed in the job only if those around me believed in me. These two years would be some of the most difficult of my life. Doubts and regrets nagged at me every day, and tortured me at night—feelings I kept secret, even from my family, thinking that also was part of the crushing responsibility I had willingly accepted.

I will tell that story, but not because I want or need sympathy. I tell it to portray an often-forgotten truth: public service is hard and can require painful sacrifices. That matters, because the pain deters most people without a powerful drive for power from participating at a high level. The world of Washington politics feels utterly foreign to a person like me, someone who came up from the PTA, as a community-activated representative in the legislature. My appointment ushered me past the brutal electoral process for the office, including the need to schmooze and beg for campaign money, skills that I'm not particularly good at. Lacking those skills alone could have prevented me from being a senator, especially from a more populous state. But even with the appointment, I still had to learn how to represent Alaska and my own conscience in the Senate, and that was the most difficult task I had ever tackled. An easier and more common way to advance in Congress is to do as you are told, following party leaders and political professionals, as a cog in a system. We all pay a price for making it so difficult to serve.

My early years in the Senate were not distinguished. I certainly applied myself, as I'd done in work or law school, and I fulfilled my obligations, but I did not stand out; I was simply average. I didn't lead or carve out an area of influence, mostly just going with the flow. Given what I was up against, that was pretty good.

My education began on Christmas Eve, four days into my service. Senator Ted Stevens summoned me to his office in the Anchorage Federal Building—summoned, not invited. I was intimidated, unsure what to expect. Stevens had just won his seventh Senate election, having been appointed in 1968, and since then he had taken a leading role in every important issue facing Alaska. Even before that, he had already established his place in our state's history, as a key leader in the fight for statehood in the 1950s. At the millennium, in 2000, civic leaders had recognized him as "Alaskan of the Century," and the legislature renamed the Anchorage airport in his honor. Alaskans knew him as "Uncle Ted," in part for his extraordinary ability to bring home federal money for the state, as the chairman of the Senate Appropriations Committee and in many other leadership roles. By now, he was known as a gruff old-school gentleman.

The must-read, unsigned Sunday gossip column in the *Anchorage Daily News* gave Ted another nickname. He was called "Senator-for-Life." Two days before our meeting, that column had revealed that Stevens's recommendation for the appointment had not been me but Alaska Teamsters leader Jerry Hood. After I was appointed, the media carried no comment from Ted. Going to meet him, I didn't know what to expect. He had a reputation for being brusque. I wondered if he would lay down the law about how I should serve, as his junior partner, a full generation behind him.

The Anchorage Federal Building stood empty that late afternoon of Christmas Eve, except for a pair of security guards, until I reached Ted's office. That suite alone bustled with activity, as staff members worked at their desks and met, as on any full workday. Ted was a tough boss. I had seen a bit of his warmer side as a high school intern in his D.C. office, in 1975, but he remained mostly an Alaska legend to me. I also knew he had a sometimes testy relationship with my father. Ted said, "I'm glad you're coming to this position with a background in the law. I don't think your dad ever understood the law."

I decided to accept the backhanded compliment without taking offense. I had no intention of going up against Ted's famously crusty, domineering personality. And, to my relief, he soon relaxed. From that first meeting, I saw a side of Ted Stevens that he didn't use much in public. He treated me with respect and interest and he offered his help, asking what committees I was interested in. My choices at the time were not strategic, and he guided me in a direction that would make more sense for our state—which proved, years later, to be extremely important. By following his advice that day, I would eventually become chairman of the Energy and Natural Resources Committee. The meeting was businesslike, not warm, but I left with a dawning awareness that the great Ted Stevens now regarded me as his colleague and equal. Also, I realized that Ted could help me only so much. I was on my own.

Verne and I had planned a two-week Christmas vacation to Mexico before the appointment intervened. We decided to go anyway, but we cut the stay to one week. I didn't really take a vacation at all. While Verne and the boys fished on the beach all day, I sat on a tiny balcony overlooking the water, writing notes to everyone who had written to me or commented publicly on my appointment. Letters to the editor had called me and my father dishonorable and an embarrassment to Alaska. They called the appointment disgusting, despicable, and brazen, and charged me with dishonestly conniving to bring it about. But I also got support from surprising places, including from the normally poison-penned columnist Mike Doogan. I felt a powerful need to respond personally to every one of them, thanking the well-wishers and promising to prove myself to those who were angry about my appointment.

We had decided not to disrupt the boys' lives by moving in the middle of the school year, and then we realized that moving them before I faced election, in two years, could force them to move twice if I didn't win. That meant that after my Washington swearing-in ceremony, when they returned to Alaska, I would be saying goodbye to my family for a long time. And that was exactly how it felt.

I rented my parents' house on Capitol Hill and worked in my father's former office—a much bigger office than a freshman normally gets—assisted by his staff plus a single member of my Juneau staff I had brought along. Somehow, I had to become my own person, not a younger, female version of Frank Murkowski. Work seemed like the solution. With his holdover staff writing all the letters and press releases, I reviewed every piece of paper leaving the office that had my name on it—and a Senate office produces an enormous amount of paper. I also dedicated many hours to reading legislation and briefings, and I developed a habit of carrying a backpack heavy with work that I could mark up at home or on an airplane. I still average three hours of homework daily, but in those days I used every waking hour.

My chief of staff begged me to slow down, because, he said, I was killing myself. But I was surviving the best way I knew how. There are senators whose brilliance or experience makes the work relatively manageable, allowing them to leave the office in time to attend evening receptions. There are also those whose colossal egos make them think they're brilliant, with the same result. I have a reasonable sense of my own abilities. I can get to the right answer, but I need to do the homework. At each step of my life, hard work solved the problems in front of me, getting me through economics, law school, and the bar exam, and giving me the sense that I could succeed and that I deserved to. With the heavy responsibility of an unearned Senate seat, the need to prove myself—to myself, firstly, and then to everyone else—had never been greater.

Not only did I skip the receptions, I skipped meals, too. In the wee hours, after the Hart Senate Office Building fell silent, I would scrounge dinner from whatever had been left in the office. My favorite was home-canned jars of smoked salmon strips, a staple in every coastal Alaska village, which constituents would bring as gifts. A letter opener worked perfectly to pop the seal on the lid, extract the tightly packed strips, and carry them to my mouth, with a paper towel to catch drips of oil. One late night, the office cleaner, Viola, came in from the dark corridor and called to me, "Lisa, is that you with that stinky fish again?" At that point, I think I knew Viola better than my own staff. It felt good to hear her booming voice and realize I wasn't entirely alone in that huge building.

Most of my new Senate colleagues were cordial and helpful from the beginning, but others sent signals that they thought I didn't belong and probably wouldn't last long. John McCain, in particular, made his disregard clear, withholding any warmth and even talking past me when we found ourselves seated together, as if I were not present. I was well aware of the contrast between McCain and me. McCain, as a prisoner of war in Hanoi during the Vietnam War, had been offered early release because his father was an admiral, but he had refused, remaining in that hell rather than accepting special treatment. I had accepted special treatment in the form of a Senate seat from my father.

I flew home to Anchorage my first four weekends. Back then, the Senate scheduled votes on Monday evenings and Friday afternoons, constricting my time at home to the flip-turn trips I had first seen my father do in the summer of 1981 in Fairbanks. The four-thousand-mile trip home gave me just thirty-six hours on the ground in Alaska. Acceding to advice that said Alaskans did not want to see their public servants sitting in the front of the plane, I always flew coach (as I still do flying within Alaska). At least the long flights allowed me more work time.

But those few hours at home didn't come close to fulfilling my needs as a mom. Verne had stepped up to be a single parent, even as he ran his business, a heavy load about which he never complained or even admitted was difficult, as he stoically supported me. I could not undercut him by parachuting in and disrupting the routine he had established, either by trying to take over the housework or by blowing it up by being the "fun" parent. Eventually, I learned that the best way I could contribute was to fill in, simply being present so he could have a few hours to himself out in the garage.

Life in the Senate would be entirely different from my time in the legislature. When I served in Juneau, full engagement and three-day weekends of homework help had been the norm. I had always known that the end of our separation was, at most, a few months away. Back then, I had talked with the boys almost every night. Now our older son, Nic, was in middle school—and they didn't want to spend a lot of time on the phone with their mom. I finally stopped trying for more than a quick "love you" on our calls. I had become external to their daily lives. By taking on a civic responsibility, I felt, I had failed in my responsibility to my family.

Loneliness overwhelmed me on nights when I was alone with these thoughts. I had committed to this job for the long term—to at least eight years, if Alaskans agreed. In eight years my boys would be gone, off to college, and that part of our lives together would be over. There was no giving up or turning back. Some nights when I was exhausted from work, in an empty house, my body heaved with sobs and I wondered out loud, "What have I done?" There was never a time when I felt that I had made the wrong decision because the job was too hard. The work was just work. But working harder couldn't protect me from the emotional sense of loss, which I struggled with almost every day. And that struggle had to be all internal—I couldn't share it with anyone.

Verne already had enough on his plate. I didn't want to add to his burden with a problem that had no solution. Nor did I know anyone in Washington well enough to discuss my feelings. I had already discovered how hard it would be to make real friends in my new position. As soon as I seemed to establish a connection with someone, out would come an ask, and I would wonder if this was really a new friend or just someone who wanted something from me. Besides, who would even understand my feelings? A seat in the U.S. Senate is among the most powerful and coveted positions in the world. For many people, it simply wouldn't be believable that I'd accepted it reluctantly and struggled with loneliness. My regrets were secret, off-limits even with my family. They had supported the decision, and I didn't want them to think I was casting blame for how I felt.

But I had underestimated them.

My sisters, cousins, and aunt were monitoring my contributions to our family email string, the messages we exchanged among my mother's female Gore relatives—the Gore Girls, or GGs, as we called ourselves. We exchanged dumb jokes, updates about our kids' accomplishments, health news, and the kind of trivial, miscellaneous thoughts that keep a connection alive. I didn't share anything about how I was feeling, but they noticed a heaviness in how I responded online. My cousin Jenny Dwyer recalled recently how the messages had worried her. She knew without asking that I must have been grieving my absence from the boys at this critical time in their lives. And she noticed, from seeing me in the media, that I was losing weight. I've never had an eating disorder, but food is not my priority when I'm busy. With her lovely calmness, Jenny decided to step in. She flew from her home in Seattle to stay at my home in Washington, wrapping me in her caring and filling me with her comfort food.

The Gore Girls got me through my secret uncertainty and regret. I wasn't the first to receive their help. We had begun gathering four years earlier, when a favorite aunt, DD Gore, let us know she was feeling lonely. Stricken with lung disease after years of smoking, she had moved from Tacoma to Palm Springs. We had gathered there for our first annual Gore Girls reunion, with women from two generations sharing fun and belonging. These women remain my best friends and have been my sanctuary and my vault. They supported me through the next two years, and many difficult times to come. They didn't judge my choices, ask me for anything, or weigh in with political advice. They simply gave me a place in a circle of love where I could listen and could be heard.

I knew I would make it through those two years supported by Verne and the GGs. I kept my eyes on the November 2004 election. The public would vote on a full, six-year term, and I would regain my family, win or lose. Either I would be back home with them in Anchorage, returned by electoral defeat to the life I remembered from my fortieth birthday, five years before, or we would all be together in Washington, D.C., and I would be serving in the Senate, vindicated by voters saying I deserved to be there.

My prediction was only partly correct.

———

Among the criticism and praise that flooded forth when my father appointed me to the Senate, one columnist considered the unique relationship I now had with Alaskans. Michael Carey wrote in the *Anchorage Daily News*, "Nobody knows what the future holds for Lisa Murkowski. But this much can be said. Newly minted Sen. Murkowski will wear the charge of nepotism like a cape until she either wins an election or is defeated by a rival." A poll taken a few months into my first year showed he was correct. My numbers were terrible. More than half of voters cited nepotism as a reason to vote against me. The governor, my father, was even more unpopular, in part for the same reason. With my vulnerability, I would draw a strong opponent—and that challenger turned out to be the previous governor, Tony Knowles.

The person who ushered me through that gauntlet was Ted Stevens. He became my true mentor, as only a master of the Senate could. With our difference in age, experience, and gender, we would not be intimate friends, but we were close as work friends, members of a team fighting for Alaska. I had a lot to learn, but Ted never treated me as junior. He guided me with respect and listened to my ideas. He never exposed me to his temper, and he never told me what to do. He liked to remind people that he, too, had been appointed, back in 1968. At the time he had also been, like me, a forty-five-year-old Anchorage lawyer with a Fairbanks background, and the State House majority leader. He would say, "Your vote has equal weight with any of the one hundred senators," which I now know is not true, but which I appreciated then.

His relationship with my father had been quite different. When my dad, Frank, was elected to the Senate, in 1980, Ted had already been there for twelve years, and the dynamic of junior and senior senator continued for Dad's entire twenty-two years in the office. In public, they presented themselves as a united team working together for the state, but in private they could be two old bulls butt-ing against each other in the same pasture. The third member of the delegation, Don Young, elected to the House in 1973—also famously loud and assertive—reportedly served as referee between these stubborn and deep-voiced men during their closed-door meetings. Sometimes the arguments got so loud they alarmed staff in the outer office. On one occasion, I've been told, Ted became so angry over a disagreement with Frank that he stood up and said he wouldn't hear any more, before stomping out and slamming the door. A few moments later, however, he came back in, barking at Don and Frank, "I can't leave. This is my office."

As the humor suggests, I don't think they disliked each other. Their main difficulty was being too much alike.

Ted's experience had made him an undisputed virtuoso of the Senate's processes, managing major appropriations bills and other legislation for the administration and the leadership without drawing attention to himself. His skill was making things happen. Part of that ability came from his relationships, which spanned both parties. His closest friend was Daniel Inouye, who had represented Hawaii in the Senate since 1963 and was also chair of Appropriations when the Democrats had the majority. Both men were heroes of World War II—Inouye lost his right arm in combat—and both became lawyers after the war. They both entered history books as leaders of their brand-new states and eventually had their names added to their states' primary airports. But their friendship went deeper than history—they called each other "brother" and unquestioningly lent mutual aid. No example could have more clearly shown me how important it was to form trusting relationships with colleagues, regardless of political party.

As the election neared, my need for Ted's assistance became increasingly obvious. My poll numbers remained stubbornly negative, while Knowles held a steady lead. Analysts picked me as the most vulnerable Republican in the Senate, at a time when Republicans held the majority by only two seats, fifty-one to forty-nine. Knowles would have all the financial support he needed, as national

Democrats saw the opportunity to pick up the seat and potentially flip the Senate. I had plenty of financial support, too. The race became the most expensive in Alaska history to that time, with the money spent exceeding the capacity of the broadcast outlets to carry the ads (almost $6 million by each candidate, plus several million more by the parties, or about $50 per voter). The heavy rotation of campaign commercials began months before the election and didn't let up. A newspaper reporter complained of the "blizzard of radio, television and newspaper ads and telephone campaigning that are starting to make the ever-in-your-face Senate race seem like a shared misery for Alaskans comparable to ice fog." (Ice fog is what it sounds like: frozen fog that fills the air with floating crystals.)

A stream of Bush administration officials came to Alaska to speak on my behalf, from Vice President Dick Cheney to First Lady Laura Bush, and on down. To my surprise, even John McCain cut an ad for me, reaching for support from veterans. But Knowles's lead held. Voters were still angry about my appointment. Moreover, my father's popularity had continued to sink, as he addressed the state's fiscal gap with painful budget cuts, including the end of a monthly payment that senior citizens had received for many years.

We would need Ted to pull me over the finish line. He campaigned hard for me and filmed a pair of influential TV ads, making the case that his power depended on keeping the majority in the Senate. "If Lisa Murkowski does not win, I might lose my chairmanship—and Alaska will suffer," he said in the ad. "I need Lisa on my team for Alaska's future." Our print ads emphasized teamwork as well, placing me in pictures with Ted, Don Young, and President Bush. Don weighed in with a memorable quote about the three members of the congressional delegation being similar to a sled dog team, with Ted in the "lead dog" position, Don nearest the sled, pulling most of the weight as the "wheel dog," and me as the "swing dog," which meant I was following right behind Ted, doing whatever he did.

Eleven days before the election, the statewide *Anchorage Daily*

News carried a banner headline: "UNCLE TED RIDES TO RESCUE OF MURKOWSKI CAMPAIGN." Polls showed the race tightening. Dog teams began to appear in ads from an independent expenditure, underlining Don Young's less-than-flattering quote about my role in the harness behind Ted. Some voters cried foul. In the words of one letter to the editor, "If Lisa is so good, then let her stand on her record, and stop making this an election between Tony and Ted." But other voters loved Ted and knew his appropriations prowess was a significant component of Alaska's prosperity—and that persuaded some to pick me despite their dislike of how I originally got the job. One wrote, "Our economic well-being is at stake. . . . Please support Lisa Murkowski. Remember, half a loaf is better than none."

President Bush won reelection, our party picked up four more seats in the Senate to hold the majority, we held the House, and I received 48.5 percent of the vote, three points ahead of Knowles, to win a six-year term.

I could catch my breath. My family would join me in Washington. But I did not have my vindication. I had won against a more popular opponent only because Ted Stevens had told voters he needed me. I had not yet proven myself to Alaskans.

My accomplishments may not have been memorable in those early years, but I had unusual qualities as a senator focused on Alaska and not caught up in the Washington world. As I did not mingle socially, people didn't always know what to make of me.

A phone call from the vice president crystallized how out of step with Washington convention I really was. In 2005, the Patriot Act was up for reauthorization, a vote that would continue the laws passed after the September 11 attacks to make it easier to prosecute terrorists. Many Alaskans—who tend to be strong defenders of civil liberties—distrusted the government's new powers under the law, and when I studied the issues, I agreed that the expanded authority for surveillance and searches could be abused. I told the Republican conference I would not be on board for reauthorization, along with just a few others, and Cheney called to bring me over. He let me know the team needed my vote and emphasized how important this would be to the administration. His pitch highlighted the political stakes, not the policy considerations. I responded, during the ten-minute call, with my own detailed explanation of why I didn't think this was a good law.

Finally, Cheney seemed to realize I wasn't bargaining. This wasn't about politics for me. After an extended pause he said, "In other words, you actually care about this from a policy perspective?"

I said, "Yes, sir. That's true."

He respectfully thanked me for my time and said goodbye. I never heard from the administration about that bill again.

Legislating, for me, is not transactional. I need to believe in the decisions I make. That alone made me something of an anomaly to some in Washington—but probably closer to what most Americans feel is the right way to govern.

As we think about how we can make our Congress work better, it is important to understand what makes it such a hard place to serve. Our electoral process screens out regular people as politicians rise through the ranks, especially in big states, favoring those who are tough, driven, or good at navigating political networks, or those who have their own wealth for a campaign. Once you're a member of the Senate, the easiest route to success is to follow your party leadership while quietly earning seniority so you can someday hold power of your own. But climbing that ladder has nothing to do with the giving spirit of the community group or the PTA—the problem-solving, people-to-people spirit—which is the essence of real democracy.

My shortcut route to the Senate gave me an advantage in holding on to those hometown values, as did my representation of a small state. I realized that difference early in my service during a conversation with Barbara Boxer, the senator from California. I mentioned how hard it was to keep my pledge to meet all my constituents when they visited Washington, and I wondered how she found time to meet with hers. With thirty-five million people to represent, there was no way she could spend time with ordinary people, and she admitted that she allocated only four hours a week for constituent meetings. My state's population was so small—our entire population of 660,000 at the time would be only the fifth-largest city in California—that I felt I owed every Alaskan a personal meeting after their long, expensive trip.

Washington is a southern and eastern city, and I come from the farthest north, farthest west state, where everything is different. Although Alaska is conservative, it is highly diverse, with among the most integrated neighborhoods in the country (as a University of Alaska professor calculated). We have a tradition of women leaders—in business, in Native organizations, as well as in politics—and the social stratification that is common in the East doesn't exist in Alaska. We have the least income inequality of any state, people dress for comfort rather than fashion, and social status comes from outdoor accomplishments rather than owning a fancy car or going to a prestigious college. Elite credentials can even be a social and political handicap.

During my first two years in office, I had made little effort to become a Washingtonian—I didn't get out much, instead spending my time working, flying, or in Alaska. Friends who were more concerned about my wardrobe than I was hunted for bargains on my behalf at Marshalls or T.J.Maxx. I didn't get to know the neighbors or even the neighborhood. Consequently, I didn't adapt much to my new home. That ignorance became a liability when we moved the family east.

In Alaska, almost everyone goes to public school, and I am a strong believer in public education. Anchorage schools are among the most integrated in the country, with many academic options, including language immersion through high school. In Washington, the public school for our area struggled with extremely low academic achievement and had almost no White students. The practical, affordable choice was Catholic school. Matt would attend St. Peter's, a block from our house. For Nic, we applied to the boys-only Jesuit Gonzaga College High School. Gonzaga had space, but Nic would have to write an essay explaining why he wanted to attend. The problem was, Nic didn't want to attend Gonzaga, or any other school in Washington. He resisted until I explained that this would be the only chance to keep our family together.

The head of the school later told me that Nic's essay was the most honest he could recall and showed no sign of parental interference. Nic began by saying he did not want to go to Gonzaga, then listed his reasons: he was happy at home in Alaska, where he could hunt, fish, and ski, and he had been looking forward to high school there, with its language immersion program. But now, he conceded, he would have to live in Washington, D.C., and so he might as well go to Gonzaga, and if he did go, he said, he would benefit the school.

Gonzaga let Nic in, and he and, later, Matt found their places with friends and sports and ultimately graduated from the school, with a good education. Gonzaga also helped us become more a part of the place we lived, where we could connect with people outside the Capitol. The social events we attended through my work seemed all the same, with people impressed by my title or who wanted something from me. But at school, friendships came together around our kids, just as they had on Government Hill.

We saw a different side of Washington when the boys joined a soccer team. Verne found an urban league with a team made up of boys from places such as El Salvador, Guyana, Ecuador, and Nigeria. They mainly spoke Spanish on the field, which was natural for Nic and Matt, although they were the only White players. The other players lived in low-income housing, and we played on dreadful fields in questionable neighborhoods. Verne and I were the only parents who attended the games. He brought the snacks. The boys on the team adopted us and made us feel safe in places where the

Capitol Police would never have allowed us to go, if they had known. And I felt deeply protective of them, too.

On one occasion we played an all-White team from an affluent Virginia suburb. Verne and I looked out of place with our team, and the parents from Virginia assumed we were one of them, with their lawn chairs and coolers. When they began losing—because our team was really good—they didn't hold back from spewing awful racist slurs at our players. I'd seen prejudice against Alaska Natives in my life, but growing up in Alaska I had never experienced this kind of ugly, blatant hatred directed at kids, and I could hardly believe the things the parents were saying. I got mad. I confronted these moms who were yelling to our boys, "Go back to your own country." To my amazement, they didn't apologize. They just seemed bewildered—as if to say, "What side are you on?" They couldn't even see the racism in their own statements.

White people in Washington were a substantial minority, but they had created a kind of bubble of affluence, an apartheid in which they didn't have to interact with the poverty of the city's majority people of color and could willfully ignore their own prejudice. Coming from integrated Anchorage, I had not appreciated the insulation of the Washington bubble, but I saw it clearly at that soccer game.

In the Senate, I had to get used to sexism less subtle than what I had encountered in Alaska. Even today, I can convene a meeting only to have a male colleague try to take over running it. Commonly, a woman senator will offer an idea only to see a man adopt it as his own and be recognized for originating it. If I got angry about that sort of thing, I would be mad all the time. But my staff sometimes tells me I am not angry enough, because credit for accomplishments is like currency in politics.

The most egregious sexism came from older southern men, perhaps unintentionally. I just smiled at their "honey"s and "darling"s as a marker of our different generations. One day early on, I was presiding over the Senate when Robert Byrd, who had represented West Virginia since 1959, took the floor to deliver his annual ode to spring. Staring directly up at me, he declared, "The presiding officer is as beautiful as the day is long." I wanted to crawl under the desk. Women senators at that time still didn't have a proper bathroom, just a converted closet off the men's room, and the Senate swimming pool was reserved for men only, purportedly because some of the older men preferred to swim nude—a mental image that definitely kept me away.

I was only the thirty-second woman to serve in the Senate, out of about two thousand members since the nation's founding. The women who went before had made their mark in this "council of old men" by being tough and playing the men's game. Maryland's Barbara Mikulski had served the longest of all the women, with a big voice and fierce directness that demanded respect and attention. I can imagine her shouting down Baltimore political bosses, despite being less than five feet tall. The women all wore dark colors, business suits with skirts, and rarely dresses. Even Hillary Clinton's conservative pantsuits stood out. My staff counseled me against wearing my bright blue jackets and other colors, suggesting I looked too much like a newscaster. They brought in a consultant to advise me on how to change my wardrobe to look more "senatorial." The consultant suggested I wear black or navy blazers and button-down shirts, with pearls or very little jewelry, to which I said, "You want me to dress as a damn page." I ended the session.

There were only about a dozen female senators at that time, few enough for a dinner party, and Barbara, the "dean" of women senators, would periodically organize us for meals under "Mikulski rules": no staff, no leaks, and no notes. Republicans and Democrats mixed. I rarely missed a dinner. These gatherings were an important time to get to know one another as women rather than as politicians. We shared stories and sometimes personal thoughts about our lives or our families. We discussed issues we were working on, the craziness of the world in which we operated, and how "if the women were in charge, things would be different." Sometimes we would eat at a restaurant; on other occasions, a senator would host at her home. My cousin Jenny helped me put on a dinner on at least one occasion, cooking salmon and setting the table for the women senators, but disappearing at the first knock at the door. (Today, I'm happy to say, there are too many women in the Senate to sit at one table, but we still gather and most attend.)

During that period, when my family had been reunited, Jenny needed support, too. In 2005, her adored husband, Pat, was diagnosed with ALS. Pat was a highly successful commercial fisherman. His crab boats and salmon tenders had educated every young person in our extended family, both as deck hands on board and with the summer wages that helped with tuition at college. Now he was losing strength and balance. He knew the disease would rob him of control of his body, and ultimately of his life.

The GGs wrapped our love around Jenny. At our annual gathering in California, we focused on her. Aunt DD took us to Mass, as she did on every visit to show us off, and the priest gave a moving homily about the difficult and confusing things life gives each of us, and how we have to peel those layers back, like an onion, to find the center of our peace and joy. Later, sitting at the pool, Jenny turned to speak to all of us. "Thank you for being the center of my onion," she said. The next Christmas, her sister Anne gave each of us a framed picture of an onion, which we all display prominently in our homes.

I was still figuring out who I was as a senator. I remained conscious after my election that voters had returned me to the Senate because Ted Stevens had asked for a "swing dog" supporting his work. I wasn't sure what being a leader would mean for me, beyond working toward the goals the Alaska delegation had long pursued: resource development, appropriations for our state, and the Holy Grail of Alaska politics, opening the Arctic National Wildlife Refuge (known as ANWR) to oil exploration. Back then, that seemed to me like enough.

But my relationship with Ted Stevens gave me opportunities to develop politically. When a district court vacancy opened up in Alaska, I persuaded Ted, against his preference, to change the selection process for recommending a candidate to the White House, giving me a voice and adding a merit-based poll of lawyers. I also began buttressing him on policy areas outside his core expertise in defense and national security. I took the lead on energy and people-based issues such as food security and family leave, and nudged him on climate change.

Ted remained razor-sharp, but he was aging. Frustrated that he had begun, as he put it, "walking like an old man," he would climb the stairs two at a time. Age increased his impatience and irascibility, as did his ever-mounting workload, which grew along with his unequaled seniority: as the Senate president pro tempore, he was third in line to the presidency. He was also a committee chair, the manager of appropriations for the Iraq and Afghanistan wars, the go-to funder of any Alaska project, and had many other leadership roles. Sometimes his staff couldn't handle him, as he might become obstinate on an issue they felt was important for Alaska. But he would listen to me. One day, his chief of staff buttonholed me and asked if I would be a back channel to communicate with him. I recall the issue was about child care, and I presented it to Ted as if it were my own. He agreed to lend his support. There would be many times when Ted's staff would call me when they needed help with him. Ted and I worked together well, and I worked well with his staff. We were a strong delegation, with Don Young in the House.

Our biggest fight together was to open ANWR, which was believed to hold a vast reservoir of oil, a potential lifeline for Alaska's economy. Opening ANWR was a generational fight. As Matt said, "I thought Grandpa took care of that years ago." Certainly, he had tried. The issue dated to the late-1970s battle over the Alaska National Interest Lands Conservation Act, which set aside for conservation an area of Alaska as large as the entire state of California. When Ted had voted for that law, he had received a promise that this area would be available for development. Twenty-five years later, that promise had never been fulfilled, but now our chance seemed to have come, with President George W. Bush in the White House and Republican majorities in both the House and the Senate.

The drama of that legislation lasted through much of 2005. We believed we had won it as the year was closing. On the winter solstice, December 21, the Senate worked late into the night on a collection of big, complex issues, including budget cuts, Pentagon funding, disaster relief—and ANWR. We needed sixty votes to send the bill to the president's desk, and we believed we had them. But the pressure from national environmentalists was intense, gathered literally in the lobby just outside the Senate chamber. When the key vote came, one Republican colleague we had counted on voted against us. Another year ended without a priority the Alaska delegation had spent a generation fighting for.

Ted was devastated and enraged. In the heat of the moment, he declared, "This has been the saddest day of my life." I felt crushed to have lost such an important issue for Alaskans, but I felt especially bad for Ted, seeing this rare opportunity taken away after so many years. I worried about him. I sent a message on my BlackBerry, saying how sorry I was.

Ted responded with a message I will never forget.

In a few days, he said, he would be sitting by a pool in Arizona with his grandchildren. And I should rest up and enjoy my family, too, because soon enough we would be back in this fight, and we would eventually win it, working together. He wanted to reassure me that I had not let him down, closing his message by writing, "You are the partner I have always dreamed of."

I felt a glow as if I had received a love letter. It was so touching to know that Ted regarded me as his full teammate, that he believed we would fight again another day, and that even after this loss he wanted to encourage me, because I had done my part well. I expected that we would have many more years to work together, and I was looking forward to it.

The year after I left the legislature, unknown to me, the FBI began investigating the corruption I had sensed around Bill Allen and the private prison deal he was advancing. That investigation, called Polar Pen, grew to entangle various legislators, lobbyists, and businesspeople, and it also involved Allen's lobbying on oil taxes. A hidden camera filmed a room in Juneau's Baranof Hotel where Allen paid legislators cash for their votes. Pete Kott, who became Speaker of the House after I left Juneau, received $8,000 from Allen through a fake flooring invoice. After defeating an oil tax amendment Allen opposed, Kott bragged, on the hidden camera, "I had to get 'er done. I had to come back and face this man right here." He pointed to Allen. "I had to cheat, steal, beg, borrow, and lie."

Allen responded, "I own your ass."

As details of blatant corruption gradually seeped out, the public demanded change.

Sarah Palin rose in Alaska politics against this backdrop. After she did well in the 2002 primary for lieutenant governor, placing a close second, my father put her on the list of people he was considering for appointment to the Senate, then appointed her to the Alaska Oil and Gas Conservation Commission. She resigned from that job less than a year later, after filing an ethics complaint against a fellow commissioner, who was also the chairman of the Alaska Republican Party. Those headlines gave her the aura of a corruption fighter. In 2004, she publicly toyed with running against me, and in 2006 she ran for governor against my father in the Republican primary.

Frank Murkowski had never been touched by a hint of corruption, but after four tough years he had lost his political popularity. Bad luck dictated that he served when low oil prices required tough choices on the state budget, including ending the unaffordable old-age payments. He also lost voters' support with his insistence on buying a small jet for use by the Department of Public Safety and the governor's office, and he never recovered from the negative publicity of appointing me to the Senate. My siblings and I knew he would likely lose, and we tried to talk him out of running. No quitter, he stuck by the unpopular but necessary decisions he had made and defended them as a candidate, despite terrible poll numbers.

Rain poured down on primary day, in August 2006. We seemed star-crossed. A campaign volunteer in front of his headquarters was hit by a bullet fragment in a drive-by shooting, which turned out to have nothing to do with us. The volunteer recovered quickly, but the chaotic incident set the tone for the day. That night, votes for Palin piled up quickly. She had a landslide victory. Dad graciously shook her hand and promised to support her in the general election. Even in private he would not tolerate negative comments about her as governor, reminding us, "It's a hard job." It was sad for all of us to see his remarkable political career end that way.

Americans who know of Sarah Palin from her national image think of her as conservative, thoroughly Republican, and adamantly pro-oil, with her chant of "Drill, baby, drill." But in Alaska she had a completely different persona. Taking advantage of the public disgust with corruption, she ran against the Republican Party, until she got its nomination. In office, she worked mostly with Democrats to pass an enormous tax increase on the oil industry and an ethics bill, her only significant accomplishments. When global oil prices shot upward, the state budget suddenly had a surplus, and she gave away a whopping $3,269 to every Alaskan—man, woman, and child—a great way for any politician to buy popularity, but not exactly a conservative move.

The explanation for this difference between Palin's image in Alaska and nationally is Palin herself. To give her credit, she was good at taking on roles. She reflected whoever was around her— whoever was writing her script. Off script, including speaking one-on-one, she quickly betrayed a weak command of issues and a shaky ability to connect sentences. She was not well informed and not intellectually curious. But as a candidate for governor, she had support from former governor Wally Hickel, and his team of experienced political operatives worked for her behind the scenes. Answering questions on her own, in gubernatorial debates, she smiled and gushed "glittering generalities," as one of her opponents, Andrew Halcro, observed. That seemed to be enough.

Each year I visit Juneau to address the legislature and usually meet with the governor for lunch at the Governor's Mansion. My conversations with Governor Palin were unique. The point of these meetings was to talk about policy and how I, as a senator, could support the state. But Palin showed no interest in policy. Instead, she wanted to talk about what it was like being a senator and living in Washington. Since her interest in taking my job was being widely discussed, it felt quite odd to have her interviewing me about my hours, staff, offices, where I liked to shop, what my days were like, and so on. She had nothing to say about governing.

We did have a good conversation, however, speaking as two women, about how lonely public life can be. We both missed having coffee with our friends, and we both found it challenging to be a mom in office. I had heard the rumors that she was pregnant, which proved to be true when she gave birth to Trig less than three months later, making that conversation feel particularly poignant. Her love for that child was obvious and captivated Alaskans. People in the state capitol found her charming, too. She brought her own home-baked cookies to legislators. In the car, she pushed her state trooper escort aside so she could drive herself. Her popularity was real.

Populists are always likable, or at least appealing in some way. They sell a personality instead of a coherent philosophy or set of core principles. Their power comes from energizing crowds, so they say whatever necessary to get applause. Sarah Palin didn't know she was helping start a movement—she was just being Sarah Palin—but she became the prototype for Donald Trump, the showman without principle. And he took populism much further, partly because he didn't need a script.

I would have warned John McCain about selecting her as his

vice-presidential running mate if I had given any credence to the rumors that he was considering Palin. I did not, because I thought the idea was preposterous. Even if they liked her image, I assumed that once McCain's team vetted Palin they would realize she was a lightweight and not up to the job, less than halfway through her first term as Alaska governor, which was her first major position.

By that time, I had gained John's respect, partly because I had won an election, and partly because I had won an argument. He would constantly, and self-righteously, criticize any "special interest" spending, as he defined it. One day on the Senate floor, he asserted that the funding we were then voting on, for the Essential Air Service program, was a boondoggle. I told him it was essential in Alaska because 80 percent of our communities were not connected by roads. Without federal support for air service, some towns would disappear. He abrasively shot back that Alaskans were always ripping off the government with special programs. I got really angry. We began raising our voices and leaning toward each other. I said, "You don't know what you're talking about," and continued my explanation. He said, "I don't have to listen to this," and turned to walk toward the cloakroom. But I ran around him and faced him down from the other direction, walking backward up the steps and continuing to speak—in fact, we were yelling by that point. In the cloakroom, he kept insisting he didn't have to listen, and I kept saying he did, until he finally retreated into a phone booth, sat down, and shut the door. I stood outside, arms folded at my chest, blood racing.

At that point, Susan Collins came around the corner. She said, "I never saw anyone back John into a phone booth."

McCain and I later laughed about the incident. Our relationship reached a different level of respect after that.

When talk in Washington turned to whom McCain would pick to be his vice-presidential running mate, my son Nic lobbied for me to put my name in the mix. I was surprised, since he didn't like living in Washington. Nic explained that if I were vice president, we would live in the vice president's residence, located on the seventy-two acres of the U.S. Naval Observatory, where, he had learned, wild deer wandered around. He fantasized that he could hunt in the morning before school. I said I was sorry to ruin his wonderful plan, but John McCain would never pick a running mate from Alaska, with our three solidly Republican electoral votes.

When McCain did pick Palin, Nic chided me. He said, "Mom, you should have tried harder."

As a woman and an Alaska Republican, I felt bound to support Palin's vice-presidential run as much as I could. Like many Alaskans, however, I inwardly cringed to see her representing us on the national stage.

The political world knew that Palin had weighed running against Ted Stevens in 2008, and she had been early to denounce him when the Bill Allen corruption investigation came to his door. I recall with perfect clarity the moment I learned that the FBI had targeted him: July 30, 2007. I was on a stopover in Minneapolis, bound for Anchorage, doing some work in the Delta Air Lines lounge. I got up to find a snack and saw, on a huge television, Ted's cabin in the ski town of Girdwood, near Anchorage. Breaking news: FBI agents were searching Ted's cabin. I was stunned, frozen, and felt sick to my stomach. I couldn't take my eyes off the screen. Only after long moments did I realize that I was standing in the middle of a large, crowded room, and people were watching me. I retreated to find another TV.

Bill Allen and Veco vice president Rick Smith had pleaded guilty and were assisting the Department of Justice with its prosecution of various Alaska politicians. Ted's son Ben, until recently president of the Alaska State Senate, had been implicated by Allen but was never charged. With the fierce protectiveness of a parent, Ted was furious that his son's name had been tarnished and was certain that he would be exonerated, but he didn't seem to take seriously the rumors that he himself would get caught up in the mess. I trusted Ted deeply, and I took his obvious lack of concern as reassurance that there really wasn't anything to worry about.

But it was true that Ted had chosen Bill Allen as a friend. Among many unanswered questions, Alaskans have wondered why. I disliked Allen, and apparently Ted's wife, Catherine, shared my distrust, but many people were attracted to his hearty laugh and good-old-boy manners. He had not risen from being an uneducated oil field welder to owner of Alaska's largest private company on his intelligence—Allen needed Rick Smith to help handle his political dealings, because he didn't get the details. But Allen knew how to make people like him and do his bidding. He fished with Ted and they shared a love of good red wine and cigars, and Ted apparently enjoyed those masculine bonds. One of the hardest challenges of high office—and one that probably grows harder as the years pass—is knowing who your real friends are.

Among Ted's best old friends was Jack Roderick, who had shared a law office with him in Anchorage before either of them got into politics. (Jack was Anchorage borough mayor in the 1970s.) As Jack related in an unpublished memoir, he challenged Ted for associating so closely with Bill Allen. This was after Ben was implicated but before the cabin search in Girdwood. Jack told *The New York Times* that everyone knew that Bill Allen went over the line in influencing legislators in Juneau.

Ted responded to his old friend with a private note, saying, "How did it happen, with Allen being an 'Alaskan of the Year' and receiving all kinds of awards as one of Alaska's most successful businessmen. Everyone knew he was bribing people? Why didn't someone tell me?"

Pete Kott went on trial in federal court in Anchorage that fall. Like everyone else, I assumed his prosecution was legitimate and the system was working to clean out corruption in the legislature, as unpleasant and distasteful as that process was. We had seen video of Kott accepting the bribes and bragging about it in the Baranof

Hotel. But during that trial, Bill Allen also testified that his company, Veco, had remodeled Ted's Girdwood cabin without being paid for the work. The courtroom audibly gasped at Ted's name, as did the entire political world. Ted had not reported any free work from Veco on his financial disclosure forms. That alone could be a violation of the law, even without any indication that Ted had done anything in return for Allen or Veco.

What we didn't know then—because prosecutors hid the fact—was that Allen was accustomed to lying to get out of trouble, and that the Justice Department had helped him get away with it. The Anchorage Police Department had been investigating him for sexual assault and for having sex with girls as young as fifteen, one of whom he flew across state lines for that purpose, while giving expensive gifts to her and her family. He then induced her to lie in a sworn affidavit denying the sexual abuse. To protect their witness, FBI agents called off an Anchorage police investigation of those crimes, and federal prosecutors later suppressed the information, keeping it away from defendants, the juries, and the court. If the juries had known the truth, Allen probably wouldn't have been believed in anything he said.

We know all this now because two major investigations looked into the extensive government misconduct in Polar Pen: one an investigation by the Department of Justice and the other by a special counsel appointed by a federal judge. Their reports, well over a thousand pages in all, detail the extraordinary actions of FBI agents and federal prosecutors who had gone off the rails, breaking the rules and, in the judgment of the special counsel, lying and intentionally distorting the trial process to win a false conviction against Ted Stevens.

In April 2008, before he was indicted, Stevens's attorneys gave prosecutors evidence that should have stopped the investigation. Ted's wife, Catherine, had paid invoices totaling $140,000—all the invoices they had received—for remodeling work by an Anchorage contractor. The project was being managed by a friend in Girdwood, restaurant owner Bob Persons. Veco employees did some additional construction, but Ted twice wrote to Bill Allen, asking to be given all the invoices, telling him to work with Persons to make sure everything was paid correctly, and reminding him of the serious consequences if he violated ethics rules by accepting anything for free.

As soon as they received copies of the notes Ted had written to Allen, federal lawyers knew this new evidence could sink the investigation they had worked on for years. No jury would blame Ted for failing to report unpaid work if he had twice requested all the bills and had paid every bill he had received. Four prosecutors and an FBI agent met with Bill Allen to question him again—although all five conveniently forgot about this meeting and conveniently misplaced all the records of it. Allen said he didn't remember Ted's notes and had never talked to Bob Persons about them; he also said numbers the government was using as the cost for the work Veco did were three times too high. After the meeting, the FBI agent told Allen the lawyers were upset with him and that the meeting had gone badly. As the trial approached, she urged him, "You better figure out or remember" Ted's notes and what Persons had said. Prosecutors also kept using the higher numbers in their case. And they never disclosed to the defense or the court what Allen had said about the notes or the costs.

Allen apparently got the message about the prosecutors' wishes, however, because he changed his story a week before the trial, in September, now saying he did remember talking to Bob Persons and that Bob had told him to ignore the notes Ted had written, because Ted was just "covering his ass." Allen testified to that at trial. At the same time, he also lied and said that this had always been his story. The government lawyers sitting in the courtroom knew he was lying about that, but they said nothing, and even underlined the lie as key evidence in their closing argument—a deep violation of their duty.

I repeat all this detail because it didn't come out until years later, well after the public had formed false opinions about the case. From these reports, it is clear not only that Ted Stevens's prosecution was egregiously unfair but also that he never should have been charged. Bill Allen withheld construction invoices for his own reasons, without telling Ted. Then he lied to implicate Ted and please the prosecutors who had given his family and company immunity in the other bribery cases. The flaws in the case were not just the result of sloppy work. The special counsel found, beyond a reasonable doubt, that the prosecutors' misconduct had been intentional, and he wrote that he would have recommended criminal charges against them if not for the thinnest technicality: the trial judge had not specifically ordered them to comply with the law.

One of the prosecutors committed suicide. The others were reassigned, and at least embarrassed, although unfortunately none faced sanctions for their misconduct. Ted Stevens's extraordinary reputation as a lifelong public servant was destroyed and his political career ended. Only Bill Allen benefited, the briber and sexual abuser of girls who had initiated all the wrongdoing. He was never prosecuted for his sex crimes or his perjury, and he and his family retained a fortune worth more than a hundred million dollars. This was a travesty of justice.

After Ted's indictment, fourteen weeks before Election Day, most of his Washington friends and colleagues abandoned him, not only Sarah Palin. Plenty of senators whispered support, but few publicly stayed by his side. Dan Inouye made a strong statement, Kay Bailey Hutchison traveled to Alaska for a campaign appearance with Ted (earlier in her career, she also had been falsely accused and exonerated), and I did everything I could. Ted stayed strong, never confiding any private feelings of vulnerability to me, and I believe his confidence was real. That was how deeply he believed in the system. I believed in it, too.

But the political situation was worrisome. Anchorage's popular mayor, Democrat Mark Begich, was running hard against Ted. The defense requested a speedy trial—Ted was adamant that his name be cleared before the election in November. The Department of Justice agreed and sped it up even more. Ted couldn't campaign while sitting in a D.C. courtroom, so I stepped up to be his surrogate in Alaska, traveling the state to speak at every event where he would have appeared.

Listening to voters in rural Alaska, I began to worry. Alaska Native people had been Ted's stalwart supporters for decades, from tiny villages in the most remote place on earth. It was easy for me to assure them that Ted would be acquitted, because I believed it. And I pointed out that in his forty years in office, Ted had done more for rural Alaska than any other person in history. But people's reactions were subdued and concerned. A young mother living in a river village in western Alaska might not know that Ted Stevens was responsible for the clinic where she got care and the sewer and water system that kept her family healthy, but she would know he was on trial for corruption. Unfortunately, when I told his campaign team about my misgivings, they pushed back hard, pointing out that the leaders of the Alaska Native corporations had all endorsed Ted. I knew that, but folks in the villages didn't.

Eight days before the election, the jury delivered a guilty verdict on seven felony counts. McCain and Palin called on Ted to resign, as did Majority Leader Mitch McConnell and several of Ted's other Republican colleagues in the Senate. I felt empty, so disappointed in my colleagues—I absolutely believed Ted was innocent. Ted planned to come back to campaign, and I would be there alongside him. Jim Jansen, Ted's longtime friend, set up a rally in his airplane hangar to welcome Ted back to Alaska, near the airport that bore his name. Anchorage was cold and dark that late October day. I wondered with Jim how many people would come, and which Alaska politicians would stand by their friend. Although a few retired elected officials were there, many did not appear, including politicians and hangers-on who had been the most ardent admirers of Ted in all his power but abandoned him as a man as soon as he needed them.

As we waited for Ted to arrive, however, Jim and I were relieved to see the hangar fill with people. There were some staffers and campaign workers in upscale East Coast clothing inappropriate for the weather, but many more who came were ordinary Alaskans—men with long, shaggy beards wearing insulated Carhartt coveralls for outdoor work in the cold. Some wore T-shirts that said, "F*#@ the feds, vote for Ted." They cheered when Ted arrived with his family, loud with gratitude for his lifetime of service and still hoping he could win. I stood proudly with Ted in front of the media's cameras. There were a lot of tears from his family, and people thanked me for standing by him—but how could they think I would not? A reporter wrote that Ted's speech was defiant but humble. Ted took blame for having Bill Allen as a friend yet insisted he was innocent, and predicted that the prosecutorial misconduct in his case would lead to his exoneration—as it indeed did, in less than six months.

"My future is in God's hands," he told the audience. "Alaska's future is in your hands."

After everything, Begich barely won that race, and only with the help of rural Alaska Natives and members of the military—ironically enough, as those had been the greatest beneficiaries of Ted's service. I didn't blame those voters for not knowing. I blamed the broken legal process that had falsely told them their senator was corrupt.

Thanks to Begich's improbable election—even after the conviction, fewer than four thousand votes divided him from Stevens—Democrats won a filibuster-proof, sixty-seat majority in the U.S. Senate and were able to pass President Barack Obama's legislative initiative without Republican votes, including the Affordable Care Act. Dishonest prosecutors working in a Republican administration had changed the course of history in favor of the Democrats. To the Obama administration's credit, Attorney General Eric Holder helped expose the misconduct and ultimately exonerated Ted. But the full facts didn't come out until almost four years after the trial.

My world had changed. Not only had I lost my mentor and essential colleague and partner, I had lost my deep and perhaps insufficiently nuanced faith in our judicial process. I began to think more about the quality of the people within our legal institutions and the importance of their temperament and integrity to fulfill their duties with impartiality and fairness. Indeed, that proved a critical part of my outlook when faced with some of the biggest votes to come, regarding a Supreme Court confirmation and a presidential impeachment.

But first, I had more learning to do, as I faced service in the Senate without my mentor, and a reelection campaign in a changing political world of increasing populism and extremism.

CHAPTER 3

If There's a Harder Way, We'll Find It

IN RETROSPECT, TODAY'S DIFFICULT era of division and resentment began in 2009. The so-called MAGA movement, this personality cult that has ripped us apart, was born, with another name, during the first two years after President Obama was elected. The virulent spread of angry populism transformed American politics.

For me, the events of 2009 and 2010 made a career as an "average" senator untenable, and I was forced to decide if I would quit public service or take a bold step to represent Alaskans in a new and more authentic way. That was when I learned the true purpose of my public service, and it's why I have something to say now that I believe is important.

This is that story. It begins in anger.

Americans had plenty to be angry about in 2009, after the financial crisis disrupted lives and spawned a deep recession. The previous year, during the last days of the Bush administration, Congress had passed huge appropriations to rescue the economy. That money saved some of the same financial institutions whose leaders had caused the disaster. Without intervention, the crisis could have been much worse for everyone, but the unfairness of these bailouts was obvious, and it frustrated ordinary Americans. I shared some of these feelings.

In February, a TV commentator on a cable news show called *Squawk Box* crystallized these feelings with a rant delivered from a bond trading floor in Chicago, calling for a new Boston Tea Party. Within ten days, Tea Party groups had cropped up around the nation, operating independently but often with ample funding from traditional conservative groups.

The Tea Party movement was real and powerful. It activated grassroots conservatives in the Republican Party with a loud, indignant voice. But, like Palin's populism in Alaska, the Tea Party was powered by emotion, not by information or reasoning. It gained strength from anger, resentment, and fear. Many Americans were legitimately afraid of losing freedoms from Obama's many proposals, especially his healthcare bill. But for some, that fear mixed with some amount of racism. Donald Trump was making a name for himself with an absurd and dishonest challenge to Obama's birthright citizenship, and Palin was egging him on.

Tea Party populism lacked a coherent political center, because it drew its energy from applause lines—also much like Palin. Tea Party Republicans were angry about government debt. They wanted big budget cuts, lower taxes, and less regulation. I often agreed, but their solutions were unworkable, and they simultaneously supported expensive and complex federal programs. Any politician unwilling to pander to those contradictory wishes felt the Tea Partiers' wrath. Rowdy crowds packed congressional town hall meetings and turned them into shouting matches. At a town hall in South Carolina, an angry constituent demanded of his Republican congressman, "Keep your government hands off my Medicare." The man wouldn't believe that his healthcare was already being provided by the government.

Sarah Palin stoked Tea Party fear in August 2009, a month after she suddenly resigned as Alaska governor, with an inflammatory Facebook post claiming that Obama's healthcare bill included "death panels" of bureaucrats who would review patients' value to society before deciding if each would receive healthcare—including, she asserted, her baby Trig, born with Down syndrome. Her statement caught fire on the internet and in the media, because it created a recognizable boogeyman to stand for the anxiety people felt about Obama's bill. But it was a lie. I did not support the bill, which I thought was too big, too expensive, and contained excessive mandates for small businesses, and also because it did little to address the cost of healthcare or the unique conditions of my rural state. But as much as I disliked the bill, I believed in telling the truth. I told an Anchorage audience, "There is no reason to gin up fear in the American public by saying things that are not included in the bill." The Tea Party would use that statement to attack me.

Emotions ran high that summer of 2009. The Anchorage Police Department asked the public not to bring guns to a town hall meeting on the healthcare bill held by Mark Begich, after people on talk radio suggested they should. I held town halls in five cities to talk about the bill. The first session was in Fairbanks, two days after my comments about Palin, in a full auditorium at Pioneer Park. I had been told to expect disruption, and I was pleasantly surprised as the evening progressed. People expressed strong feelings, but everyone was courteous. The event was ending when I overrode the moderator and took one more question, from a bearded man in the back of the room. He spoke up with the angry, confrontational voice that was being heard from the Tea Party activists across the country—and attacked me for calling out Palin's death panel falsehood. As we left, I thought it had been a good event, except for that one jackass at the end, who turned out to be a lawyer named Joe Miller.

That was my first encounter with the man who would nearly end my political life.

———

After his defeat in 2008, Ted Stevens gave a gracious and moving farewell address to the Senate. The chamber was full, with senators sitting motionless and silent. Ted had not yet been exonerated, and while he insisted on his innocence, he spoke warmly, with gratitude, not rancor. "I have two homes," he said. "One is right here in this chamber, and the other is my beloved state of Alaska. I must leave one to return to the other." Summing up the past—his accomplishments, chairmanships, and many battles—he said, "That's it, Mr. President, forty years distilled into a few minutes." Thinking of the future, he turned toward me, sitting a few desks to his right, saying he was confident I could carry on the work for Alaska. My feelings must have shown on my face. He left his prepared remarks and said, "My steadfast partner in the Senate, Senator Lisa Murkowski, to whom I owe so much, and I admire so much. She really has been a true friend and a true partner and I really wish her well in the future here."

Without Ted in the Senate, and in a political world that was changing rapidly, I seemed to have graduated from the stability of elementary school to the uncertain first day of middle school. I was the senior senator from Alaska now, although I doubt anyone thought of me that way, with only six years of service; nor did I really think of myself that way. Don Young, a member of the House since 1973, was our delegation's senior leader. My new Senate colleague Mark Begich, the former mayor of Anchorage, was ambitious and talented but politically precarious, as a Democrat from a very red state. Many people believed, indeed, that I also had become too liberal to represent Alaska, especially during the Tea Party era, and with my reelection coming up in the next round, in 2010.

Throughout my time in politics, I have been more moderate than most Alaska Republican Party leaders, but when I started, I used to sit at state conventions with other moderates who thought like me. Those seats had changed. Moderate Republicans grew old and retired or disengaged because they felt they no longer belonged. My inspiration in politics, Arliss Sturgulewski, ultimately disclaimed the Alaska Republican Party, changing her registration to nonpartisan. She said, "I didn't leave the party, the party left me."

Warnings began reaching me of disquiet in the Alaska party as I voted on Obama's appointments to the courts and his administration. I've always believed—and I think the founders intended—that the Senate's role in advice and consent for presidential nominees should focus primarily on the qualifications for the office. The president deserves to pick his team. As the Senate became more polarized, and confirmation votes fell largely on party lines, I more often found myself voting against my party on nominees. If the president put up a qualified nominee, I would consider supporting that person rather than, as the majority of my Republican colleagues did, issuing an automatic dismissal because he or she was an Obama nominee.

My primary job has always been to fight for Alaska. The federal government owns over 60 percent of Alaska's landmass and controls most of our waters and fish, our timber and the petroleum and minerals underground. With a Democrat in the White House, I needed to give the administration a reason to care about our issues. Votes on nominees put me in a position to argue for what my state needed. Giving a confirmation vote to an Obama nominee could build a bridge to an official who would control our destiny. When Alaska needed help later, my phone calls would be answered.

There was a price to pay for being receptive to Obama's nominees. Political operatives chart voting records to illustrate where each senator stands in relation to the president, and my advisers saw my location on those maps moving too close to Obama for the comfort of our state party. These concerns had less to do with Alaska and more with political labels. The anger driving the party allowed no room for nuance or compromise, or even for positive proposals. The Tea Party didn't know what it favored, but it certainly knew what it was against—Barack Obama, his agenda, and anyone who helped him.

Most votes in Congress are not matters of deep conscience. While there are no "easy" votes—every one of them affects people, as well as our own integrity—it is all too easy to weigh the pressure of party on the scales of these decisions. On both sides of the aisle, leadership supports senators by providing policy guidance and a clear strategic path. Sometimes we come out of our conference lunches with pocket cards of talking points on the party's positions and helpful statistics backing them up. Even when senators start out as independent voices, we can fall into the groove of following party leadership, because that is such a clear, well-worn path. I did that more often than I like to admit to myself, during those two years leading up to my reelection. Objectively, there was nothing wrong with that choice, as a Republican senator following Republican leadership in what I said and the positions I supported. But these positions weren't ones I had earned. Rather than immerse myself in both sides of issues to reach a conclusion, I was accepting my own team's side. For many in Congress, going along with the conference seems the wiser, safer path, but I was like a student handing in math assignments with correct answers that didn't come from her own homework.

In 2009, Mitch McConnell, then the Republican minority leader, asked me to run for conference vice chair, part of the leadership team. The post would rank fifth in our party, and I was honored to be asked. But a somewhat less flattering reality explained why. Kay Bailey Hutchison had departed from the leadership as she began her campaign for governor of Texas, and without a woman to replace her, our Republican leadership would be composed entirely of White men—not a good picture when stepping in front of the cameras. Other than Kay and me, only two other Republican women were serving in the Senate at the time, Susan Collins and Olympia Snowe, both of Maine, and both moderates like me. I ran unopposed and stepped up the ladder of the Senate. I had always known that the key to helping my state would be to accumulate seniority and positions of power. As conference vice chair, I would also demonstrate that I could be a Republican team player as I faced reelection.

But, again, I paid a price. No rule says that a member of the leadership must vote with the conference position, but some adherence is implicit in the job, since it is the role of the leaders to hold the conference together to achieve the objectives party members jointly support. I came out of conference meetings with the other leaders to represent our positions to the news media. Taking a contrary view would have been counterproductive to the team and would have undermined the purpose of holding the role. Accordingly, I adopted a new tone, taking on the stereotypical conservative rhetoric blasting the Left and calling every environmentalist an extremist. After spending six years as Ted Stevens's Senate understudy, I thought it made sense to join the team and move upward in the system, even if I sometimes had to alter my true voice to sound more partisan.

Ted himself had mastered the system, with an extraordinary list of chairmanships and leadership positions. But when Ted joined the Senate, in 1968, partisanship had a different meaning than it did in the Tea Party era. He constantly demonstrated that with his relationships, especially with the friendship of Daniel Inouye. Filibusters were extremely rare back then. The Senate, even when I'd arrived, had remained a truly deliberative body, with bills that worked their way through committees before arriving on the floor as hard-fought compromises. Senators from far ends of the political spectrum prided themselves on working together, as when Ted Kennedy and Bob Dole passed the Americans with Disabilities Act in 1990, a time when Democrats controlled both houses of Congress and Republican President George H. W. Bush was in the White House. In 2009, the Tea Party wasn't the only force driving greater partisanship in Congress, but the division it engendered made it much more difficult to cooperate with the Democrats, especially President Obama. For a senator, moving up within the party became even more important, because more decisions were made within private meetings of party conferences, not in committees or on the floor.

I didn't fully realize it at the time, but Alaskans sensed that I wasn't being authentic. My team was marketing me as a true red-blooded conservative to win over voters in the upcoming closed

Republican Party primary, a bloc now fully engaged with the Tea Party. And I was allowing my politics to play along, representing just that slice of my constituents instead of all of them, as had always been my ideal. These were good people who worked for me, and they were doing what appeared necessary to fight another day in the arena in which we found ourselves. I was on board with that: to serve Alaskans, we needed to stay in office and accumulate influence. But a senator has only three things of great value: her vote, her reputation, and her integrity. By moving to the right for the primary election, I risked cheapening those three things—of which my integrity is most dear to me. American voters have become cynical, believing politics is just about doing whatever it takes to get elected. I had never bought into that, but now, perhaps, I was contributing to it.

The last person in the world I would have wanted to call me out on this did. "She's voted like a liberal the last six years and now she wants to recast herself as a conservative." It was that jackass from the back of the Fairbanks town hall meeting on healthcare, Joe Miller, who in April 2010 had announced that he would challenge me in the primary. He was deep into Tea Party conservatism, telling reporters on the state capitol steps that he wanted to halt the nation's "headlong plunge into socialism." But my Democratic opponent made the same point—the mild-mannered mayor of Sitka, Scott McAdams—saying I had abandoned my core as a moderate to tack to the right.

This mattered most not because of where I stood on the political spectrum. It mattered most because I was in danger of losing my greatest asset—being who I truly am—and letting down the people who had believed in me.

That spring, I sat down with a group of family, friends, and political supporters at one of their homes in Anchorage for the express purpose of asking if this was true. Had I gone too far to the right, betraying my true identity? Around the living room, in turn, each of those I had invited nodded yes. Andrew Halcro, my old friend from the legislature, said, "We get that you have to go along to get along, but you're Lisa Murkowski, and this is not you."

———

No one thought Joe Miller had a chance, least of all me. I met him for the first time in 2010, at a Memorial Day observance in the Mat-Su Valley, an hour north of Anchorage. The organizers had invited me to speak to a crowd of a couple of hundred people. In the audience, I saw Miller with his wife, Kathleen. Miller was a slender man with a dark, close-cropped beard and an upright bearing suggestive of his West Point education. Six weeks after declaring himself a candidate in the Republican primary, he remained completely unknown. I greeted him and asked how his campaign was going. The answer was poorly. He had been unable to raise enough money even to travel, so he was campaigning only by car, which kept him out of the roadless majority of Alaska. That day, after a long drive and attendance at the warm outdoor event, he hadn't even been introduced by the master of ceremonies, much less allowed to speak. I wished them well and told Kathleen that I knew this campaign process would be hard on both of them and their eight kids. She thanked me and said she would pray for me, and I said I would do the same for them.

There was no reason to fear Joe Miller in the primary, or McAdams in the general—the latter had reportedly signed up for the race on a whim, and his campaign was nearly nonexistent. No Democrats had wanted to run. My poll numbers were high, with approval near 70 percent, and my campaign account was full. Given the size of the federal government in the Alaska economy, voters understood the importance of my seniority in the Senate for the state's continued prosperity. Moreover, my campaign team had plenty of experience, with consultants who had previously worked for me and for my father decades earlier. I planned to concentrate on my Senate work and let the professionals do their job.

My disengaged attitude was only one similarity to the 2002 legislative race, in which Nancy Dahlstrom almost beat me. Another similarity: I was in the sights of powerful people with a grudge who saw the primary as the way to take me down. Sarah Palin endorsed Miller at the beginning of June, which got the attention of the Tea Party Express, a well-funded political action committee run by a campaign consultancy in California. It threw its support behind Miller two weeks later, saying my defeat would be its top priority. In Utah, the group had just helped defeat the very conservative Senator Bob Bennett for nomination to a fourth term. Bob was my dear friend and a senior member of our caucus, with a distinguished record and deep Utah roots. The Tea Party attacked him for being part of the problem in Washington because he had been willing to work with Democrats on healthcare and had voted in favor of President Bush's fiscal crisis bailout, the Troubled Asset Relief Program (TARP). Both could be said of me, as well. The Tea Party Express issued a victory message that said, "You're next, Lisa Murkowski."

My gut told me Alaska was different. I wasn't meeting a lot of angry people in the grocery aisles or on community visits. The individuals who popped up in the media as representing the Tea Party came out of nowhere—no one knew who they were. Palin might be a Tea Party darling nationally, but after she abruptly quit her job as governor of Alaska in 2009, she was no longer popular in our state.

On top of that, some of Joe Miller's positions were fringe and unpopular. He called himself a "constitutionalist." He wanted to phase out Social Security and Medicare and to abolish the Department of Education, because it was not explicitly listed in the Constitution (which, I pointed out, is also true of the Air Force). He took the side of urban sport hunters against the subsistence rights of rural Alaskans, a stand deeply threatening to Alaska Natives. And he had problems with his personal story, too. Despite his Yale law degree, his work record was spotty, and embarrassing issues about his past had begun to surface soon after he'd entered the race. He surrounded himself with questionable people. In July, at the Bear Paw Festival parade in Eagle River, near Anchorage, he marched with a campaign Humvee and a group of twelve men wearing his T-shirts and openly carrying AR-15 rifles and semiautomatic pistols, some of whom turned out to be members of a private militia (one was later convicted of conspiring to murder judges and police officers). I couldn't believe people would take him seriously.

I've always avoided any negative campaigning, and my team felt that it would be counterproductive even to talk about Miller—he was so unknown, we would only be bringing attention to him. I stayed in Washington except for the Senate breaks around holidays and my flip-turn trips on weekends. I also had an ace in the hole. At the end of July, with the primary election less than four weeks away, Ted Stevens recorded a powerful testimonial for me. He had been exonerated and his conviction cleared, and he once again stood as a historic giant for Alaskans, especially Republicans. My communications director, Steve Wackowski, who had been a close aide and friend to Ted, went to Girdwood to film the ad. (An Air Force reservist, Steve was often known by his military handle, "Wacko.") When they were done filming, Ted invited Wacko to join him on a fly-in fishing trip the following weekend, at a lodge owned by the GCI telecom company. A week later, Steve had his bags ready to go by the door, but I needed him on the campaign instead.

That first weekend of August started my full-time campaigning in-state, beginning with a packed Saturday at the Blueberry Arts Festival in Ketchikan. We were scheduled to attend the Tanana Valley State Fair, in Fairbanks, on Monday with a *New York Times* photographer, so Steve came along, as did another aide, Rachel Kallander. Timed so close before the primary, the fair is always a good place to measure the community's political temperature, and I watched for how many Murkowski buttons I saw compared to Miller's. A lot had changed since Memorial Day. The straw poll held annually by the League of Women Voters booth went in Miller's favor, 313 to 212. We laughed it off, since that poll is notoriously easy to manipulate by sending supporters to stuff the ballot box.

But we also knew—or should have—that it's the more energetic and organized campaign that does the stuffing.

We were staying the night at my sister Eileen's home, the house I grew up in on the Chena River, with the boxcars and barn. Eileen was away, but her daughter Kimberly was home for the summer and cooked our dinner. It was a lovely evening. With the sun high, we drank wine and discussed the campaign. But at about nine P.M., Steve received a worrisome call from a newspaper reporter about a plane that had gone down in the Bristol Bay region in Southwest Alaska—a plane that had taken off from the GCI lodge. We stopped drinking. I called an old high school friend at GCI, someone who had been at the lodge but had not gotten on the plane, and learned that Ted Stevens had been on board. We sat in silence, waiting for terrible news. We didn't know it yet, but the single-engine de Havilland Otter, with eight passengers and the pilot aboard, had hit a mountain that afternoon on an outing away from the lodge to fish for silver salmon. For three hours, no one had realized the plane was missing. Brave helicopter pilots had dropped medics in fog, wind, and closing darkness that evening, some distance from the crash, and they fought their way through brush and tangled alders to get to the plane, but no rescue would be possible until the next morning.

In Fairbanks, we waited for news in Eileen's living room. The sun finally set after ten-thirty P.M. and the sky mostly darkened, as it does for a few hours at that time of year. Sitting in the gloom, we talked about Ted, his legacy, our memories, and the injustice done to him by the Justice Department, and then we would remember the others, also possibly dead, who were friends as well. Many Alaskans have stood this kind of vigil, as small plane crashes are, unfortunately, so common. Many of us have known more than one person who has been lost that way. Indeed, Ted had survived a crash in 1978 that killed his first wife, Ann. He had worked hard in the Senate to make flying safer, as had the pilot of the Otter, Terry Smith, who was an Alaska aviation legend.

Finally, Wacko reached friends at the Air National Guard Rescue Coordination Center in Anchorage, folks he knew from his own military service. He told them he was with me and that we needed to know. They confirmed that Ted Stevens was dead. We later learned that four others had died as well: Dana Tindall and Bill Phillips, both of them my friends of many years; Dana's sixteen-year-old daughter, Corey; and the pilot, Terry. The others were seriously injured. I knew everyone on the plane. I was utterly shocked, utterly devastated. New feelings came over me that I would never have expected, as I imagined the world as it now existed. I realized that Ted had never left me as my Senate mentor, until now. The load had shifted. I was a different person.

I said, out loud, "Now I am all alone."

We went to bed and tried to sleep, feeling it was our responsibility to be rested for whatever would happen the next day. The state would be in shock. Someone had to be in charge. In the morning we canceled my Fairbanks schedule and flew to Anchorage, where I met the media at the airport, on a brilliant sunny morning, my emotions evident for all to see. The reporters were in tears, too. They quoted me saying, "He was a great man and his memory will be honored for as long as I am on this earth."

I suspended the campaign and pulled all our advertising. The state was in mourning. Instead, we turned to helping the recovery and the family, with special aircraft needed to bring back the bodies and with support setting up Ted's services, in Anchorage and Washington. My staff and I did everything but bake casseroles. Miller stood down his campaign for a few days, too.

The service at Anchorage Baptist Temple, then the state's largest church, was like nothing ever seen in Alaska, with more people in attendance and more dignitaries than had ever been gathered, including five governors, twenty current or former senators, and Vice President Joe Biden. I vividly recall, as I rode to the church in a car behind the hearse, seeing people standing along the road for miles, in the damp weather, to see Ted's procession pass. In my eulogy, I talked about all the lives Ted had touched in Alaska, and the affection and grief that Alaskans were showing in response, with signs in Utqiagvik, an impromptu community gathering in Cordova, and even the heartfelt testimonial given by an Alaska Airlines flight attendant over the intercom during my flight from Fairbanks to Anchorage.

After the service, some of us gathered for dinner at the Crow's Nest restaurant, atop the Hotel Captain Cook, overlooking the city, and I was seated with my friend Bob Bennett, who was finishing his lame-duck term after his Tea Party defeat in Utah. Bob wanted my undivided attention, and I listened to him. He wanted to warn me. He said he had campaigned just as hard as he always had, but that the Tea Party had changed the rules. His experience and accomplishments had become liabilities rather than assets, because their movement was driven by anger against the status quo and all those who held authority. His willingness to compromise and reach solutions became suspect by people who viewed bipartisanship as betrayal. I listened, but I wasn't concerned. Alaska wasn't Utah. I continued to believe that Alaskans wouldn't fall for Tea Party populism.

The next day, a Thursday, our campaign started up again, after having gone dark for ten days. The election was four days away, the following Tuesday. Those of us who had been close to Ted found it difficult to put our hearts into our work. I debated Miller on statewide TV that night, our last face-to-face encounter. He was strong and articulate, focusing on my weaknesses with conservative Republicans: my pro-choice stand, my vote for TARP, and his false charge that I had supported Obama's healthcare bill. In fact, the airwaves had been full of that charge, partly from his campaign, but mostly from the Tea Party Express, with a big media buy blanketing the state that had gone unanswered from my side through the entire period of mourning Ted's death. Alaskans believed the Obamacare charge, and my poll numbers dropped steeply while Miller's rose. A talk radio personality in Anchorage, Dan Fagan, began dedicating his show, all day, every day, to blasting me over Obamacare and for not being conservative enough.

I don't think anyone thought we were going to lose, but my campaign was nervous. We had run an incumbent campaign as if there were no opponent. In doing so, we had allowed the ever-rising Tea Party to define us. We had held back significant money in our campaign account, saving it for after the primary. And we'd gone dark during the key weeks when voters were making their decisions.

With only one weekend left, my consultants wanted to act, and their chosen solution was to play our hole card, the ad Steve Wackowski had filmed of Ted Stevens strongly endorsing me, taped just three weeks earlier. I absolutely refused, and refused to even raise it with the Stevens family. I would not put them in that position at the depth of their grief, and I would not take advantage of my friend, who had not even been buried yet (he was laid to rest the next month in Arlington National Cemetery). I have never doubted that decision.

That weekend would be our wedding anniversary. Verne and I had a tradition of taking an anniversary camping trip with two other families whose kids had grown up with ours. It shows just how confident I remained that we didn't cancel it—we camped and the kids fished on the Kenai River, and then attended a campaign rally in Soldotna the next day. A lot of my supporters probably had the same attitude. Turnout is usually low in these late-summer primary elections in Alaska, when everyone is enjoying the tail end of the fishing season and getting kids ready for school, not paying much attention to politics or the news. And my supporters assumed everything was okay—as our low-key campaign had implicitly communicated to them.

On election night, a rowdy crowd of supporters and staff gathered at our campaign headquarters in a strip mall in Midtown Anchorage. The first votes came in showing Miller in the lead. I assumed these had been ballots from some very conservative precinct. But then the next batch was from Anchorage, which we considered a stronghold, and his lead held. Hour by hour, I watched each new count come in without a change in the trend—so focused on the numbers that when I looked around, I realized the party was over. The room was practically empty but for my family and our closest friends. That was when the reality hit, that we had lost the night. I was stunned. But I still thought we would win when the absentee ballots were counted.

When I got home, both boys were in bed, and I told them, with a kiss good night, that we could lose this election. They said no—they were confident of the absentees, and I really assumed they were right. A couple of days later, I flew to Colorado to help Nic move into a new off-campus house, and then I flew to Washington for Matt's first day of school. I returned to Anchorage a week later feeling anxious but cautiously optimistic about the final counting of the absentee ballots.

When the news arrived at the headquarters, it was not good. The team huddled to talk about what to do—could the very last overseas ballots change the outcome? My numbers guy came back and said no. Although the count was not final, I realized the race was over. I had not prepared myself for this, and I didn't know what I would say, but I knew the honorable thing would be to concede. Who had Joe Miller's phone number? Wacko called his counterpart at the other campaign and gave me his phone. I stepped outside. My sister Carol followed me out the back door to give me moral support, standing by a green dumpster in the asphalt alleyway. I told Miller that I would be announcing my concession shortly and congratulated him on his victory.

He did something I would never have imagined. Instead of thanking me or being conciliatory, Miller was abrupt and immediately demanded to know if I would endorse him. When I said I wasn't ready to think about that, he went into a hard sell, telling me how an endorsement would benefit the party, and so on. I replied that I would have to think about it. He asked if he could have my cell number so he could call me about it again. I said no and hung up. I turned to Carol and said, "I can't believe this guy."

My perceptive mother, a great believer in good manners, has pointed out that Joe Miller might have ended up a senator if he had been more polite on that call. I might have reacted differently in the weeks ahead, as supporters pushed me to run, if my emotions had been sad and resigned that afternoon, instead of how I did feel: searingly, white-hot angry. Over the weeks ahead, I would keep coming back to that moment and the way his arrogance made me feel.

But first, I had to face my supporters. We had called in the media. I asked my team to smile and not be too downcast as they surrounded me for the cameras. I highlighted the bright side to the reporters—while I would not be returning to the Senate, I would be able to get a season ski pass and use it all winter for the first time in a decade. But my supporters' faces were heartbreaking. Their fake smiles only accentuated their sad expressions and red eyes.

Then Miller made his victory speech. He told the media he had talked to me on the telephone, had thanked me, and had congratulated me on a good race. Carol and I looked at each other. We could not believe it.

———

The decision I made over the next three weeks was among the most consequential of my life, and not only because of the outcome. This decision changed me and how I represent Alaskans. The decision belonged to them. My connection to them and my true responsibility became much clearer—and it has stayed that way.

The first sign we were not done came the morning after I conceded, when our core group of family, staff, and volunteers arrived at the office to dismantle the campaign. The phones would not stop ringing. Voters were calling in to say they were sorry, they hadn't bothered to vote because they thought I would win anyway, or they hadn't been able to vote in the closed Republican primary. Others confessed that they had voted for Miller to send me a message, never suspecting he could win. All begged me to keep fighting. I went on about my work, but the calls didn't stop. The phone rang constantly for days.

Lest I seem overly impressed with my own popularity, I knew that much of this groundswell came from fear, not love. Alaskans had benefited from decades of solid, mainstream representation in Congress, well aware that these positions meant much more to Alaska than to states with economies less reliant on federal decision-making. Joe Miller, with his anger and extreme positions, could blow that successful consensus apart. Moreover, his focus on draconian cuts to federal spending, if successful, would threaten an economic lifeline for our state, particularly in rural Alaska. Besides, he struck many people as a little strange and scary.

Nationally, my primary defeat was being headlined the political shock of the season, with the assumption that my career was over. Joe Biden cheered me on a call, demanding, "Goddamn it, what were those people thinking?" (In fact, I got more calls from Democrats than Republicans, as many of my colleagues remained silent.) I phoned Mike Castle, the Republican House member from Delaware running for the Senate, and warned him, just as Bob Bennett had warned me, to beware of his Tea Party primary opponent, Christine O'Donnell. The Tea Party Express had made her its next candidate. He gave this advice as little weight as I had given it, and O'Donnell went on to beat him, despite her many problems, then lost in the general election to Democrat Chris Coons after running her famous "I am not a witch" TV commercial.

Many Alaskans were unwilling to accept the outcome of the primary, especially knowledgeable people inside politics. In 1990, Governor Hickel had won after bypassing the two-party system, running on the ballot line belonging to a fringe group, the Alaska Independence Party, whose candidate withdrew after the primary to give him the spot. Perhaps, the thinking went, I could do the same kind of switch with the Libertarian Party, which possessed the only other ballot line in that year's Senate race. I would have money for a run. We had been so overconfident that our campaign account still contained $1 million in cash.

Without my involvement, intermediaries began talking to the Libertarians before I even conceded, suggesting I could carry their banner. They were interested. My opposition to the Patriot Act appealed to them. Carl Brady and some other established Republicans from my father's generation encouraged me to make the jump. I told Carl I could not be a Libertarian—I simply disagreed with too many of their positions. He asked that I at least consider the move, and I agreed to meet in person to discuss it, but said I would not change my mind.

Two days after I conceded the race, Wacko warned that a firestorm was about to erupt: Andrew Halcro had released a poll that showed I would win if I put my name on the Libertarian ticket. Their party candidate and chair told a newspaper reporter they would give me the party line if I would adopt at least some of their positions. I showed up at Carl Brady's office, where two more titans of my father's generation were waiting: Jim Jansen and banker-philanthropist Ed Rasmuson. They said I had to save Alaska from Joe Miller, they would help fund a run, and they would get the Libertarians to go along with the plan. Soon, however, I realized that the meeting was an ambush: Libertarian Party chair Scott Kohlhaas came into the room. Evidently, I had been brought here so they could squeeze me into making this decision. This, I was told, would be my only chance to remain in the Senate. I made my final decision on the spot. To Kohlhaas I explained that I was not and could never be a Libertarian. Their party platform called for complete legalization of drugs; before entering politics, I had led Alaskans for Drug-Free Youth and, in 1990 I had helped pass an initiative to re-criminalize marijuana. I told my father's friends that I would rather lose my seat than risk my integrity by carrying a flag of convenience, and I left the meeting.

Then a funny thing happened. I felt good. I realized that I had been tested with the lure of remaining a senator. I had been offered that opportunity in exchange for being untrue to myself, and untrue to my identity with Alaskans. And I had passed the test. I was okay with myself and whatever might come next.

Having ruled out a party switch, however, I knew that the probable cost was the end of politics for me. The only remaining route to reelection would be a write-in campaign, but the difficulty of winning a write-in was notorious—indeed, most political professionals considered it impossible and crazy to attempt. No statewide write-in had ever succeeded in Alaska. Nationally, a Senate seat had been won by write-in only once, in 1954, by Strom Thurmond of South Carolina (and in very different circumstances, after the death of the party's nominee). To vote for me, voters would have to correctly spell my nine-letter name, and then also fill in a bubble next to the write-in line so that the computer scanner would register the vote. It was believed to be simply too difficult. If there was a harder way, this was it.

There were a lot of good reasons not to try. A political candidate is responsible for the enormous money and effort supporters put into a campaign. Doing that for an impossible cause would be a terrible waste. And running a spoiler campaign, with no chance of winning, could distort the outcome, by taking my supporters out of contention for the real choice to be made.

I called my brother Mike, who was living in Miami at the time, as he had always given me good advice in life and politics. He said a write-in was likely impossible unless I myself was confident of success. I could only win, he said, as an "evangelist for the cause," believing that victory was within reach. In other words, voters wouldn't believe unless I did.

Strong discouraging signals came from my party and former allies. My Republican colleagues in the Senate rapidly lined up behind Miller and pledged him full support, including sending money and top advisers to Alaska. John McCain planned a campaign trip for him. Campaign professionals with national experience would be unavailable to me, including people I had worked with for years, as soon as I declared a run against the Republican nominee.

And there was another threat. My chief of staff in Washington, Karen Knutson, let me know that a move had arisen—presumably from Joe Miller's camp—to strip me of my seniority in the Republican conference. That would mean losing the power I had gained through eight years of working my way up through my committees. It would put chairmanships that much further away, and make my ability to serve Alaska the same as a freshman's—and the same as Joe Miller's. Floating the threat was supposed to deter me from running or, if I did run, to punish me for defying my party.

I couldn't worry about that. I needed to concentrate on Alaska to make my decision. If I didn't run, the seniority wouldn't matter. If I did, it was true, I *would* be going directly against my party.

I swore to myself that before I would consider running, it had to be for the right reason. I didn't want to be the kind of candidate who simply cannot accept an election loss. Certainly, I felt disappointed by the voters' decision, but I had been honest about getting my season ski pass—my life would go on without the title of "Senator." In many ways, it would be better.

My family surrounded me as I considered what to do. I tried to keep my circle small.

I've often been criticized for taking too long to decide about big issues or being too easily swayed by the people I talk to along the way to my decision. Since making decisions is a critical part of my job, I think it's strange that people fault me for putting *too much* thought into my deliberations. Facing a major vote or a decision such as the write-in, with many lives potentially affected by the outcome, I take the time necessary and listen to as many voices as I can. Since I remain open to what each has to say along the way, a strong argument can sway me, but I also recognize that my final decision will come only when I have fully processed the input. Maybe I look indecisive, especially compared to those senators whose views are so set that no one even needs to ask their positions. But I would say I am careful and serious, not indecisive. I honestly hold my mind open, sincerely weighing the evidence until I've gathered all the relevant information I can.

But for the next ten days, Alaskans insisted this was their decision, not mine. Regular people from every walk of life, most of whom I had never met, showed me that this mattered to them. Staff and family members gave me many dozens of emails a day from people urging me to run, and not only one-liners—many were long, heartfelt pleas for me to take on Joe Miller. It felt very real. Perhaps that sounds like typically self-serving political rhetoric. In truth, I would not have run but for these messages and some unforgettable encounters over those days.

The unexpected double blows of Ted Stevens's death and my defeat weighed heavily, and when I was by myself I could feel a dark sense of loss. But then something would spark a sense of defiance—and even joy. One gloomy evening, alone in my Anchorage apartment, I reached out to my cousin Anne and we agreed to meet for dinner at a restaurant called Kinley's. When I walked in, I received a standing ovation from one of the tables, and diners surrounded me, urging me to run. Our waiter, Patrick, also insisted that I had to run. I thanked him. A few minutes later, he came back with his contact information and added that he would quit his job and volunteer for my campaign full-time.

Anne said, "Lisa, you have to do it."

Soon after, I was having coffee with an Anchorage staffer, Bob Walsh, sitting in the sunshine in front of the Fire Island Bakery, near downtown. A woman rode by on a Schwinn bike with six baguettes in a basket, then turned around at the corner and came back. "I just realized who you are," she said. "I have never voted for a Republican in my life, and I am begging you to run a write-in."

Bob smiled and said, "How can you not hear that?"

On the glorious Sunday of Labor Day weekend, I sat in the rose garden on the downtown Delaney Park Strip, on a long call with

Karen Knutson, trying to cheer her up about our loss, and to get a feeling from her about what others were saying in Washington. People there saw a write-in as political suicide, but they thought I might be crazy enough to try it. I agreed: it would be crazy. As we talked, I watched a dozen teenagers playing a game that involved running around with brooms between their legs like hobby-horses—a goofy sight, but they seemed to be having fun. I decided it was time to get out of the sun and get an A&W root beer float. As I was departing, still talking to Karen, someone in the group recognized me and asked to take a group picture, which we did. They explained that they were a Quidditch team, playing the game from the Harry Potter books, only with brooms that did not fly. They were giddy, fun teenagers from Service High School, hot and sweaty from running around in the sun. I told them I was deliberating on a decision and spontaneously asked what they would do in my position. They debated the question like a political team. Finally, I asked for a show of hands. Run or don't run?

One of the kids said, "I don't know why you're asking us. We're not old enough to vote, so we don't count anyway."

"Whoa, stop right there," I said. "You count the most. You're Alaska's future. If I don't do it for the young people of Alaska, why do it at all?"

To this, one of the other kids replied, "That's exactly why you should run. For us."

I won the show of hands unanimously. I told them I would need their help if I did run. Then, as we parted, Karen spoke; I realized that she was still on the line and had been listening the whole time.

After a long pause, she said, "You have to run."

"You were just telling me it's impossible," I said. "Everyone has given up on me there."

She responded, "But you can't give up on Alaska."

All of these encounters were persuasive, but one more meeting brought promises that would prove critical. The Alaska Federation of Natives asked me to meet with their board. AFN has represented

Alaska Natives since 1966 and holds a huge, state-spanning convention every fall. When I arrived, some twenty of the most influential Alaska Native leaders were sitting around a single table, including the CEOs of each of the twelve regional Alaska Native corporations. These corporations own forty-four million acres of Alaska and today include all ten of the ten largest-grossing Alaska-based companies.

AFN president Julie Kitka started by saying that I had been a good senator, Joe Miller would be bad for rural Alaska, and they hoped I would consider running. Then she turned to those seated around the table, and each person spoke, one by one, making the case in a clear and persuasive way. I felt almost unworthy as I heard the praise of these distinguished representatives of a dozen cultures.

When it was my turn to speak, I thanked the leaders for their confidence in me. But I also stressed what the political professionals had said: that winning a write-in would be nearly impossible. If it could be done, it would take a broad coalition of Alaskans, not just the leaders. The Native corporation CEOs had supported Ted Stevens in his last run, I reminded them, but that message never got to the voters in their remote villages. Stevens lost those precincts and lost his seat. "I cannot do this alone," I said.

Georgianna Lincoln took the floor. She is Athabascan from the Yukon River village of Rampart, a leader in the Doyon regional corporation, and had been a widely respected state senator, the first Alaska Native woman elected to that body. She is known for her dignity and her resonant voice.

She stood up, her body straight, gray hair streaming all the way down her back. She said, "I will get out in my region. I will go to my villages. I will talk to all my people. I will work with you."

She turned from me to the room.

"I will stand with Lisa Murkowski," she said. "Who else will stand with me?"

Every chair slid back, and every person in the room but me rose to their feet.

The power of that demonstration was overwhelming. I still feel chills, fifteen years later, as I think of it.

I had a ticket to fly back to Washington, and Anne invited the whole family to dinner at her house the night before my departure so we could make a final decision. To run or not to run? Time was running out, and the wheels were moving forward on a write-in campaign. A meeting with family would be the right forum in which to settle it, to bless the efforts or cancel them. Anne grilled salmon in her backyard on that unseasonably warm autumn evening. About ten of us gathered around her table for a long, spirited conversation. I needed to know how these most important people felt, back at the center of my onion.

We were divided. About half said yes, half said no. Some didn't want me to go through the heartbreak of a near-certain defeat. The conversation around the dinner table went on for hours, and I had an early plane to Washington. Anne brought out an excellent bottle of champagne she had chilled to celebrate the decision. Now she said we needed to decide so we could drink it, either for a run or because we would stand down. But the conversation went on for another hour.

Finally, Carol suggested flipping a coin. Anne did the flip: heads we run, tails we don't. She caught the coin and put her hand over it. But she couldn't bear to look. Only Carol was brave enough to peel her fingers away: Heads!

We raised our glasses to the unknown ahead, drank the champagne, and went to bed.

In the morning, Kevin Sweeney arrived to drive me to the airport. Kevin was director of my Alaska office and had agreed to manage the write-in campaign. He would be assembling the team and planning an announcement of the write-in at the Dena'ina Civic and Convention Center, in Anchorage, on Friday; it was now Tuesday.

In the car, Kevin begged me to cancel my trip to Washington. He knew me well. He had been working with me for six years. He predicted that the negativity I would encounter in Washington—the nattering nabobs of negativity, as he put it—would tarnish the energy and enthusiasm I had picked up from Alaskans. This race should be driven by Alaskans, not Washington, he argued, and our best hope was the energy coming from the defiant conviction that we could do the impossible.

I wish I had listened to him.

The last encouraging word I heard was at the airport before I boarded the plane headed east. A janitor rolling a big garbage can on wheels came up next to me and said, "You have got to run. You have got to give people like me a chance."

———

Back in the Capitol, my workplace over the last eight years, I felt like a ghost. People were awkwardly avoiding me. The Democrats were somewhat warmer than members of my own caucus, but even they behaved as if I'd lost a family member and they didn't know what to say. Many of the Republicans seemed aggrieved and threatened that I was considering a write-in, which they regarded as quixotic and egotistical—"ill-advised," as Mitch McConnell put it—for they believed my run could split the Republican vote in Alaska and hand a Senate seat to the Democrats in a year when we had a chance to regain the majority. (That concern showed a complete misunderstanding of Alaska politics—the smart money saw my entry as relegating Democrat McAdams to third. His only slim chance was for me to stay out of the race.) Some people I had worked with and considered friends were distant, sympathetic at best. Others welcomed Joe Miller and were openly glad to see me go. The Tea Party wave had emboldened those who wanted a more unyielding Republican Party controlled by populist conservatives incapable of compromise. It was they who were actively scheming to strip me of my seniority, although that would not come to a vote until after I returned to Alaska.

Had the hope I'd sensed in Alaska been an illusion? Washington

was—and is—its own world, a place that believes it sets the rules
and defines the reality for everywhere else. Hope and idealism can
feel like orphans here. Maybe the optimism in Alaskans had merely
been evidence of their political naïveté. Even my two staffs seemed
to be living in different worlds. The Alaska team fed on the energy
felt there, and they remained excited and confident about a run.
The Washington staff was supportive but tentative, and some were
already circulating their résumés. Steeped in the world of how
things really work—how campaigns get money, who they spend it
with, and why candidates win—they did not believe in the same
way. The usual sources of campaign funding would be closed to me.
National pollsters, consultants, and media producers would all
avoid me, and without those resources, victory seemed out of reach.
A winning campaign needs money and professionals—and that
meant people from D.C.—or so say the experts. I felt the downward
pull of the mood, and, more than that, I knew that the experts are
usually right.

In fairness, I thought I owed it to my conference to let my colleagues know what I intended to do. At our regular Thursday lunch,
behind closed doors, I rose to talk about my decision. I confirmed,
as they all knew, that I was considering a write-in, and that I was
leaning toward doing it. I apologized for the spot this had put them
in, as my process dragged on and reporters asked their opinions
about what I should do. And I apologized, as well, because I knew a
good Republican was supposed to endorse the winner of the primary and go away. My comments were awkward with so many
apologies, as if I were doing something wrong—as the party's true
believers believed I was. Even some colleagues who behaved as
friends were working against me, as I later learned. My demise—
either electorally or if they succeeded in stripping my seniority
away—would move each up a notch and closer to committee chairmanship.

I was leaving the room, downcast, when George Voinovich of
Ohio intercepted me and said, "When I'm struggling with a deci-

sion, I go across the street to St. Joe's and I pray." That seemed like good advice. I crossed Second Avenue to St. Joseph's Roman Catholic Church, climbed the steps, and opened the heavy Gothic door to the empty church. Midafternoon light came through the stained glass. I found myself looking up at the statue of Mary standing on a bank of clouds. Underneath, writhing serpents seemed to grasp for her ankles to pull her down. I thought, "I've got to get out of Washington before the weight of negativity pulls me down."

I had more meetings that afternoon. Each was more discouraging than the last, especially with people who supported me and liked me but didn't want me to run a futile race and get hurt. My last meeting was with Mark Begich, my junior Alaska colleague. Although we are from different parties, we worked well together on Alaska issues, and he understood our state's politics. Begich went through an analysis, looking at many scenarios, all of which showed that I had no chance of winning a write-in, and that by running I would ensure Joe Miller's victory. He knew, as I did, that Miller was unsuitable for office and a threat to rural Alaska. Mark thought McAdams had a chance and was trying to build a campaign for him. Obviously, his analysis was self-serving, but I found it persuasive, coming after what everyone else had said. I left the meeting convinced. I could not win. That was why campaign professionals wouldn't work with me. That was why fundraising had dried up. That was why everyone said, *Give up*. No one had done it successfully in fifty-six years. Because it couldn't be done.

I had asked the staff to stay late that evening so I could share my announcement. I could feel their excitement when I walked back into the office. They thought I was going to tell them I was running a write-in. Instead, I told them I could not—I could not lead them and our supporters into a pointless loss. Their desolate faces broke my heart. I did it next with the Alaska staff and my campaign team, via videoconference, shocking them to tears, as they truly believed we could win. Our big announcement had been scheduled for the next day, at the Dena'ina Center, and they were planning that event

as a huge campaign kickoff rally, with live media. I told Steve Wackowski to cancel the venue and to set up a small media briefing instead. Then I went home to tell Verne we couldn't do it. Standing in
the living room, wrapped in his arms, I cried tears of defeat.

Verne and I split up the list of family members to begin making
phone calls. For the most part, my sisters and cousins said, with
disappointment, that they understood my decision and would support my choice. I then called my dad.

After I laid out the situation, he said, "You don't quit at anything.
You've never been a quitter."

I grew defensive. I had called to tell him my decision, not ask
advice. I explained that this wasn't about me or about quitting, this
was about facing up to reality and protecting my family and supporters from false hope.

He wouldn't accept it. As we went back and forth, his voice remained infuriatingly calm, while mine continued to rise.

"You love Alaska too much," he said. "You won't give up on
Alaska."

I said, "I can't do this," then shouted, "I'm done!" as I hung up on
him.

"What was that all about?" Verne asked from across the room,
where he had been making calls.

I was crying again, this time in anger.

"He won't let me quit."

I called Carol to share my frustration at our dad.

"Well, but he's right," she said. "You do care too much."

Early the next morning, as Verne and I were leaving for the airport,
Matt came downstairs in his fuzzy striped bathrobe to say goodbye
(he would stay with the neighbors over the weekend while Verne
was with me in Anchorage). I told Matt a write-in would not be
possible, and I hugged him and apologized for letting him down.

Matt said, "It's okay, I know you're going to do the right thing."

Off we went to the airport, but Matt's comment stuck in my head and bothered me. Did he mean the right thing was not to run or that he thought I would change my mind again and run? Or did he mean, I finally realized, that he simply trusted me to make the right decision?

If he trusted me, perhaps I should trust myself.

And with that thought, Verne and I boarded a flight to Minneapolis, where we would change planes for Anchorage. Exhausted, we sat in silence. I felt Alaska coming closer and Washington falling behind me. Alone with my thoughts, in that window seat in coach, I knew what to do.

Halfway through the flight I quietly said to Verne, "We're going to do it."

He asked if I was sure, and when I said yes, he simply said, "Okay."

As soon as we landed in Minneapolis, still taxiing, I called Mitch McConnell. I told him I was running and would resign from my leadership post effective immediately. He wished me well.

During the layover, Verne and I sat in the Delta lounge and made phone calls to reactivate the campaign I had deactivated the night before. It was still early morning in Anchorage, and we woke up everyone we called. Making the situation worse, the night before, after I'd told everyone to pull the plug on the campaign, the whole team had gone out to the bars for serious drinking (it had also been Kevin Sweeney's birthday). So I don't blame Kevin for asking, in his bleary, hungover voice, if I was kidding. When I said I was serious, he said he was going to hang up, and if my decision hadn't changed in fifteen minutes, I should call him back. After a few more calls, I dialed Kevin again and told him we needed to rebook the Dena'ina Center and go ahead with that evening's rally. During those fifteen minutes, he had called Wacko, who apparently had never canceled the Dena'ina or any of the other plans after I had told him to the night before. As Wacko later explained, he had hoped I would change my mind, and if I didn't, he wanted me to tell those eager Alaskan supporters, to their faces, that we couldn't win this thing.

Instead, we had one wild, exciting day to put together a rally and a campaign. I called my former state director, Mary Hughes, and Byron Mallott, a Democrat and Tlingit leader who was a powerful speaker, and both agreed on the spot to be campaign co-chairs. We would have leaders from both parties and from Alaska's past and present on stage. At six P.M. the live TV feed would go out on the evening news. I wrote my speech sitting at a small counter in the women's bathroom at the Dena'ina Center as people gathered, knowing this would be one of the most important and widely heard addresses I had ever given. Then, as I came out into the soaring lobby atrium, I heard the roar of a huge, uproarious crowd coming from the hall, and I knew we really were on our way.

Arliss Sturgulewski told the crowd, "Isn't it fun to yell like heck for something positive!" The room was buoyant, and no one could keep from smiling and cheering. Union leaders and Native leaders, old-school Republicans, teachers, construction workers, environmentalists and developers—a huge crowd, everyone shoulder to shoulder—were all shouting, "Run, Lisa, run!" I felt it, but my comments were also tinged by the emotions of the last weeks—the journey from complacency, through loss, to determination and, now, excitement. We were taking on the impossible.

As I quieted the cheers, I opened by saying, "You make my heart whole again, and I thank you."

And then I talked about what made this campaign different, and what made Alaska different: the cause that would make this effort worthwhile, and worth all the risk and possible regret—the cause that is still my call to service. That was our belief that our democracy should not serve one group or one kind of people. Our government doesn't belong to a single party or those with a certain skin color, culture, or social class. I truly believed that was our fight, against those who sought power through division and for those who would build together, for all Alaskans. I recalled Ted Stevens and what he had stood for, and his famous saying: "To hell with politics, just do what's right for Alaska." I would not let that fall away.

"More often than not, when you're dealing with tough decisions, the right thing to do is very often the hardest thing to do," I told the raucous audience, quieting them with the emotion in my voice. "It is the hardest thing to do. The easier route for me personally and for Verne would be to accept the results of this primary and put my family first, and I gave that very, very serious consideration. In fact, as of last night I was still wrestling with this. Still uncertain as to whether or not I could continue this race. But I looked into my heart. And I said, 'Where is my heart?' And my heart is Alaska. And I cannot leave you."

CHAPTER 4

Voters Prove We Don't Need Parties

W E HAD TAKEN A giant leap. It would be up to Alaskans to catch us. The first good sign came the morning after the announcement, a Saturday, when we showed up at our headquarters to get to work. People were already waiting outside the locked doors. The answering machine was already full with offers of help. Within hours, two hundred new supporters came through, eating up our entire supply of yard signs and bumper stickers. That was promising, and we immediately ordered many more. But it wasn't enough. A campaign is more than yard signs and stickers, and a write-in is even more complicated.

A state like Alaska, with only about seven hundred thousand residents, cannot produce the kind of funds necessary for a modern Senate campaign, because too few donors can afford large contributions. We don't have wealthy oil tycoons like Texas or old-money fortunes like the East Coast. When Alaskan candidates need millions of dollars, they turn to sources outside the state. But I needed to stay in Alaska through the six-week campaign, without fundraising trips Outside (we use "Outside" to mean anywhere but Alaska). Besides, we had been cut off from national funding sources because of my primary loss. We would have to run our campaign on the cash we already had, the roughly $1 million we had retained from the primary, as well as small contributions from Alaskans. And we might get help from independent expenditure groups, which had looser fundraising rules but were legally barred from coordinating with us. One other potential source of funds was ruled out by me: spending my own money or going into debt. I had made clear that if Alaskans wanted to return me to the Senate, it was up to them.

The lack of party support also denied us the infrastructure to reach people. We would have to build our own network of supporters and contacts statewide. And we would need a new campaign team. I had learned in Washington that national campaign professionals wouldn't touch us—media people, pollsters, and such. In Anchorage, I recognized we would need new staff, too. Many supporters believed that we had lost the election because of a weak effort, and they wanted a completely different approach with different people.

Except for our money in the bank, we were starting from scratch. And the election was only forty-six days away. We would have to do everything at once, and fast. If Alaskans stepped up as they had said they would, this would be their Senate seat and, for the first time, truly mine. If not, our leap would turn into a fall.

Five days after my announcement, the Republican conference scheduled a meeting to decide if I should keep my seniority, determining if I would remain in line to chair the Energy and Natural Resources Committee, among my biggest political assets for Alaska. Miller and the Tea Party's supporters in the Senate campaigned hard against me, especially South Carolina's Jim DeMint, who declared that I had "built a record of betraying conservative principles." The Republican leadership and the National Republican Senatorial Committee were already backing Miller with heavy spending and professional expertise.

Instead of traveling to D.C. to defend my position, I stayed in Alaska. The conference would have to decide without me, because I was where I needed to be.

The meeting was closed, and the vote held by secret ballot. The public learned what happened mostly due to an angry fundraising appeal DeMint sent out on Miller's behalf, denouncing his Republican colleagues and saying, "One senator after another stood up to argue in favor of protecting her place on the committee—a position she will no doubt use in her campaign against Joe Miller, the conservative Republican nominee." He was right. I won the vote and kept my position, although I would never know all the details, and that win *was* a good reason for Alaskans to vote for me.

I would remain a Republican, but to win I would need Democratic votes. With control of the Senate in the balance, would Democrats support me? To probe this question, I met in Alaska with a group of moderate Democrats I respected. Members of that group gave me clear advice along with their support. They said my campaign could succeed if I ran not as a Republican or as a Democrat but if I could just run as Lisa. I next asked about strategy: Who could I get to create that kind of campaign? The name they shared: Cathy Allen.

Cathy had run big Democratic campaigns in Alaska—including on the opposite side of a mayoral campaign I'd helped manage shortly after college—before she'd moved to Seattle to strategize for women candidates globally. I knew she was smart and driven, and I was a little intimidated by her. When I called, I said I was probably the last person she was expecting to hear from. She said, "No, I was actually hoping you would call." She was soon in Anchorage, putting together our strategy, working with our rapidly expanding campaign corps with grace and good cheer. I honestly was amazed by that, because we had thrown her into a room with her traditional adversaries as well as longtime friends—folks who had opposed each other on Republican and Democratic campaigns for years—and they all seemed to click with Cathy and with one another.

Few others had national experience. Our media team would be led by John Tracy. He had been Alaska's most respected TV newsman for many years, before buying an advertising agency with a business partner. Although he had never worked on a campaign, he knew politics as a journalist. Cathy and John collaborated well together, defining the message that he would turn into TV and radio spots. John pulled in the best of the local producers and videographers. Kevin Sweeney led with an analytical mind and plenty of political instinct, but without ever having run a statewide campaign before. The all-Alaskan campaign developed a distinctly local Alaska vibe, and I liked it. This was exactly how our campaign should feel and what it should be about.

We decided not to hire a pollster, even a local one. There was little time, and we thought we knew what we needed to say without polling. Our slogans wrote themselves. One popped up on a hand-made sign at our announcement rally: "Let's make history." We would legitimately make history if we won, and that challenge inspired us. Another slogan explained the way that could happen: voters would have to fill in the bubble for the write-in line on the ballot and write my name next to it. Every chance we got, we said, "Fill it in, write it in." And another slogan was just fun: "Too legit to quit." These simple messages began showing up everywhere, and not only on material we produced. Alaskans were doing it themselves, as the campaign bloomed organically all around us.

————

We were eating breakfast in the Snow City Cafe, in downtown Anchorage, when a woman excitedly approached our table. She said she was a Democrat and worked in a building across the street at a state government office. From her purse, she pulled a bundle of bumper stickers bearing a slogan she had made up slamming Joe Miller. She had printed them up herself and had been handing them around, without coordinating with anyone. This was her own personal pro-Lisa campaign. It was only one of many.

People had continued showing up at our campaign office, volunteering, in big numbers, and working for many hours. With a month left before the election, a group turned up and asked if they could stand on street corners waving our signs. We said, "Why not?" They continued that energetic effort every day of the campaign, working different corners. Every day a team of young people sat at laptops in a back room at the campaign headquarters, which we started calling "the Nerdery." They engaged with social media and the comment sections of online news articles, gathering public opinion and responding in real time. By the end of the campaign, they had sent a quarter million emails to voters and posted innumerable times. A massage therapist showed up, saying she knew nothing about politics but she could help keep the staff relaxed—and she gave chair massages around the office. Casseroles and cookies appeared at all hours, too, so our team was well fed; more important, we all had a sense of being part of something the whole community was pitching in to support. It felt more like a movement than any political campaign I had ever been a part of.

Volunteers organized their own workshops to make big plywood signs for the roadsides in Anchorage and towns around the state. A group from the firefighters' union came up with a jingle and made a video of their guys in their firefighting gear singing, "Fill it in, write it in, bring Murkowski back!" At the headquarters, Kevin Sweeney put up an ideas board where anyone could pin a suggestion, and we committed money to make the best ideas happen. That was how we got the spelling-aid T-shirts, which were printed with the letters "Mur" followed by a picture of a cow and a pair of skis. (Later, the vice president would pose with us holding these shirts.) More than just being fun, this openness felt exciting. We were a band of Alaskans from every walk of life—of all ages, from all political parties, and also of every race and tribe, with representatives of businesses and unions, LGBTQ activists, churchgoers, and anyone else who wanted to help. Most of these people had never been involved in a campaign before.

The coordinators managing all these volunteers were also volunteering, including some with thriving professional careers who took the time off to keep our irregular army of helpers all going in the same direction. With that organization and all the help blossoming from everywhere, we were able to stretch our money in new ways. When I traveled for the campaign, we didn't have to pay for many hotels or restaurant meals—there was usually a supporter's cozy guest room and a family dinner arranged for me and my travel partner, Rachel Kallander. Her high energy kept me upbeat on the trail throughout the campaign.

With our tight budget, we decided not to rent offices around the state, but supporters in some communities found their own spaces. Many others did their own campaigning, too, often without asking us. I tried to smother my anxiety—what were these people doing in my name, often without my knowledge?—while at the same time enjoying the validation. After our leap, we were really taking off. Indeed, things were happening that barely seemed possible.

We lacked the money or time for much travel to rural Alaska. There are more than two hundred rural villages around the state, each with a relatively small number of voters. And going to a village can be an all-day affair. To get to a typical village in, for example, western Alaska, you first take an Alaska Airlines jet from Anchorage to a hub community such as Bethel, followed by a riverboat ride or small plane flight to a dirt airstrip, and you always run the risk of a long weather delay, including the possibility of being stuck in a village for days, unable to leave. Because there are few votes to chase, most statewide candidates never bother to go to these rural areas, but getting to Alaska Native communities is important to who I am as a senator and is one of the most rewarding parts of the job. I have visited just about every community in Alaska, something very few people can say.

During the write-in campaign, Alaska Natives organized themselves. The CEOs and other board members of the Alaska Federation of Natives, who had stood up for me at that dramatic meeting in September, now fulfilled their promises to help—and more. Led by Gail Schubert, the president and CEO of Bering Straits Native Corporation, they funded an independent expenditure group called Alaskans Standing Together. Earlier that year, the Supreme Court's

Citizens United decision had unleashed groups to gather and spend unlimited campaign cash, so long as they did not coordinate with the candidate's own campaign. The Tea Party Express dumped $660,000 into beating me, and traditional Republican groups in Washington added another $1.1 million between them. But Alaskans Standing Together devoted $1.7 million all on their own, and they used it far more effectively.

Part of that money went to advertising—our team kept having to cancel ideas for ads when we turned on the TV and saw that the independent group had beaten us to it. But even more impact came from the way Alaskans Standing Together worked in the villages. The leaders of each community let people know that this election was important for protecting their way of life and for keeping someone who had always listened and worked hard to meet their needs. They campaigned in person over coffee and via VHF two-way radios.

While all that was going on—out of our control and almost out of our awareness—I was learning a lot about running a different kind of political campaign. On the Republican side, we were accustomed to campaigns that reached out to individuals, one at a time, with volunteers typically organized by Republican women's groups. Now I learned how the Democrats did it. The unions came to our side. Their pragmatic leaders explained that Joe Miller would be a disaster and they didn't think Scott McAdams had a chance. That meant we would get their contributions but, more important, we got their members' attention. Phone banks and direct mail let unionized workers know about the endorsements and activated more volunteers to help. The teachers supported us, too, and communicated to their members in every school district across the state. So did other normally Democratic groups.

People said I was courageous for taking the leap on this campaign, but that's not right. Making the decision was hard, for the many reasons I've already described, although not because of worry about my political career—it was over if I didn't run. Many of the people who supported me, however, did show real courage, especially at the start, when they crossed over from their traditional allies—and with the Senate potentially in the balance—to pour their hearts and hours into a campaign for a Republican. Likewise, many Republicans took a risk by sticking with me even though I was not the party nominee. Some from both parties went way out of their comfort zones and against their traditional teams, and I've never forgotten that. Thinking of their courage has often helped me in the years since be a senator who represents Alaskans rather than representing my party.

The Stevens family also showed courage. Lily Stevens, Ted's youngest daughter, joined me on the campaign trail and traveled on her own, paying all her own expenses. Sue Covich, his oldest daughter, cut a TV ad, at the family's insistence, explaining my decision not to use Ted's endorsement ad during the primary, after the plane crash. Sue's face told the whole story—her grief remained fresh—and the emotion of the minute-long piece built to her introduction of an excerpt from Ted's video. With the date, July 30, on the screen, Ted said, "I trust Lisa and her commitment to keep fighting for us. She's working for Alaska every single day. We need Lisa now more than ever." Then I joined Sue on the screen, saying, "I thank Sue and the Stevens family for the years they shared their father with Alaska." John said the guys in the editing room had tears in their eyes.

Ted Stevens remained much on my mind, even in these fast-paced days of constant activity and public appearances. After the sadness, I had drawn strength from his memory, as I sought his advice in my private thoughts. I could almost hear him telling me, "Shake it off, get moving, and don't let your state down." There had been no time for Alaskans to come to grips with what had happened: two years earlier, Ted had been our "Senator-for-Life," then he was convicted and lost his office, was exonerated, and then suddenly killed in the crash. We hadn't put that story away—we were still living it—and, at least to me, the campaign felt like our partial answer to those tragic and unfair circumstances.

———

Joe Miller created a lot of his own problems. Our campaign was less than two weeks old when he went to Washington to raise money and announced on Twitter that he would also be house hunting, picking out office furniture, and choosing a name plaque for his door. Our team grabbed a quick screenshot before the tweets were deleted. They made the national media, underscoring Miller's arrogance. He blamed the tweets on a staffer, whom he said he had fired. But that was an old excuse. He had already used it a month earlier, and supposedly had already fired that staffer, during the counting of the primary ballots, when the political world was speculating that I might run as a Libertarian. Then he had tweeted, "What's the difference between selling out your party's values and the oldest profession?"

Miller might never know the impact of that offensive tweet in Kenmore, Washington, a suburb north of Seattle, where my cousin Jenny Dwyer read it aloud to her husband, Pat, over their morning coffee. Pat's ALS had progressed, and he needed an assistive breathing device and a wheelchair. Each morning Jenny showered, shaved, and dressed him, and worked him through forty-five minutes of range-of-motion exercises, before reading the news to him. She said, "Miller is calling Lisa a prostitute." Pat got mad. Despite his physical weakness, he remained sharp, intuitive, and bold. Now he was motivated as well. Even while trapped in a failing body, he believed he could take on Joe Miller.

He told Jenny, "It's on."

And so began what we called Kenmore Opposition Research. Pat's disease limited him to using the computer with a single finger, with his hand propped over the track pad, but he proved gifted at finding damning information in public records and the media. He set a pattern that first morning, as Jenny recalled, sitting at a laptop on their kitchen island, working with his single finger, while directing her, using another laptop a few feet away. They found a rich hunting ground. Miller's embarrassing and hypocritical actions waited in plain sight for a well-designed search.

Miller had posed as the ultimate Republican, yet he had switched parties multiple times and had missed voting in various elections. He liked to spout sanctimoniously about eliminating public benefits, but he had repeatedly collected those same benefits for his own family. He portrayed himself as a rugged Alaskan, yet he received farm subsidies in Kansas, and from a program he said he opposed. And he had gotten an Alaska state agricultural loan for land he never farmed. He worked as a lawyer, with a law degree from Yale, and yet applied for a low-cost hunting and fishing license meant for people who are indigent. He opposed federal healthcare funding as unconstitutional but used it for his own family through Medicaid and benefits for his children. He had hired his own wife to assist him as a federal magistrate, then fired her because her hiring had broken nepotism rules. She had then collected unemployment, benefiting from another program he said was unconstitutional. And so on.

At first Pat and Jenny were freelancing. They came up with good stuff, sent it to the campaign, and Steve Wackowski and the Nerdery ran with it, putting out press releases on some of these nuggets, quietly slipping others to reporters, and spinning many out on social media, with our volunteers' many fingers pushing them to go viral. After the first successes, the Kenmore operation became a key part of the campaign. Pat and Jenny would develop leads and strategize at bedtime about what they would pursue the next day. But often, Jenny's sister Anne would call from the campaign in the morning with an urgent assignment, and they would run down that trail all day.

Pat uncovered at least five major Miller issues during the campaign. Those disclosures helped start a rolling snowball of scandals. The news media had not dug deeply into Miller's past during the primary. Perhaps they were put off by his pedigree, with his West Point and Yale diplomas, and his short but distinguished service in the Army. Besides, the primary race had been a sleeper, with no one expecting an upset. Upon examination, however, his résumé in Alaska raised questions, and Miller became secretive and unwilling to respond to reporters' basic inquiries. That further aroused their suspicions and, as the national media's interest in our race increased, energized many journalistic investigations following up on Pat and Jenny's research.

Sometimes the crazy pressure of a modern political campaign serves a purpose, as a crucible that burns out those who can't stand the intensity of the public attention that would be part of their job if elected. Miller melted down under the glare. In mid-October, he held a disastrous press conference in which he declared that for the rest of the campaign he would answer no more questions about his background or any personal matter. He particularly attacked the Alaska Dispatch, a well-funded journalistic website that had broken many of the stories about his scandals.

Miller seemed most concerned about inquiries into the job he had left a year before, as a part-time lawyer for the Fairbanks North Star Borough. Two days later, Jim Whitaker, the borough's former mayor, talked to the media, saying that Miller had been "less than honest" at his press conference. It turned out that just two years earlier, Miller had been suspended from that job over an ethics violation, and for lying about it. The story was farcical. While working with Sarah Palin to take over the Alaska Republican Party (unsuccessfully), Miller had waited for his colleagues to go to lunch, then used their computers to vote in a straw poll supporting his party coup. To cover his tracks, he erased each computer's internet cache, deleting the other lawyers' saved passwords and websites. Unfortunately for him, this meant they immediately knew something was wrong when they next logged on. Then he lied about it, over and over again.

This led to the weirdest incident of the campaign. The editor of the Dispatch, Tony Hopfinger, attended a Sunday afternoon forum Miller held at a middle school in Anchorage. Afterward, as Hopfinger followed the candidate down a corridor, asking about the computer scandal, Miller's security detail grabbed him and threw him in handcuffs. Other reporters were there, of course. While they filmed and asked questions, the security agents pushed them and tried to block their view of Hopfinger, handcuffed on the floor. I've never hired security in Alaska, or anywhere else. These guys were dressed in black, with earpieces, like characters from an action movie. The story blew up nationally and became a punch line.

For the most part, we didn't get involved. Miller was proving himself unfit for office, and he didn't need our help. He continued fighting in court against the release of records about his Fairbanks computer scandal, producing a steady flow of headlines, until he lost the case and all the embarrassing details came out—just days before the election.

Around then, at one of our last debates, Miller complained about all the negative press he had received, blaming it on the vast sums my campaign had spent on opposition research. I didn't mention that the work of Kenmore Opposition Research hadn't cost us a penny. Jenny and Pat had been delighted to do it. As Jenny later said, it had made Pat's life a bit brighter, as he had once again felt needed, back in the game, and occupied by something other than his disease.

———

As hard as everyone was working, I was determined to work harder. We had given our press secretary carte blanche to book anything— the only time that had ever happened, Wacko said—and we were inundated with interview requests. We had an interesting story. A credible write-in is rare; a write-in by an incumbent senator is unheard-of. But the national media also focused on us because they saw our race as a test of the Tea Party movement and its potential to take over the Republican Party. Palin had become that movement's face, and she was frequently mentioned as a promising candidate for the 2012 presidential nomination. Palin had endorsed Tea Party candidates all over the country, but nowhere had she gambled more political capital than in her own state. Some in the media were playing my write-in campaign as a face-off between Palin and me, with national stakes.

The morning shows wanted me ready by six or seven A.M. eastern time, which was two or three A.M. in Anchorage. Hardly had I gone to bed when Wacko would knock on my door and say, "Put on your lipstick," and I would be up, dressed, and ready for television long before dawn. We drove through dark and empty streets to a TV station for a video uplink to the *Today* show or sat in the living room of a house where the staff had assembled a studio for *Good Morning America*. The trick was to think "morning" rather than "middle of the night."

Normally, local media matters more than national outlets. Moreover, I knew Alaskans saw this as a race with Miller, not with Palin. Since her resignation as governor, Palin had lost her popularity and felt largely irrelevant to our state—there was talk about whether she even lived in Alaska anymore. If this was about Palin, I didn't believe that getting up to please East Coast journalists was really worth it.

Fortunately, I had smart people on the campaign to educate me. For the audience Outside, we needed to communicate some of the excitement and momentum building in the state, so that we would be credible to potential donors. We made some progress with that, but most political people nationally didn't appreciate the grassroots miracle we were seeing at home. It can be hard to believe in such things if you're not a part of them.

For Alaskans watching that national media, however, these appearances did hit home. Alaskans are proud of being different, and we like to be recognized for the exceptional qualities of our state—not the embarrassment of Sarah Palin or other reality TV stars but the sense that we are unique and independent. The national coverage showed Alaskans in a positive mirror, as we tried to do something that had never before been accomplished. The coverage demonstrated that people Outside were noticing, and reminded Alaskans of the reality of our slogan "Let's make history."

We campaigned on the excitement of achieving something hard together (living out the family motto). We also had another campaign theme, one even more important, but slightly less inspiring: correct spelling. We would be making history partly by showing that you could teach an entire state to correctly spell and legibly write a Polish name in the privacy of the voting booth, something political professionals said could not be done. The Alaska Division of Elections wouldn't allow voters to use stickers with my name, because they could jam up the ballot-counting equipment. But exactly what we could do was unclear, because the issues had never come up in a serious way in Alaska.

Our lawyers studied precedent for how the write-in ballots would be counted. Would the name have to be spelled perfectly, or would the voter's intent be enough? The courts had never ruled on that in Alaska. The Alaska Division of Elections gave us no clarity. Without knowing the answer, our only prudent course would be to assume that every ballot had to be perfect, and to concentrate on getting voters to make them that way. Otherwise, we could find ourselves, after the election, litigating with Joe Miller about misspellings and bad handwriting, and hoping the courts would be lenient with our voters. We had already heard rumors that, anticipating those fights, the other side was trying to recruit another candidate into the race to create confusion, someone named Lisa with a last name beginning with M. Shortly before the election, talk radio host Dan Fagan did just that. After learning that the Division of Elections was keeping a reference list of potential write-ins for use during the ballot-counting process, Fagan induced 150 of his listeners to sign up as candidates to generate maximum uncertainty.

The Alaska Native independent expenditure tackled this spelling problem in rural villages. English is a second language for some Alaska Natives, especially elders, who might still speak Yup'ik or Iñupiaq at home. For many others, limited schooling might leave them unsure of how to manage the write-in vote. I later met some of the village leaders who helped—I'm thinking in particular of one older woman who proudly told me about how villagers gathered in their tribal hall, taking a break from bingo night, to painstakingly practice how to fill in the bubble and write the name "Lisa Murkowski" on the line provided. Communities also played bingo with special MURKOWSKI cards and distributed temporary tattoos showing a correctly filled-in ballot line. These scenes were repeated dozens and perhaps hundreds of times in villages across the state.

For the rest of Alaska, we leaned on our slogan "Fill it in, write it in," which we used in dozens of mailers and TV and radio spots, keeping the spelling of my last name prominent. Our advertising professionals did everything they could to push out that simple message. But the best solution came from home.

Verne and I were attending the memorial service for Terry Smith, Ted Stevens's pilot in the fatal crash, when someone handed out colored rubber bracelets embossed with Terry's name, like the Livestrong bracelets popularized by cyclist Lance Armstrong. Verne suggested we could give away bracelets with a colored-in oval and my name spelled correctly, the way it should look on the ballot. Brilliant! We ordered enough to put one on the wrist of every registered voter in Alaska, and then some. We sent the bracelets out through all our new networks, to our regional offices, the unions, the organizations that had rallied to us, and to any supporter going out to communities. Pretty soon, we were seeing people everywhere wearing our blue-and-gold bracelets. We heard about them being on every wrist in the rural bingo halls and gymnasiums where folks were learning how to vote.

John Tracy did brilliant work producing commercials on this theme. We ran some traditional ads, but most of our commercials focused on how to vote for me. The strategy worked. Not only did Alaskans learn to spell "Murkowski," but they also absorbed the subtext that voting for me was such an obvious choice that all we needed to talk about was the mechanics of doing so—not why to vote for me, but only how. That fed the growing sense that we were doing something together, as Alaskans, making history.

John's best ad, which won awards and was copied many times around the country by other campaigns, showed an elementary school spelling bee. A young girl stood at the microphone.

FEMALE MODERATOR: The word is "Murkowski."

GIRL: Can you please define that?

MALE MODERATOR: Alaska's senior senator in Washington who represents all Alaskans.

GIRL: Could you please use that in a sentence?

FEMALE MODERATOR: To reelect Lisa Murkowski, you must fill in the oval and write in her name.

GIRL: Murkowski. M-U-R-K-O-W-S-K-I.

Applause.

MALE MODERATOR: That is correct.

Girl sits down.

SECOND GIRL: You get all the easy ones.

First girl waves to someone in the audience. It is the candidate, who waves back and turns toward the camera.

CANDIDATE: I'm Lisa Murkowski and I approved this message.

The ad was so darned cute, everyone loved it and wanted to see it. And it added to the bandwagon effect. While Joe Miller melted down, we projected total confidence.

John took advantage of Miller's bizarre errors with another ad. After Miller made headlines with his militia-style security-detail handcuffing of journalist Tony Hopfinger, John unearthed footage of the Eagle River Bear Paw Festival from the midsummer, when Miller had marched with an ominous bunch carrying military weapons. The ad suggested that Miller wanted an authoritarian

America, and lingered for long seconds on those scary men marching with their guns. Then it switched to my own upbeat campaign
event on green grass, as I reached out to hug an old friend. The an-
nouncer said, "It's time for a return to common sense."

On Halloween I went out trick-or-treating with my three nephews, aged four to six, who were dressed like Miller's bodyguards, in
dark suits and ties, with sunglasses and earpieces, "protecting me."
It was fun, and it got picked up by the media. Everyone seemed to
be enjoying a laugh at Miller and his security details.

We still had, at that point in our nation's life, enough shared belief in the media and our institutions that most of us saw Miller's
paranoia as ridiculous. We've changed since then. As John Tracy
said recently, looking back, our ad—showing Miller as an authoritarian, with his supporters marching with military weapons—might
not work anymore. We've elected more and more people like Joe
Miller, and a segment of our population now seems attracted to that
kind of imagery.

But in 2010, John's ad did work. By the end of October, I felt a lift
that was carrying us over the top. National media had descended
heavily on Anchorage. We were one of the biggest political stories
in the country, partly because this was all so fresh and new, and
partly because we were showing that good-government moderates
could fight back against the Tea Party crazies who had seemed
ready to take over the GOP. Perhaps some people sensed, as I did
not, that this election would be an opening battle in a long war with
angry populists, one that is still going on today.

Our Alaska Native support powered us into the final stretch. Late
in October, all three candidates came to Fairbanks for the Alaska
Federation of Natives convention, the state's most prominent political stage. Miller had just filed a Federal Election Commission
complaint against the Native independent expenditure group Alaskans Standing Together, calling it an illegal "PR front group" for me.
The complaint went nowhere, but it further alienated Native leaders. He had already attacked my use of appropriation earmarks to

help rural Native communities and had denounced a federal con-
tracting set-aside program originally created by Ted Stevens to support Alaska Native Corporations. He called Indigenous Alaskans "a
special interest" and suggested that their support for me was somehow corrupt.

Myron Naneng responded with anger. He was the leader of the
Association of Village Council Presidents, a consortium of fifty-six
tribes in the Yukon-Kuskokwim Delta. Myron declared, "You don't
call the first people of Alaska special interest. We were here first."
He made a motion on the convention floor to endorse me. Byron
Mallott gave an extraordinary nominating speech. The endorsement passed with a loud voice vote, followed by a standing ovation.
It was only the second time AFN had ever endorsed a candidate. I
rose to thank the convention, promising, "I will fight for you as long
as I am able. I love you all!"

The next day, the convention had planned to have the three Senate candidates debate, but at the last minute, AFN chairman Albert Kookesh canceled that and gave the stage to me alone to speak,
while Miller and McAdams were left on the convention floor shaking individual hands. Albert frankly explained to the media that
this was a political decision. AFN had endorsed me, and he saw
no reason to help anyone but me to win the election. Everyone in
the hall seemed to be wearing our rubber bracelets and temporary
tattoos. As I spoke, I saw many friendly faces from communities
around the state. Miller was back to where he had started, at that
Memorial Day event, forced to listen to me speaking to my friends,
while he was left anonymous in the audience.

We didn't have our own polls and the public polling was all over
the place, but each of us had our own way of judging where the voters were going. About a week before the election, Wackowski and I
made a campaign swing through the Mat-Su Valley, including
Wasilla, where Sarah Palin had been mayor, at the deep-red center
of her Tea Party brand. The day went well, and we ended it by dropping into a Wasilla bar, where the legendary Alaska folksinger Hobo

Jim was playing his guitar. When Jim saw me, he stopped singing and said, "Hey, look, everybody—it's Lisa Murkowski." To my amazement, the place went wild, as everyone clapped, high-fived, and took pictures. Wacko and I looked at each other. If this was the reaction in Wasilla, something really was happening.

On the final weekend of the campaign, I was feeling confident that we would win. Miller's embarrassing employment file had come out. Paul Jenkins, a leading conservative columnist, wrote, "As the Joe Miller Looney Tunes Express chugs toward Tuesday, somebody needs to point out the obvious: No rational person, nobody in complete command of his or her faculties, could possibly vote for Miller." Republican leaders began backing away from him. John McCain canceled his campaign trip to Alaska. Contributions began flowing rapidly into our campaign from the same Washington sources who had told me six weeks earlier that I should not run and had no chance.

On election night, the raucous crowd was deafening, chanting, "We made history!" Computer-counted election returns showed "write-in" winning decisively. Rural Alaska had come in with overwhelming support for the write-in—over 70 percent in some areas. In the village of Newtok, the community threatened by erosion I had recently visited, "write-in" won 116 out of 119 votes cast (the other three were split between McAdams and the Libertarian—Miller got none). The tribal administrator said he had worn his rubber Murkowski bracelet on Election Day and had reminded everyone on the two-way VHF radio to "fill it in and write it in."

That scenario had been repeated across the state.

It was a glorious night, but we could not declare victory, because no one had seen those write-in ballots. Errors would disqualify some of them. And Miller and the Republican Party brought in lawyers to challenge as many as possible.

A week after the vote, the Division of Elections set up a counting center in Juneau with forty tables, one for each district, where an election worker would inspect and count each ballot while being watched by an observer from each campaign. The observers could challenge ballots on the spot. Kevin Sweeney went to the table for District 38, in Southwest Alaska, an area of the state that includes Newtok, where traditional Yup'ik language is strong and many voters have weaker skills in writing English. As he watched the ballots go by, he felt a growing sense of pride, which became a feeling of elation. Almost every ballot was perfect.

Miller's observers had to challenge at least one in nine ballots for a chance to change the result. Reporters watching saw an alarming number of ballots being moved into the pile of those disputed. John Tracy recalled a Fox News reporter going on the air, repeating the concern that my victory might not hold because there were so many errors. After that live report was broadcast, John approached the reporter and asked if he had looked at the challenged ballots—anyone could stand by the tables and watch as they were sorted. The reporter did so, and in his next update, he changed his prediction. Miller's people were objecting to legible and correctly spelled ballots, calling them out for trivial reasons—because the *o* in "Murkowski" wasn't closed, the *i* was dotted by a heart, or the voter had written, "Murkowski, Lisa" or "Lisa Murkowski, Republican." And even assuming those silly challenges were validated, the number still would not be enough to change the result.

Two weeks after the election, the Associated Press called the race for our side. Unfortunately, Miller refused to concede, charging that the state's vote-counting machines were "suspect" and vowing to fight in court—a sad preview of things to come. Our attorneys were among the unsung heroes of this story, as they had to fight out the tedious case, ballot by ballot, until it was finally resolved in late December, establishing my final margin of 4 percentage points over Miller. I closed the book on the campaign before that, with the AP call. I spoke to supporters and the media at the laborers' union hall in Anchorage, still feeling amazed and enjoying the energy of the packed room.

"Tonight, after eight weeks, I think we can say our miracle is here," I told the crowd over chants of "We made history!"

I knew this election was special, but not because of me. This had been a unique moment when a state had expressed its will in a very deliberate way. This vote had meant something more than the typical checking of one of two boxes. This was proactive and intentional voting.

"Can you imagine, over a hundred thousand people who wrote in the same name—think about what that means," I said. "There's no apathy when you have to take out that bracelet, and you have to look at it upside down, and you have to figure out how to spell it. Alaskans knew exactly what they were doing, and they showed their intent with every letter they put down on that ballot."

Reporters and insiders immediately began asking me about "payback" and what I would do in exchange for the help I'd received or in revenge against the party insiders who had tried to eliminate me. (I held no grudges and later even nominated Joe Miller's son to West Point.) The questioners missed the point. This outcome was something totally positive. I had been given something precious.

"I don't know that it's a question of owing anybody," I said. "It's doing the best job that I possibly can to represent everybody. And that's a challenge. It'd be a heck of a lot easier if all I was going to do was represent the Republicans. . . . I'm in a different spot than I ever have been before. Which I think is a good spot for the Democrats and for the independents and for the Natives and the laborers."

Alaskans had given me a new way of seeing my responsibilities and who I was really working for. A new freedom. They had given me new muscles to do my work.

I began using them right away.

———

We all knew we would never be involved in anything like that campaign again. Many campaigns are exciting, and a few end in upsets, but this had been something truly special, as different kinds of people put down their usual roles to work side by side with former adversaries and achieved something that most people thought impossible. We had seen the threat of Tea Party populism, and the potential damage to Alaska of its extremism and chaos, and we had started our own movement to turn that tide, successfully, in this place and time. For most of us, the sweetness of our victory mixed with a little sadness, because it was over and everyone was returning to real life.

Everyone but me, that is. I was returning to Washington with an entirely new outlook, a new mandate from this diverse, grassroots coalition of Alaskans, and new respect accorded me by my colleagues. Mainstream Republicans had been afraid of Sarah Palin and her potential to win presidential primaries, but now analysts said our victory in Alaska had damaged her aspirations. Many of her candidates had not won, and their lack of viability might have cost Republicans the Senate. She had helped four Tea Party candidates win Senate primary upsets, and now the last of those four, Miller, had lost in the general election. In the Senate, we had gained six seats, mostly with conventional candidates, but came up just short of winning the majority. (Over in the House, however, Republicans had given President Obama a "shellacking," to use his word. Many of the sixty-three new Republican members helped form the Tea Party Caucus, which later morphed into the Freedom Caucus, an uncompromising right-wing group that has often paralyzed Congress.)

We held a small reception in Washington for those who had stood by me—although not as small as it would have been if attended only by those who really did stand by me. I commented on Minority Leader McConnell's recent statement that "the single most important thing we want to achieve is for President Obama to be a one-term president." I told the gathering I disagreed with the idea that beating Obama should be our top priority. I was ready to work with the president on anything that helped Alaska. My most important goal would be to serve those who had elected me.

Four major votes came up in the lame-duck Congress as the Democrats sought to salvage what they could before the new Republican members were sworn in. I talked about the politics of these votes with my staff, but after what had happened in Alaska, I didn't get the usual political advice. Instead, Kevin Sweeney said, "I would much rather defend the positions and the actions you take because you believe in them. The reason we won the write-in campaign is because you were genuine, because Alaskans believed you and they trust you. And even though they don't always agree with you, they like you. And that genuineness only comes through if you do what you believe is right."

Those four votes were on the DREAM Act, protecting undocumented immigrants who had arrived as children; for President Obama's compromise to extend the Bush tax cuts; for ratification of the New START nuclear arms control treaty; and for the Don't Ask, Don't Tell Repeal Act, ending the military's dismissal of gay servicemen and servicewomen. On this four-item wish list for President Obama, I was the only Republican to vote for all four. My votes were not intended to be a statement, but they got noticed. I was following Kevin's advice. I simply looked at each issue and did what I thought was right.

Don't Ask, Don't Tell was particularly personal. Gays and lesbians had been barred from the military since World War II, but in 1993 Congress had passed President Bill Clinton's policy declaring that they could serve so long as they stayed in the closet. I may have agreed with that at the time. I was raised in a conservative Catholic family. My journey to understand equal rights gained personal insight when I was involved with the Government Hill PTA and we had a controversy in our school community about a same-sex couple that included a teacher. As a school leader and a friend, I felt it my responsibility to support her. That was the beginning of my recognition that gays and lesbians should be free to love whom they choose.

Aunt DD's lung disease had advanced when she finally decided to share her secrets at one of our GG reunions in Palm Springs. All of us women of the younger generation were on hand to support and love her during that tough time, as her health worsened. We could tell how nervous she was, as she had something she needed to tell us. DD had spent much of her career in the U.S. Naval Reserve, rising to be a captain in 1981, the only woman at that time to reach that rank. But she served in a system that had never allowed her to be herself. Now, long after she'd retired from the military, and in the safety of our female reunion, she could finally be true to her identity with her family. We just laughed, said we'd figured out a long time ago that she was gay, and hugged and loved her. It didn't matter.

DD lived to see the passage of the Don't Ask, Don't Tell Repeal Act, and I was proud to take that vote.

The write-in victory had given me a new kind of power. Internally, it gave me new strength to act for myself. As a member of the Senate, it had made me a critical player on many issues. The parties were divided by only a few votes. At the same time, partisanship had continued to intensify, with more senators feeling bound to vote the party line—out of fear of the Tea Party, on the right, or the extreme liberals, on the left. As a senator willing to examine issues independently and vote my conscience, I became someone to talk to, because with me, persuasion had a chance.

Sometimes colleagues trapped in a straitjacket of partisanship would come to me for help. In 2011, during the first debt-ceiling crisis, McConnell and other leaders approached me to vote against our party position. They knew the United States should never default on its debts, but they could not escape the strategy of brinksmanship initiated by the Tea Party in the House. I said, "So you are whipping my vote for the other side?" They sheepishly nodded. I voted to help save our nation's good credit.

On another occasion, DeMint himself approached me. After years of denouncing me and others for adding earmarks to the bud-

get, he now needed something for his own state that I had the political freedom to give him: money for dredging Charleston Harbor.

I said, "Isn't that an earmark?"

"Yes," he admitted, but he assured me that the port would be important for the country. He wanted me to put his earmark in the
budget so he could take the credit without breaking his own self-
righteous rule.

I declined.

The circumstances of my return to the Senate were unique, as
was my special freedom, but as I think about how American politics
have gone wrong, I see a useful lesson here. There was nothing
complicated about my new status. It was simple as sincerity. De-
Mint and the Tea Party fought earmarks, but earmarks are merely
appropriations advanced by an individual member for a particular
purpose. Passing an earmark is not corrupt; doing so for the wrong
reasons is. Tea Party voters were justified in their frustration with
Washington, but their populist prescriptions—no earmarks, no
compromise, strict party discipline—were irrelevant or counterproductive. What I had discovered, as I entered my new life as a
senator, was that I could be loyal and attentive to the people of my
state, and that would be enough.

CHAPTER 5

The Real Alaska and How It Shapes My Politics

FALL COMES TO THE interior with special crispness, as the northern sun rapidly loses strength and the birch trees turn brilliant yellow against the dark boughs of the black spruce. In the fall we go to Healy Lake. First you drive 130 miles southeast of Fairbanks on the two-lane Richardson Highway, past Delta Junction, then continue on a gravel side road about ten miles to the boat landing on the Tanana River. You navigate the unruly Tanana to the calm of the Healy River, until finally reaching the broad, six-mile-long lake. As you boat across the lake, green water reflects the rounded golden hills of autumn, with the jagged, snowcapped mountains of the Alaska Range beyond. The journey takes a day. Once I get there, I never want to leave.

Duck season opens on September 1, and I am out there at dawn. I enjoy the hunt, and I am good with a shotgun. It's not so much the success of the hunt that I enjoy, but rather just being in this special and beautiful place with my family. I stay busy around the camp, constantly feeding and poking the fire, which is my specialty, and drying wet socks on the ends of sticks. I often don't sit down while others are reading, cooking, or doing jigsaw puzzles. I like the physical work, splitting and stacking wood and tending to the camp—

our place is rough, without electricity, plumbing, or cellphone reception—and at the end of a visit I'm always reenergized, with sore muscles and bruises reminding me of those outdoor efforts that clear my head. Healy is where I fill up my reserves.

In the fifty years since Dad bought the place with some hunting buddies, not much has changed—even the pots and pans are vintage. We have had to move the cabin up the bank as the lake water has slowly risen over the years. Back in the 1970s, the girls didn't go duck hunting, but that changed when we were older and realized the fun we had missed. Duck camp is now all about family, and there is a wonderful picture of our babies laid out in a row on the bank. For many years, we've crammed into the one cabin, enjoyed noisy family dinners, and stood together around the campfire, talking, laughing, arguing, and sharing, deep into the night. In September, you wear wool and fleece against the nighttime chill and the fire warms your face. All that goes on, with comforting continuity, from one decade to the next, as the birch trees grow and our ancient riverboat shows new welds from repaired leaks. Each generation overtakes the last, and now the babies we lined up on the bank are married adults bringing on new babies.

We have not changed. But the land is changing. Even the seasons are changing.

The changing climate has been evident in Alaska for decades, as those who pay attention to the land know. Native people pointed out the differences to me, things they perceived in the thousands of variables on the land and in the water they knew intimately from hunting, fishing, gathering, and traveling. Shorter, warmer, and low-snow winters interfered with their tundra travel and hunting. Many parts of Alaska are swampy, and summer travel there is practical only by riverboat or airplane. To go cross-country you need a snow machine, as well as snow-covered ground and frozen waterways over which to travel—but that season is shortening. Soil that has been frozen for thousands of years, called permafrost, is thawing, and that has collapsed roads, ruined ice cellars, and even rerouted rivers. Sea ice has thinned, shrunk in area, and now lasts for less of the year, making hunting more dangerous and contributing, with rising seas and stronger storms, to rapid coastal erosion that threatens northern communities. Berry crops have failed, insects have swarmed, migrations have been delayed, fish populations have been displaced, and warmer ocean water has caused fish and bird kills. Clinics in Arctic communities have had to learn about heat stroke.

Today and for more than a decade past, most reasonable Alaskans have had no doubt that a dramatic shift is happening, although debate remains about how much of the warming has been caused by human activities. Some respected scientists in our region were tracking long-term climate oscillations in the North Pacific, which they said could be partly to blame. I was unconvinced that the time had come for a drastic government action limiting carbon. In 2005, at a hearing in Anchorage, I told a scientist from the National Center for Atmospheric Research that I wanted to know the cause with a level of certainty. He said, quite directly, that human activity had caused "nearly all the warming" in recent decades.

Whether I agreed or not, the accumulation of evidence demonstrated that something very serious was happening. Climate change was real and present in Alaska, not a theoretical threat. If we were causing any significant part of it, we had a responsibility to act.

In February 2006, I became one of the few Republican senators who spoke publicly on this. In a speech at Catholic University's law school, in Washington, I said, "I believe it is reality that man is contributing to the current warming trend. Accordingly, it is appropriate, and quite frankly our responsibility, to take steps to curb the growth of greenhouse gases."

According to the strange logic of politics, my new position exposed me to more criticism from environmentalists than if I had stayed quiet or expressed skepticism. They accused me of hypocrisy or cynicism whenever I advocated for my state's oil industry or voted against a carbon-reduction proposal I considered unready for passage. *Mother Jones* ran a take-down headlined "LISA MURKOWSKI: CLIMATE CHANGE DOUBLE AGENT." I'm not aware of a similar article about the more than forty Republican senators who denied or ignored the problem.

I've received this sort of criticism many times. Unfortunately, it is common to feel that those who agree with you have legitimate reasons for their views, while those who disagree are misinformed or dishonestly motivated. I'm often applauded for voting my conscience when I side with the Democrats, only to be condemned by the same liberals as a sellout when I side with the Republicans. I want to tell these people, *I am voting my conscience, not your conscience.*

Politically, my path is a hazardous one. It's human nature to take for granted those who agree with us—"naturally she agrees with the correct point of view"—while being strongly opposed to those who disagree—"something must be wrong with her, since she supports something that is wrong." The clannish partisanship of our current politics exacerbates this narrow-mindedness, as it encourages us to see those who disagree as enemies rather than trying to understand their genuine motivations. When I do the hard work of taking each issue on its merits, I rely on Alaskans to do something hard, as well: to pay serious attention to my reasons or, more likely, to trust me and believe that I really am who I say I am, with their best interests at heart. The latter also helps keep me honest, as trust like that is hard-won and easily lost.

In Washington, I am more often misunderstood. When I vote contrary to expectations, people look for an explanation in the context of the Washington they understand. What transactional deal did I make? What lobbyist or interest was I trying to please? The answer is "None." Unfortunately, explaining my real reasons doesn't always help. Cynical insiders know not to believe the phony rationales politicians give for their votes. I understand why voters no longer believe politicians, but I feel frustrated that an honest explanation isn't good enough to convince them.

Fortunately, I represent Alaska. When I am home, I hear about real needs, not political slogans or the latest Washington controversy. Constituents talk to me about transportation, fisheries, energy and mineral development, housing, clean water, and public safety. People are practical. In rural Alaska, my help is especially necessary. Locals don't have great financial means, their communities lack a tax base, and their representation in the state legislature is small and shrinking due to demographic changes. There are many villages where I may be one of the few statewide officials (or the only one) who has ever visited or has access to the resources to solve problems. That's why I serve—to improve the lives of Alaskans. I am personally fulfilled as I do so. We won the 2010 write-in because enough voters sensed that, especially Alaska Natives.

This cultural and political chasm between Alaska and Washington is the central challenge of my service. Alaska really is different. And I am different because I am Alaskan, to my core. Many Americans Outside hold grossly distorted views of my state, based on reality TV exaggerations or mythic imagery generated by environmental campaigns, advertising, and Hollywood. One of my goals in writing this book is to bridge this gap of understanding. I cannot explain what I do in Washington without explaining Alaska.

The 2023 battle over the Willow oil field was a powerful example of this disconnect. The field is under the National Petroleum Reserve in Alaska, a swath of Arctic Alaska set aside for this purpose in 1923. It lies east of Utqiagvik (formerly known as Barrow), the northernmost community in the United States, and the home of the Iñupiat. Their whaling culture has thrived there for thousands of years. ConocoPhillips had owned valid oil leases in the area for decades, but environmental organizations were fighting a last-ditch battle to persuade President Biden to block development, calling it a "climate bomb." No one knows more about living with climate change than the Iñupiat. Their world has been melting for years, with sea ice withdrawing and permafrost thawing. Whaling had been more dangerous and difficult for two decades due to less reliable ice. That winter, a young mother and her baby were killed by an emaciated polar bear outside the school in the village of Wales, where the bear's sea ice habitat had frozen very late that year.

During the fight over Willow in Washington that January, a long-time family friend, Iñupiaq leader Oliver Leavitt, died. I flew home to his service in Utqiagvik, two hours by jet from Anchorage, to the northern edge of the continent, where the land and the frozen sea meld into a single flat white surface. Sunrise remained a week away during the sixty-five-day night.

The weathered plywood houses on this white tableland suggest a community in poverty, but that's only because building here is so expensive—Utqiagvik is thriving, at the center of the North Slope Borough, which holds North America's largest oil field. The Native-owned Arctic Slope Regional Corporation is headquartered here. Its oil-related businesses helped ASRC become the largest company based in Alaska. I recalled Oliver's stories about his childhood, when he gathered driftwood to heat his family home. He said he liked school because it was the only building in the village with heat. In one lifetime, he had gone from that hardship to helping start the borough and serving as the chairman of ASRC. But he didn't lose the old ways. He was captain of a whaling crew, building his own umiaq boat and each spring dragging it over the sea ice to camp at the lead of open water, then paddling after the immense bowheads with a hand-thrown harpoon. This sustainably managed hunt, and the shared food it provides, is the heart of the Iñupiaq culture, which I have come to love. I have been out on the sea ice with crews as they broke trail to the open lead, I have helped move the large slabs of whale meat piled on sleds pulled behind snow machines, ever aware of polar bears watching, and I have eaten the maktak (raw skin and blubber) at the Nalukataq festival when the whaling was done.

We gathered in the school gym decorated with pictures of Oliver, showing his low, sturdy build and the thick cheeks that bulged when he smiled. The eulogies and gospel singing were in English and

Iñupiaq. The service lasted five hours. "We are a product of the school of Oliver Leavitt," said Richard Glenn, an Iñupiaq scientist and business leader. "He trained us in life. He trained us in work. He trained us in the knowledge of the Arctic environment." Willie Hensley, the intellectual father of the Native land claims movement, said, "Our nation's capital became his hunting ground. And he was good at it." The current chair of the ASRC board, Crawford Patkotak, said, "He was a staunch fighter for rights to resources." The gym where we sat had been built with those resources. Oliver liked to talk about the battle with the oil companies, in the 1970s, to create the borough, which could impose property taxes on the oil fields, bringing good schools to generations of Iñupiaq children, helicopters to the search-and-rescue squad to save lost hunters, and flush toilets to every house. Community leaders had tapped a nearby natural gas field to warm homes. These changes added years to the life expectancy for the Iñupiat.

I put everything I had into the battle to open Willow. I had a lot of political capital to invest, as President Biden was calling on me frequently for help in the narrowly divided Senate. We met many times, and every time we met, I told him Willow was my highest priority.

So am I a hypocrite? Are the Iñupiat? No, we know that people need resources and will continue to consume oil for some time—and if we don't produce that oil in Alaska, there is plenty coming from the Middle East, Russia, and other unstable parts of the world. Willow will supply two-tenths of a percent of the world's daily oil consumption, barely a click on the knob adjusting Saudi Arabia's output. That country has failed to budge world oil prices with production changes ten times larger than Willow's total output. And yet Willow would operate with more environmental protections and less carbon footprint than oil fields in most other parts of the world. It also would employ thousands of Alaskans. (As I was employed one summer, when I paid for a year of law school by working at Prudhoe Bay.) Only by reducing demand for oil, through conservation and carbon-free energy production, can we mitigate climate change.

Despite these facts, activists target Alaska oil, because it is symbolic. They highlight the irony of our state's impact from climate change while we pump oil out of the ground. But Alaska is not a symbol. Real people depend on these resources. I accept the responsibility to reduce carbon emissions, and I have worked for clean and renewable energy and conservation, especially in Alaska—although the emissions of our tiny population are nearly insignificant. But, at the same time, I also fight for Alaska to retain as large a share of the remaining oil market as possible. There is nothing hypocritical or cynical about those dual positions. The transition will be lengthy and costly as the technology advances.

My job was to work alongside leaders like Oliver for our Alaska communities, and all the good things natural resources bring. And when we won on Willow, I celebrated with great pride. I was honored to help free the resources needed by the Alaskans I serve. We knew we were doing the right thing.

To understand my politics, and to understand me, first understand this true picture of Alaska.

———

My earliest memories come from the small Southeast Alaska coastal fishing and timber community of Wrangell, where my father, as a young man, was the town banker. Wrangell sits in the lap of an island mountain among other mountainous islands, all covered in misty rainforest trees and moss. To get there, you take a boat or an airplane. When I was a kid, we left Wrangell on a Grumman Goose amphibious plane or rode the ferry. Today, Alaska Airlines flies north once a day to Petersburg and south once a day to Ketchikan. The ferry system is still there, but less reliable, and the ride to the highway connection in Bellingham takes forty-eight hours.

As kids, we were safely enfolded in the arms of this island community. On weekends, the family piled into Dad's seventeen-foot wooden boat and ventured out of the harbor to find a rocky beach where we could picnic and play. An infinite maze of channels among uninhabited islands surrounds Wrangell, all part of the Tongass National Forest, and as children these beaches were our unexplored country for personal discovery where we felt as comfortable and safe as in our backyard. When I was nine years old, we moved to Juneau, but the essence of growing up remained the same, with the sense that this wild place of land and water was not something separate from us. It was our home.

In Juneau, the main industry is state government, but most of Alaska's small towns connect to resources the way each year's blossoms connect to a perennial Sitka rose. The town blooms brightest when the fish are running strong, then goes largely dormant, waiting through the winter like a rose hip for the cycle to repeat. People in these towns know where their food and their paychecks come from. The waitress on Main Street is connected to the ecosystem, pouring more coffee and getting bigger tips when the salmon runs are healthy. Oil, minerals, and timber, although not as seasonal, similarly connect us to the place. Tourism may be the industry most like fishing. Visitors arrive like schools of spawning salmon in the spring, and guides and shop owners put out their offerings like set netters on the beach, seeking to catch just a few from the passing run.

My father's generation shared an unquestioned consensus that the land is home and its resources are to be used, and from their perspective, indignation was an understandable reaction to the arrival of the Outside environmental movement. The pollution and degradation that had inspired activism in the Lower 48 hadn't touched Alaska, which had not even been entirely mapped by the 1960s, but the new environmentalists—stereotypically long-haired kids and elite easterners—wanted to lock up resources and transform our home into a park. Outside policymakers paid no price for indulging them, but for Alaskans the stakes were high. For example, when President Clinton canceled long-term timber contracts in the

Tongass National Forest, the primary industry disappeared in several Southeast Alaska towns, including my hometowns of Wrangell and Ketchikan. Alaskans had fought for statehood in the 1950s to gain control of land and resources and now felt betrayed. For half a century, we fought for public lands, oil, timber, minerals, and fish, as Alaskans asserted their rights to the resources that had been promised and that sustained them.

Americans have long debated the true ownership of this vast, unpopulated land. The United States bought Russia's interests in Alaska in 1867 for $7.2 million, but the Russians had explored little of the land. Migrants from the rest of the States arrived in Alaska with the Klondike Gold Rush, in 1898, the last time Native people outnumbered Whites. In 1959, when Alaska became a state, the federal government pledged 103 million acres of land for the new state government to own. That event energized the Alaska Native land claims movement, as Indigenous communities saw the risk of losing their traditional lands, but they didn't reach agreement with the federal government until 1971, with passage of the Alaska Native Claims Settlement Act, which transferred 44 million acres of Alaska to corporations owned by the Native people then living. Today, 60 percent of Alaska belongs to the federal government, 28 percent to the state government, 12 percent to Native corporations, and two-tenths of 1 percent is owned conventionally by private parties.

Our landmass is a fifth of the rest of the nation's and more than twice the size of the next largest state—Texas—and our shoreline of forty-six thousand miles is more than that of all the contiguous states combined. Our coasts touch two oceans and three seas, ranging from the temperate rainforest on the Gulf of Alaska to the flat, treeless, and icy shores of the Arctic Ocean. Our mountains are the highest, we have more lakes and rivers, more wildlife, larger forests—the extremes go on and on. Yet small states like Connecticut have more miles of road (as do forty-three other states), we have no interstate highways, and you cannot drive to 80 percent of our communities. Alaska's cities have become exceptionally diverse, and proudly so, as immigration has mixed all races and nationalities into our demography, mostly within the last thirty years. But Alaska Natives remain the largest minority, at 17 percent of the population, which is the largest proportion of Indigenous people in any state.

These facts make Alaska different from the other states, but Alaska *feels* different, too. Every Alaska kid encounters surprising firsts when traveling to the Lower 48, such as seeing farm animals or fruit trees for the first time or, for those of my vintage, riding for the first time on a divided highway or watching live television for the first time. In 1975, when I went to Washington, D.C., as a high school intern for Senator Stevens, I was fascinated to be in the minority among all the Black people who lived there. We were staying at Trinity College, and I took my first ride on a city bus with the other interns heading to the Capitol. They were shocked when I struck up a conversation with an African American man seated nearby and asked him about his hair, which was in cornrows, something I had not seen up close before. I was curious. As we talked, I asked to touch his hair, and he agreed. The other interns were horrified. I didn't know enough to realize that my genuine curiosity had broken a taboo.

In truth, kids like me had a lot to learn about Alaska, too. Wrangell would seem quite rural to most Americans, as would most Alaska towns and cities, but "rural" has a whole different meaning in Alaska, referring to the barely populated, largely inaccessible majority of the state, where primarily Indigenous people carry on age-old lifeways, largely subsisting off the land. Alaskans sometimes call that rural-plus area "the Bush." Those living on the road system often don't know much about Alaska Native villages—there are more than two hundred of them—reachable only by small planes, boats, four-wheelers (as Alaskans call ATVs), or snow machines (as Alaskans call snowmobiles). Kids in the 1960s and '70s knew even less. As a youngster, I recall seeing the drab, boxy gray buildings of the Wrangell Institute, but I don't recall ever meeting the children there or knowing anything about their lives. Now I've heard many heartbreaking stories about this notorious Bureau of Indian Affairs boarding school, where children as young as eight years old were sent, having been taken away from their parents and villages, and stripped of their Native language and culture.

Prejudice often grows from ignorance, and even today most non-Native Alaskans have never been to a rural village. It can be less expensive for an Anchorage resident to travel to Europe than to a rural Alaska village—and, for the most part, going to a village really isn't practical without an invitation and a host, as most communities have no accommodations, restaurants, or any businesses other than a central tribal or village store, which is usually smaller than a typical gas station convenience store, with exotically high prices.

My friend Andrew Halcro unintentionally demonstrated the consequences of this situation not long after we were both elected to the State House in 1998. He became the chairman of the Community and Regional Affairs Committee—overseeing rural issues— without an accurate understanding of how Native people lived. He embarrassed himself by making some ignorant, offensive remarks and by losing his temper on the House floor with a Native member, Albert Kookesh, from Angoon. But Andrew redeemed himself, gaining new respect, when he apologized and admitted that he needed to learn more. Despite being a lifelong Alaskan, he said, he had been to a rural community only once, as a high school wrestler. After the incident on the House floor, he met with a group of Native leaders, and they opened his eyes to their need for more self-determination as tribes and the poor treatment accorded them by the state government. Andrew said he understood for the first time the prejudice in Alaska society, a problem we called the urban-rural divide. Sitting next to Albert Kookesh on an airplane returning to Juneau, Andrew said, "I never knew."

Albert said, "This is what I live with every day."

"There really are two different worlds," Andrew observed.

Alaska's urban-rural divide has narrowed since the 1990s. Many Alaskans work to bridge the two worlds. As a legislator, I accepted an offer to take my family to rural Alaska offered by the Alaska chamber of commerce. Verne, the boys, and I flew to Unalakleet, four hundred miles northwest of Anchorage, on Norton Sound, facing the Bering Sea, to spend a few days with Chuck and Virginia Degnan. He was a Native leader and former legislator, and she was a teacher. The boys' excitement and astonishment began when the plane landed on a gravel runway, and grew as the Degnans brought us to their home on four-wheelers, which Nic and Matt got to drive. Verne and the boys found heaven fishing in the Unalakleet River. The community welcomed us like family. We met people who impressed us deeply, who we would never forget, including Reuben Mixsooke, an Iñupiaq subsistence fisherman who took us upriver in his boat. Reuben, an Army veteran, had lost both his legs to a land mine in Vietnam but had figured out how to adapt his boat and his four-wheeler—he had no wheelchair—to support himself on the land in the traditional way and in a village without accessible facilities.

When I ran in my first Senate election, in 2004, we planned a big river trip as part of the campaign, taking the boys and my mother-in-law, Dorothy McCoy, up the Kuskokwim from Bethel, 260 river miles to Stony River, stopping over the course of a week to meet voters in ten villages along the way. The trip was a comedy of errors. We ran hard aground on a sandbar within the first hour. Waiting for the tide change in eight hours was not an option once we realized that we had no food on the boat other than Pepsi and powdered sugar doughnuts (much to the delight of my boys!). We were eventually able to lighten the grounded boat by carrying the women by piggyback across to a mid-river island, with Dorothy laughing until she cried as she clung to a man who had stripped down to his jockey shorts. Our trip continued over multiple days with more mishaps, including running out of gas and discovering that none of our fancy communications devices worked in the remote area. Finally we sheared a prop above Lower Kalskag, which ended the journey short of our intended destination, leaving us with a rich stock of memories and stories that people in the villages are still laughing about.

When it comes to rural Alaska travel, if no one gets hurt, it doesn't matter when you arrive. Village time reflects the conditions around you, reminding you that you are not always in charge. The connections to people and the place are what matter, the caring and respect for elders, honor for people of life-proven ability, and, always, the community, which comes before any individual. Food is a gift we never refuse, although you can take just a small, symbolic bite of something like fermented whale blood, which isn't my favorite—because to refuse, would be a grievous insult. Sharing is fundamental in these cultures. In the far north, people survive collectively. Respect enables that, and conflict is avoided. In Iñupiaq culture, no one will directly disagree. Instead, if someone makes a statement that is incorrect, the next speaker will take the floor and tell a long story with a different moral at the end.

I learned to listen. Long pauses are times for consideration and for a speaker's emphasis to be held—even with a thirty-second silence—and hurrying to fill that gap with your own words only shows your own lack of awareness. In the Tlingit culture of Southeast Alaska, the oratory of impressive speakers is held in high esteem, and meetings always begin with lengthy speeches, given by men in a strict hierarchical priority, an order they understand without any explicit direction and that no one would dare interrupt. This lasts a long time before a visitor is asked to comment—and basic courtesy requires following those rules. In the Athabascan region, there is also great formality and dignity, but not the tradition of speechmaking, and the rules aren't quite so clear. One must be careful and attuned to the moment. The Yup'ik politely invite a visitor to speak first and then comment in line with that lead, often with raised eyebrows alone. And the Iñupiat overflow with kindness and welcome, full of cheer as they assiduously avoid conflict. There, younger people always cast their eyes down—to look a person in the eye is an assertion of status, which properly belongs to the elders. And always, in all these cultures, respect is paramount. Particularly for elders.

The most important skills for a visitor are patient, thoughtful listening and never to push. More is happening than appears on the surface. Fortunately, I am naturally a person who waits to hear what others will say, so I observe as well. Active listening is key to connecting with Alaskans.

Villages are tribes, more like extended families than our American sense of a village as a smaller version of a town or city. You don't just show up. And it matters who invites you, regardless of your status in the outside world, and who travels with you and who introduces you—it matters deeply, in ways an outsider can scarcely understand. Subsistence opportunities trump all other schedules in rural Alaska. Fish runs, bird and animal migrations, berries—those are the source of life, and there are no second chances if you miss the season. When my father was a senator, he brought a delegation of several senators to the Arctic village of Kaktovik in the heart of ANWR during peak berry picking and learned firsthand the priority of subsistence. No one was at the airstrip to meet the official party. When they arrived at the community center, they again found no one, but there was a note: "Welcome, senators. The berry picking is good today. Have a nice trip."

That story is not an example of rudeness; it is an example of the vast distance between two cultures. And it goes both ways. With goodwill, we have nevertheless struggled to equip children in rural Alaska with the education they need to navigate both our culture and their own. Getting Washington to understand Alaska has been even more difficult. Early in my Senate tenure, in 2003, I could not get the Bush administration to listen to me when I explained that its signature No Child Left Behind Act simply would not work in rural Alaska. The law, which was finally acknowledged as a failure ten years later, was intended to improve public education through competition, using standardized testing to label schools based on "adequate yearly progress," or AYP, and allowing families from failing schools to go to the nearest successful school instead.

I looked at a map to figure out where in Alaska this policy would be most ridiculous, and I settled on a St. Lawrence Island village out in the Bering Sea, 165 miles from Nome, closer to Russia than the Alaska coast. In Savoonga, the traditional Siberian Yup'ik student body would be unlikely to make AYP. Besides the educational challenges in the village, there were so few students that if a single child missed the test day, the entire school would automatically fail. I had never been there and I didn't know exactly what we would find, but I knew the law would make no sense, just based on the geography. I invited Secretary of Education Rod Paige to go with me to see.

At first, Paige refused, saying he was too busy for the five-thousand-mile journey. I asked Ted Stevens for help, and he called the White House, strongly suggesting they tell Paige to go. Paige wasn't happy about it, but he joined me on a trip to Nome, where we boarded a small plane to Savoonga, a flight of an hour and fifteen minutes. He grew quiet, looking out over bright water, strewn with icebergs in May, as we flew far out of sight of land. This, I reminded him, would be the trip made by children from St. Lawrence Island every day to go to school in Nome, the nearest alternative, if their tiny village schools could not reach AYP. The airplane would be their school bus. He said, "I think I'm starting to get it."

We rode snow machines from the landing strip to the school. Principal Dave Bauer had come from the Midwest and was finishing his second school year in Savoonga. I asked how his family liked living in such a remote village, and he responded that his wife had never even visited, because there was no place for her to stay. Without housing available, the principal lived in the school, sleeping on a mattress in a broom closet (he planned to leave at the end of the term). A special ed teacher was living in her classroom, on a mat the janitor laid out behind her desk each night. The secretary was dumbfounded. He also learned about the students' health, as the children could use running water and toilets only at the school, since none of them had that at home. And he saw the heavy impact of fetal alcohol syndrome, which affected more children than he had ever seen in a school.

To his credit, Secretary Paige was deeply moved, and after getting over his shock, he became animated about taking care of Savoonga.

"When you said 'rural' to me several days ago, it meant one thing," he told reporters. "When you say it to me now, it means a different thing."

On the trip back he said he would consider an Alaska exception from NCLB. To deal with the housing, health, and sanitation issues, he would convene the secretaries of Housing and Urban Development, the Interior, and Health and Human Services, as well as the administrator of the EPA. Those four cabinet members did meet to talk about little Savoonga, and we did make progress on teacher housing, which is continuing.

I learned a key lesson for getting things done in Washington for my Alaska constituents. Washington people needed to see for themselves. Our Alaskan lives were too different, too far from their experience, too far from home, for them to really imagine the impact of our problems.

I suppose that knowledge has helped keep me more grounded in Alaska than in Washington, even after all these years. These are two completely different worlds. And Alaska is more real to me.

The independence that Alaskans gave me in the 2010 election made me an increasingly unusual member of the Senate, as the body became more partisan and the traditions that encourage compromise broke down. Respect and cooperation cannot be forced, they must be given willingly, and that is how the Senate worked for two centuries. Although the filibuster was always available, for example, senators almost never used it to block presidential appointments, resorting to it only in exceptional circumstances, nor was it routinely used on other matters. The existence of that tool for the minority kept the majority honest, but most of the time senators worked things out without resorting to the confrontation of filibuster and cloture, the supermajority vote that ends a filibuster.

In 2005, Democrats had filibustered enough of President Bush's appellate judge nominations that Majority Leader Bill Frist threatened the so-called nuclear option, allowing a simple majority to win a cloture vote, which would give the majority party the power to stop a filibuster against a judge, rather than the sixty votes needed under the rules. A bipartisan group of seven Democrats and seven Republicans, the Gang of Fourteen, got together to find a compromise, and informal rules emerged to allow nominees to go ahead without filibusters or the nuclear option (I think that was the first Senate "gang"). The system worked for a while, but with Obama in the White House and the Democrats in the majority, in May 2011, the Republicans filibustered confirmation of a liberal judge for the Ninth Circuit Court of Appeals. The controversy was identical to the one six years earlier, but with the parties reversed. And besides swapping their roles, the two sides also swapped their rhetoric, each saying what the other side had said last time, and with equal indignation.

I simply refused to participate. I was the only Republican to vote for cloture, to stop that filibuster. (Even Republican members of the original Gang of Fourteen helped blow up their own agreement.) Alaskans wanted me to vote on the merits of judges, not block considering them because the president was from another party. But I didn't make a big deal about it. I had no intention of calling out or alienating my Republican colleagues. I simply adopted my own, internal rule, in accordance with the way I believed the Senate was intended to operate: I might vote against a nominee, but I would not support a filibuster of a confirmation vote. My party, however, kept obstructing Obama's nominees, and near the end of 2013, Democratic Majority Leader Harry Reid invoked the nuclear option for all judicial appointments except the Supreme Court. The filibuster had been abused, and now it was gone.

Today's erosion of faith in the courts developed, in part, from these events (as we shall see in the chapters ahead). The threat of filibuster served a purpose. The alternative—each party approving its own judges without considering the other party—made the judiciary more political, as it freed party leaders from the need to attract support from across the aisle. The president, advised by senators, could choose judges appealing only to the party's base, the most ideological and extreme of their supporters. Most of us say we want judges who follow the law, without a hint of which political party originally put them in their robes. With the loss of the process in the Senate, the moderate majority lost its leverage to make that happen, and Americans began losing respect for the judiciary, a key pillar of democracy and the rule of law.

My new freedom after the 2010 write-in victory also helped me see the issue of same-sex marriage differently, as I thought of Alaskans rather than of my party. I was in Kenai, at the big community picnic called Industry Appreciation Day, when I met an interesting woman at the Veterans Affairs booth, Victoria Green, and we got into a conversation about families. Victoria had taken in a foster child, Mercedes, whom she loved, and she wanted to take in Mercedes's three siblings, too, but she had run into difficulties with the foster care agency. Victoria's partner, a member of the National Guard who would soon be deployed, was a woman, and the system would not consider the couple as a mutually supporting family unless they were married—which was disallowed by a state constitutional amendment I had supported years earlier. We had a deep discussion and later stayed connected. My staff helped Victoria and her partner; they were able to foster the other children, and they later adopted all four. Several years after we met, in 2013, I nominated her for an "Angels in Adoption" award, and the family received a trip to Washington.

The entire family joined me for lunch in the Senate Dining Room. The children, wiggly but well behaved, joyously brightened my busy political day. I told their mothers they had created a beautiful family. But Victoria pointed out that the family was, in fact, precarious. The kids were legally hers, not her partner's, and only she could deal with the school or the doctor. And if anything happened to her, the children would all be taken back into the foster care system. In that moment, I was overwhelmed, seeing these two women, whose love was so obviously strong, and the safe and loving family they had made for these kids, who had never known that stability before. The government's rule was just wrong. I told them, sitting at that table, that I would work to protect them and their family—it was time for marriage equality.

My staff freaked out. Our party had used this issue to mobilize voters for years, and only two other Republican senators had publicly supported same-sex marriage. The Supreme Court was considering the issue, and nothing was before the Senate to vote on—there was no reason to choose this moment to go out on a limb. I told the staff I didn't need to know the politics or the polls, I only needed help making the announcement. I did it in an Anchorage TV interview and a lengthy essay we posted online about Victoria's family. "They embraced the joy and sacrifice of four adopted children living under the same roof, with smiles, laughter, movie nights, parent-teacher conferences and runny noses," I wrote. But, I explained, "if one of them gets sick or injured and needs critical care, the other would not be allowed to visit them in the emergency room—and the children could possibly be taken away from the healthy partner." Two years later, the Supreme Court's *Obergefell* decision settled the matter.

Winning the 2010 write-in also gave me the confidence to help break a legislative logjam in Congress. I saw an opportunity, working from the middle, to bring together senators with complementary goals on federal lands. The Senate had not passed lands bills in years, and now I was ranking member of the Energy and Natural Resources Committee—the top Republican—and could bring together a bill with many issues that individual senators wanted. Working far away from the bright lights of the partisan flash points, we could fix problems that mattered to local people, especially in my own state.

The chairman of the committee, Democrat Mary Landrieu, of Louisiana, was fighting a losing reelection campaign and was not fully engaged in committee tasks, so I worked with our counterparts in the House. We put together a bill by cleaning out a basket of hundreds of senators' and representatives' orphaned land proposals, which had accumulated over years of congressional inaction, and picking out those bills that could fit together in a single package. Some were for development, some for conservation, and many would just help communities with problems. Nothing was too small—we even got support from Al Franken of Minnesota by including a one-acre land transfer for a school district in his state that had been stalled for a decade. We balanced the pieces carefully. In Alaska, for example, we set aside 150,000 acres of the Tongass National Forest for protection, but we also exchanged 70,000 acres to a Native corporation for timber harvest, keeping the local forest products industry alive. This kind of legislating is hard. You have to work with each individual member of Congress to learn his or her desires and dislikes, and build a level of comfort around the whole effort as legitimate and honest.

In 2014, Republicans won control of the Senate. I was ebullient about winning the majority. I would take the chair of both the Energy and Natural Resources Committee and the Appropriations Subcommittee on Interior, Environment, and Related Agencies, which oversees spending for those agencies. These were the prizes Ted Stevens had set me up for strategically in our first Christmas Eve meeting, twelve years earlier. Getting onstage at Anchorage's Election Central gathering, I picked up a chair and lifted it over my head like a trophy. Oliver Leavitt told a reporter, "She's always been a tough lady, but now she's a tough lady with a big stick." I got an even larger compliment from a Sierra Club executive, who expressed fear over my new power, saying I would be "formidable."

The next month, in December, my lands bill, with its fifty seven individual pieces, finally passed. Each piece was small, but the entire 167 pages, affecting thirty-six states, was among the biggest legislative accomplishments of the year. Just before Christmas, President Obama signed it.

In January, I took the gavel as chair of Energy and Natural Resources and sat down to meet with my ranking member, Maria Cantwell of Washington. On our side of the aisle, she had a reputation as a liberal and a committed environmentalist, a tough opponent. Ted Stevens had feuded bitterly with Maria. She had led the devastating defeat of the ANWR drilling bill in December 2005. He had vowed on the floor of the Senate to campaign against her the next year, and he had (although since Ted and ANWR drilling were both unpopular in Washington, he may have unintentionally helped her). Maria and I had a social relationship through our dinners for women senators, but she wasn't easy to get to know. Now, however, I needed to figure out how to work with her, because I wanted to run a bipartisan committee that could pass legislation into law.

We sat down to talk about our most important priorities. Mine was oil exploration in ANWR. Hers was to make ANWR a wilderness. I respected her despite our differences. She was a hard worker, determined, and knew her stuff. Nothing would happen either way on ANWR with a Republican Senate and Obama as president, so I suggested we set that to one side. What else could we agree on that would be good policy for our country? We started thinking about an omnibus energy bill, like the lands bill I had just passed. No energy legislation had passed Congress since 2007, eight years previously, but the country faced unprecedented and rapidly evolving energy challenges, including climate change. We couldn't fix everything, but we could do some important things, and prove that Congress was still able to address America's problems.

Next, we sat down with our staffs. Every Senate committee has two, one for the majority and another for the minority. Committee staffs tend to be professionals with deep expertise on their subject matter, and some of the best have decades of experience. Sometimes, however, after so many years in the partisan trenches, they can become harshly determined fighters for party positions. We had some true professionals, and they were ready to follow the committee leadership in whatever direction we chose. Maria and I sat them down and let them know we were working together now. The two staffs would travel together, build the energy bill together, and cooperate as a team. We made a tradition of weekly morning coffee to talk with our staff directors about their assignments and how we could get things done.

Maria proved to be a good partner. Like me, she didn't mind putting in the hours, and she could be trusted to keep her word. We figured out how to collaborate. We partnered on rounding up supporters for our bill from each side of the aisle. Many senators had their own dormant energy bills, like the lands bills I had assembled into that successful package, and each of those pieces was a potential offer to bring in the vote of a senator. Over sixteen months of work, we would include provisions giving ownership to most members of each party. That would give us a base of support upon which we could build the larger policy pieces capable of advancing the nation's energy system, while taking steps to address climate change, including how to integrate renewable energy.

Before tackling this project, we had carefully studied the issues and had drawn up a blueprint for our bill. Working with our talented bipartisan staff and with support from the secretary of energy, Ernest Moniz, we attempted to thread the needle on the tools to address climate change that we could encourage in legislation without driving away those senators who still refused to be part of the solution. Our country was not prepared for the transition to renewable energy because we lacked the ability to move and store enough electricity. We could invest heavily in battery technology and energy transmission—science and infrastructure—and those expenditures would produce economic benefits even in states represented by senators who insisted that climate change was a hoax.

We introduced our package in May. The following December, we passed tax credits for solar and wind energy, as well as an end to the ban on exporting oil, as part of the federal spending package. The strategy that I advanced to lift the forty-year ban on oil exports led to the transformation of the U.S. energy industry as a whole, as exports helped make our country the world's top oil producer (but it did not affect Alaska, which was not subject to the ban). And then, in April 2016, our omnibus bipartisan energy bill finally came to the Senate floor. I monitored the vote sheet while some of the most liberal and conservative senators came to offer congratulations. Maria Cantwell and I exchanged high fives. The final vote was eighty-five to twelve.

The work continued as we negotiated in a conference committee with the House, which had passed a version oriented to Republican priorities only. That began in July, with not much time left in the election year. Again, the process was additive, bringing in more positive pieces. By the time we were done, the bill contained a conservation proposal for sportsmen's groups, a package of fifty individual lands bills, and Maria's legislation addressing fire mitigation and water management in the West. The conference version included provisions for 74 senators and 224 members of the House. But the House side brought up late changes and objected to a provision sponsored by Maria, raising an insincere argument. As the end of the year approached, we worked through the issues one by one. The election took place and the bill sat in the lame-duck Congress, on the House side, waiting for action.

In December, we got word that the House might adjourn without voting on the completed conference version of the bill. Adjournment would kill it and waste our two years of efforts to pull together support. Maria and I were working very late in the Capitol, and we decided to go over to the House and find someone to help get the bill over the finish line. We saw that the House Christmas tree was dark, with its cheesehead ornament on top—Paul Ryan, from Wisconsin, was Speaker of the House. The House had closed out and members had departed, but even so, at two A.M., Maria and I marched up and down the halls of the House, knocking on office doors and calling out the names of congressmen. It was frustrating and we were ridiculous, but we weren't ready to give in without trying everything.

But we failed. The House left without taking up the bill. I'm still not sure why Ryan closed out without voting on the bill, although the rumor in the Capitol had it that he wanted to catch a train to New York for a Christmas party. In January, with a new Congress and a new president, we would have to start all over again.

————

In Washington, people couldn't figure me out. *Outside* magazine declared that, as chairman, I was "The #1 Anti–Public Land Lawmaker" and quoted an activist from an Arizona environmental group saying, "Extraction is her top priority, whether it's drilling, fracking, or logging. She's not looking at what's really good for the future of Alaska." I think that was backward. But I had learned that development supporters also assumed I was automatically on their side. When a deadline came up for the federal government to demand additional settlement payments from ExxonMobil for its *Exxon Valdez* oil spill, oil industry people thought I would automatically oppose the reopener so the company would not have to pay more. But I had been to Prince William Sound and I knew that, twenty years after the spill, oil could still be found under the cold rocks of some beaches. And the big spring herring runs that had crashed after the spill had never returned, with scientific evidence suggesting that buried oil could be a culprit.

I am not on the development team or the environment team. I am dedicated to the economic *and* environmental health of Alaska.

I did carry on some of the battles fought by my father and Ted Stevens, for ANWR oil and Tongass timber, for reasons I am proud of. Both jobs and the environment sustain us, and I refuse to believe they are mutually exclusive. But while we want to move beyond these legacy issues and conflicts, the federal government needs to keep its side of the bargain on commitments already made. Alaska relied on promises made in the Statehood Act, in 1959, and in the Alaska National Interest Lands Conservation Act, in 1980, and contained in other laws, for how we could use and develop our state, regarding access, revenue from petroleum, and many other issues. The federal government cannot now change the terms, offensively suggesting that Alaska must be protected from Alaskans, who get too little credit for our care and stewardship. The beauty and purity of our great land is the main reason most of us live here.

Now we also find ourselves on the front line of the global disaster of climate change, and our people need help. We have about seventy Alaska Native villages threatened by flooding, erosion, and thawing permafrost, including a few where lives are at risk during fall storms that tear away the ground from under homes and buildings. Newtok was one of the first where the hazard became undeniable and the struggle to move began early, as I discussed in the introduction. Its region, known as the Y-K Delta, between the Yukon and Kuskokwim river mouths, is a patchwork of lakes and wetlands, in places solid only by virtue of being permanently frozen. The Bureau of Indian Affairs chose this ill-considered site for the village in the 1950s, when it built a school there, forcing families to settle from traditional homes. By every measure, the federal government owes it to these people to help them move to a new, safer place.

The move would be expensive and require a coordinated effort led by the community—not outsiders—to build a new village, with a new school, post office, homes, power plant, water and sewer system—everything from scratch—on solid uplands nine miles from the original site. But while we were working on that, homes in Newtok were physically falling apart—old, overcrowded homes—as the frozen ground beneath them turned to mush, collapsing their footings and opening huge gaps in their walls. The Ninglick River carved Newtok toward oblivion. Sometimes only a few feet would go in a year, but a big storm could take many yards of the newly thawed ground in a single night. The water supply was failing and the sewer lagoon was condemned, taking away the place villagers had dumped their honey buckets. They began dumping them in the only place available, the river. Then waves and high tides would bring the filth back. Children got sick.

Newtok had one advantage, in that climate change brought the attention of the media, with reporters periodically dropping in to highlight the problem. Most of my village constituents are invisible, their living conditions unknown to the outside world. In Buckland, in the northwest Arctic, I attended a school assembly with the whole community. I was watching children dancing when an elder sitting near me in the bleachers leaned over and said, "Lisa, all I want before I die is a flush toilet." This was Dora Hadley. I often have replayed that encounter in my mind, because her request was so basic. I went back to Washington thinking that, whatever I accomplished during my Senate service, I would at least get Dora a toilet.

People in Washington, and most of America, take for granted safe drinking water and access to sewer systems, which protect us from disease. In many rural Alaska communities, illness preys on people, especially children, when they lack clean running water and use buckets for toilets. In some villages, it is still the job of the young boys to haul those buckets of human waste to the sewage lagoon. During the pandemic, we told everyone to wash their hands, but in many villages, they had to go to the village school to do so. To address these problems, I have often put earmarks in the federal budget for village projects. But in the minds of Washington insiders who don't understand rural Alaska, earmarks are nothing but wasteful pork-barrel spending for shady special interests. Ask the people of Buckland if they think basic sanitation is wasteful spending.

My motivation to get Dora's toilet was pure. But I did receive gifts from the community. Standing at that community presentation in the middle of the gym, I was given a sweatshirt with the school's beluga whale logo—the beluga is part of the local diet. And then the mayor handed me a large heavy-duty garbage bag containing a bigger gift: a huge black wolf pelt, with dried blood from the recently killed animal. This was legal, as a tribal gift, and, of course, I was grateful and thanked the mayor. The rich black fur was magnificent. But what was I going to do with a raw wolf pelt in Washington? In Fairbanks, on the way home, I asked for advice from my sister Eileen's husband, Leon Van Wyhe (who has, sadly, since passed away). A solid old-time Alaskan, Leon gruffly took the pelt off my hands and said he would handle it. The next time I came through, he had it ready for me, expertly tanned. I asked what I owed, but Leon said no money had changed hands—he had traded the cowling of his old Ski-Doo snow machine with his friend who had tanned it, who owned the same model. And now I had to figure out how to report *that* on my Senate ethics report.

The folks in Buckland got impatient. They didn't understand what it takes to get the Senate and the Washington bureaucracy to build an Arctic water and sewer system. By the time Dora approached me and I got involved, the project had already been going on for a number of years and had consumed millions of dollars, without anything being built. Many agencies were involved, but none was in charge. I convened all the state and federal agencies and picked a lead, and we found more money. Finally, the project began to move—but it took a total of twelve years to complete. When the system began working, I went back to Buckland. The first toilet was in an elder's house. We strung a blue birthday ribbon across the toilet bowl, and each member of the village came in, dozens in turn, to cut the ribbon with me and flush.

We don't often get perfect wins. Success uncovers another problem. Buckland's new system proved too expensive for many residents to use. Moving Newtok is hard not only because of the cost of housing and infrastructure, which is my job, but also because of the emotional, social, and financial costs for the people who live there. I try to remember that I am not responsible for everything. Alaska Native peoples are wise and know more about surviving on their land than anyone else. They are lucky and enviable in the richness and enveloping connections of their cultures and communities, which I have been honored to know as a frequent visitor. As Alaska's senior senator, helping as much as I can is enough for me.

As for climate change, I can't afford to worry about symbolism, irony, or what *Outside* magazine thinks. We have to solve this, but oil and natural resources will remain Alaska's economic lifeblood for some time. And I will use any tool in Congress for Alaskans' benefit, within the bounds of ethics and the law.

Most likely, I will never be understood in Washington. The best gift that Alaskans have given me is that I don't have to answer to Washington.

CHAPTER 6

Staying Strong in Trump's Washington

I NEVER LET DONALD TRUMP get to me. I never voted for him and I ignored his threats, voting against him at key moments, yet I won some of my biggest legislative victories during his first term. Trump's MAGA movement captured the spirit of the Tea Party— a disruptive, angry spirit, oblivious to nuances and deaf to other points of view. He perfected that style of politics, but I had been resisting it for years. As an Alaskan, I knew who I was and who I worked for. I supported many of Trump's policies once he became president, particularly on energy. I had to work with whoever was in power to serve my state, but I didn't have to bend my principles. Indeed, my willingness to go against the party gave me additional strength. If I "mastered Trump's Washington," as *The New York Times* asserted in a headline in 2018, that was how I did it.

Trump struck me the wrong way from the first time I heard he wanted to be president. How could ordinary Americans relate to a rich businessman from New York City who always wore a suit and tie? Then we learned of his repeated bankruptcies, his dishonest business dealings, and his failure to pay contractors. I had never seen his TV show or read his books, so I didn't appreciate the image he had created. His candidacy at first looked like a stunt. He posed on a golden escalator in the gaudy lobby of his New York skyscraper and lashed out against Hispanic immigrants, calling Mexicans rapists. It was offensive, simplistic nonsense. No one in my circle thought he had a snowball's chance in hell of getting the nomination. I didn't pay much attention.

But Trump was connecting with people. I got my first sense of that a few weeks after he entered the race, at an Independence Day celebration in the small coastal town of Seward. After the parade, I lined up for a hot dog and chatted with folks around me—true "retail politics." The hot dog vendor recognized me and asked who I would support for president. I gave him the political runaround, saying it was still early. He responded very directly. He said Trump was the only one who was authentic and could fix things, the only one who would stand up for people like him, and warned me that I had better get on board. I defused the situation by pointing out that he was out of mustard, but privately I acknowledged the intensity of feelings Trump could elicit. I didn't need polling data for that.

Within months of entering the race, Trump became a front-runner in polls for the Republican presidential nomination, but most political insiders expected his support to collapse when voters learned more about him. In the first debate, in early August 2015, Megyn Kelly of Fox News challenged him about his frequent attacks on women. "You've called women you don't like fat pigs, dogs, slobs, and disgusting animals," she said. "You once told a contestant on *Celebrity Apprentice* it would be a pretty picture to see her on her knees. Does that sound to you like the temperament of a man we should elect as president?"

That was the right question. And it should have stopped Trump.

But in response, he said, "I think the big problem this country has is being politically correct." And then he said America had become a loser and he would make it win. The next day he went on CNN and attacked Kelly, suggesting that she had been menstruating.

In March 2016, Mitt Romney courageously challenged Trump in a speech during the primaries, clearly and strongly calling him out as a fake, a phony, and a con man. He pointed out Trump's unwork-able policies, his many failures in business, his weird admiration for Vladimir Putin, his dishonesty, vulgarity, and personal immorality. Romney also said something else that resonates with me—and that still confuses me about my friends who were willing to ignore Trump's faults.

"Now, imagine your children and your grandchildren acting the way he does," Romney said. "Would you welcome that? Haven't we seen before what happens when people in prominent positions fail the basic responsibility of honorable conduct? We have. And it al-ways injures our families and our country."

I believe that the person in the presidency must be held to the highest standard of honor and dignity, regardless of political views. Those qualities have been one of America's strengths through our history. We have had presidents who fell short, making mistakes or exposing their own flaws after they were in office, but the voters always did their job, rejecting those who lacked moral character. That judgment is part of our responsibility of citizenship. Electing a president we respect is good for our children, as Romney said, and it is also good for our democracy, contributing to our faith in the institutions of our government even when we disagree with the in-dividual decisions—a key to the peaceful transfer of power over the 250 years of America's success.

Trump's immigrant bashing also offended me. Immigration should be controlled and legal, of course, but much of the MAGA rhetoric attacked not the process or the law of immigration—which we have had ample opportunities to fix—but the people themselves. And, for some reason, that rhetoric was directed only at people of color. Immigrants from Africa, the Middle East, the Pacific Islands, Latin America, and Asia bring new vitality to our economy and culture. I learned at Government Hill Elementary that these Amer-icans by choice can be the best Americans, full of idealism, with the energy and determination to succeed. Their skin color makes them no more a threat than Trump's German grandfather, Scottish mother, or Slovenian wife.

Alaska's diversity exploded in the last thirty years, but immigrants have strengthened my state from the beginning. Filipinos powered the fishing industry in territorial days, Japanese supported the timber economy in the 1960s, and Koreans opened small businesses all over Anchorage. Moving to Alaska takes initiative even for native-born Americans, so imagine the courage of those choosing to make Alaska home from Venezuela, Sudan, or Laos. These are strong people. Families from American Samoa and Tonga have thrived in Utqiagvik, where from October through May the average daily high temperature never rises above freezing—while on those Pacific islands the average daily low never falls below sixty-five degrees all year long. Strong people, indeed.

Despite my unease, as Trump gathered momentum in the primaries, I didn't speak up the way Romney did. I was running for reelection, again challenged by Joe Miller, and I deflected questions about who I was supporting for president. Speaking out against Trump at that point would have done our state no good. Nor would it have slowed Trump—I wasn't a national figure like Romney, who had been the 2012 party nominee, and his speech hadn't changed Trump's trajectory.

Occasionally I'm asked if I would run for president. I immediately dismiss the idea. I usually say I love Alaska too much, and the president has to love all the states equally. The truth is that I am a patriot and I love my country, but in my heart I am an Alaskan first. Perhaps that explains, in part, why Trump never rattled me. He took over the party and the government, but he didn't take over the source of my power, which was Alaska, in my heart.

————

Supreme Court Justice Antonin Scalia died in his sleep on February 13, 2016. Before the day was over, Majority Leader McConnell released a statement saying that the seat should not be filled until a new president was inaugurated, in eleven months. Our conference had not been consulted about this snap decision, but many Republican senators quickly expressed agreement in public. I was in Alaska for my annual address to the legislature and was caught off guard by McConnell's announcement. I did not believe the framers had intended for senators to hold open a Supreme Court seat for close to a year until they had a president more to their liking. Advice and consent were supposed to be based on the nominee's qualifications, not pure politics. For the most part, that was how the confirmation process had worked for two centuries. Scalia himself had been confirmed by a unanimous vote. To foreclose a nominee before the person was even named would nakedly politicize the process.

After my speech in Juneau, I told reporters, "I do believe that the nominee should get a hearing."

At that time, Judiciary chairman Chuck Grassley was saying he would decide on whether to hold confirmation hearings after President Obama announced a nominee. When President Obama nominated Judge Merrick Garland, Grassley said he would not hold hearings, and I announced that I would respect the will of the committee. (I was not a member.) As a chairman myself, I knew the importance of having your conference back your decision. I did meet with Garland, as I always do with consequential nominees. While the conversation was interesting, the meeting was perfunctory. The nomination was already dead.

In May, soon after Trump's final primary opponent withdrew, his campaign released a list of judges he would appoint if elected president. In combination with McConnell's strategy to hold a seat open, the message was clear. Voters were electing a Supreme Court justice as well as a president, and a vote for Trump would be a vote for a justice Republicans had preselected. The strategy proved to be effective politically. For traditional conservatives repelled by Trump's populist stands and coarse style, the promise of a court seat gave them a reason to hold their noses and vote for him.

Trump never hid his disdain for the justice system. Within a month of becoming the presumptive nominee, he launched a racist attack against a U.S. district court judge, Gonzalo Curiel, whose parents were Mexican immigrants. Curiel was presiding over litigation against the so-called Trump University, a real estate seminar that regulators said defrauded students. (Trump ultimately settled for $25 million, returning students' tuitions and paying a fine.) Trump claimed that Curiel was biased because of his heritage. "I'm building a wall. It's an inherent conflict of interest," he said. Speaker Ryan called Trump's statements "the textbook definition of a racist comment." At that early stage of his rise, Trump was forced to issue a statement saying he had been misconstrued, but within months, most Republicans would be afraid of challenging his offensive remarks. We gave him that power to destroy norms by failing to stand up to him from the start.

Trump's election in 2016 hastened a historic decline in the institutions of American justice. The judiciary, like the other two branches of our democratic republic, depends on the respect of the people for its authority. The philosophers of the eighteenth century saw, and our framers understood, that human beings need sovereign authority to hold violent anarchy at bay. The miracle of our constitution was to establish a system of checks and balances to substitute for a monarch in that role. The system was built on faith. So long as we believe in our institutions, we can accept their rule, even when we disagree with individual decisions. By degrading that faith, first in Congress, then the presidency, and finally the courts, we punctured the fabric that protects us from the chaos of uncontrolled conflict.

Trump would come to preside over anarchic violence and an attempt to overthrow the democratic system, disregarding the rulings of the courts about his bogus claims of a stolen 2020 election. But the partisan war over the Supreme Court did not begin with him. It preceded him by years, as senators eroded the institution for political wins in confirming their own party's preferred judges. Likewise, Trump did not create the conditions for his political success. He stepped into a degraded process custom-built for his self-interested style of disruption, following the path Palin and the Tea Party had blazed for him in the Republican Party.

Trump wants to be seen as special and uniquely capable. He seems to have a deep psychological need for that kind of approval. In fact, he has opposite qualities. In my dealings with him as president, it was evident that he could not have planned his own rise or engineered the transformation of the Supreme Court. He isn't that smart. As former attorney general Bill Barr has said, Trump lacks the ability for strategic or linear thinking. He isn't able to form or follow through on complex plans. Instead, Trump was extraordinarily lucky. He appeared at a moment when Americans had lost touch with the civic virtues that hold us together as a nation. A movement had arisen among Americans who were angry that the government wasn't representing them, dissatisfied by agencies ranging from the Internal Revenue Service to the federal lands agencies to the federal courts. People who felt no one listened to them finally, with Trump, had someone who spoke loudly about the unfairness and dissatisfaction they felt.

Trump did not create this situation. He hit like a lightning bolt, which normally is a momentary and ineffective flash, but this time touched tinder-dry ground and ignited a landscape primed for a spreading wildfire. Our institutions had been firebreaks against the spread of demagogues. The tradition of senators denouncing unacceptable conduct from our leaders was another firebreak. The tradition of senators' civility and compromise with their political opponents was yet another. The tradition of senators evaluating nominees on their merits was, too. Too few of us had been tending the firebreaks. And when the lightning struck, most senators ran rather than staying to fight the flames.

———

On a Friday a month before the 2016 election, *The Washington Post* released tapes in which Trump could be heard bragging about assaulting women by grabbing their genitals and kissing them against their will, among other degrading comments. He had been captured on a live mic while appearing on the celebrity news show *Access Hollywood* a decade earlier. "I just start kissing them. It's like a magnet. Just kiss. I don't even wait. And when you're a star, they let you do it. You can do anything. Grab 'em by the pussy. You can do anything."

When I saw the video I was on a campaign visit to Dillingham, a Southwest Alaska fishing community. I had just come from a community meeting where a woman had stood, in tears, to tell the story of her daughter being lured to Anchorage for sex trafficking, and to ask for my help in stopping that criminal threat to rural Alaska girls. I was horrified and disgusted by the video. The tape essentially confirmed that Trump was the creep his own words and attitudes had already suggested he was. My next emotion was relief, because he would not be president. By all the normal rules of conduct, he would drop out of the presidential race or would be forced out.

Without consulting anyone, I immediately told a local reporter that Trump should withdraw. The next morning my office released a statement saying so. Although we hadn't spoken, my Alaska colleague Senator Dan Sullivan released a similar statement at the same time. Elected in 2014, Dan had supported Trump and had spoken at the Republican National Convention, but he was the father of three teenage girls and was sensitive to Alaska's epidemic levels of sexual abuse.

Somehow, I had avoided committing to supporting or opposing Trump through the course of the campaign, even though I was on the ballot—an extraordinary omission for a senator running in a presidential election year. Now many other senators joined me in denouncing his *Access Hollywood* comments. Two dozen members of Congress called for him to drop out of the race. Many other Republican leaders, however, denounced the comments without calling for Trump to quit, or they withdrew their endorsements but said they would still vote for him (whatever that meant). Some even defended him. Sarah Palin was among the first to excuse Trump's comments as "locker room" talk. She said she had heard worse. Others soon followed that line, saying the comments weren't so bad after all.

At the presidential debate on Sunday, two days after the tape came out, Trump brazenly attempted to turn the issue against Hillary Clinton, somehow blaming her for her husband's infidelities. His campaign had seated Bill Clinton's accusers in the audience. On television, we could see Trump stalking around the stage, using his bulk to loom threateningly over Hillary. I talked to the GGs and other women about what we saw. We all recognized what was happening. We had been there ourselves, facing a misogynistic man's show of physical dominance.

Trump survived. At a lunch with colleagues back at the Capitol, I sat disheartened as I heard the voices around me repeating the locker room excuse, saying "Boys will be boys" and otherwise minimizing what Trump had said. I felt sick. Did they have any awareness of how women feel? And was I really that out of touch with how men speak and behave? Some of those who had initially called for Trump to withdraw or who had revoked their endorsements were now backtracking to stay on his good side. Trump would strike back at some of those who honorably stood by their original condemnations. Senator Kelly Ayotte of New Hampshire, up for reelection, told me her advisers wanted her to keep her head down, but she took a principled stand on the *Access Hollywood* comments. Trump targeted her, and she lost.

We had hit a new low, one I had never imagined was possible. I thought of my sons. I would never have accepted them saying anything like this, in a locker room or anywhere else, nor do I believe they ever would. I'm proud they have grown into men of good character. But I'm disturbed by the environment they face, in which dishonor and misogyny are excused and even elevated. When I realized that the culture had become degraded to the point that a man like Trump might become president, I felt sad and uncertain for them in that world.

None of us can control where the culture goes, but each of us can do our own part by being firm and honorable in upholding positive values. Building up norms and traditions is harder than tearing them down, but it is not impossible. This work depends on each of us. We're all called upon for the courage to do what is right every day, not only senators. One of my simple rules along those lines has been to withhold my vote from any candidate of bad character, regardless of the politics. When I went into the voting booth in 2016, I could not vote for Trump. Nor for Hillary Clinton. I admired her as a woman, but I also saw that the policies she proposed as a candidate would be similar to Bill Clinton's, and his presidency had been an economic catastrophe for our state. I wrote in the name of Ohio governor John Kasich.

On election night, I focused on my own race. We celebrated in a large space with a stage in downtown Anchorage called 49th State Brewing. Our results came in quickly. At about ten-thirty P.M. I was standing with my campaign manager, Steve Wackowski, getting ready to go on TV about my victory, when word came in that Trump had won the presidency. The news shocked us, like all of America and, apparently, Trump himself. In a few moments, I would be among the first public officials to react to this political earthquake. I said to Wacko, "Oh my God, what do we do now?" In my interviews, I said Trump's victory meant a new chance to open oil development in ANWR and the National Petroleum Reserve in Alaska (the future site of the Willow oil project). That was all true.

For the first time in ten years, Republicans would control the White House and both houses of Congress. I would continue as chair of Energy and Natural Resources, where I was still pushing for passage of the energy bill we had been working on for two years. Alaskan goals that I had pursued for many years, and that my father and Ted Stevens had pursued before me, now seemed attainable. But the person who could help these things happen, sitting atop the administration, was one I had denounced and declared unfit for the office. Somehow, I would need to win Trump over to my priorities despite my opposition to his candidacy and my distaste for him personally. And I needed to do so without compromising my principles or entering into the transactional politics he seemed to prefer.

Over the Thanksgiving holiday, Verne and I went to Hawaii to visit my mother-in-law, Dorothy (or Tutu, as the boys called her). Then, as now, I would go to her home on Maui for respite, encouragement, and new energy. Our relationship has always been extraordinarily close, and we talk about everything. On one occasion, we spent a whole morning talking about the color pink. At ninety, Dorothy remained vibrant and life-loving, still swimming in the ocean or walking on the beach every morning. She carried herself with perfect posture, shoulders back, presenting herself to the world with confidence.

In Washington, we had been busy with the transition, as possible names for Trump's cabinet fluttered about. The secretary of the interior fell under the purview of my appropriations subcommittee, with responsibility for managing five hundred million acres of public land, the federal relationship with Native Americans, and resources including wildlife, oil, and minerals. During the visit with Dorothy, I joined leadership calls about cabinet selections. Rob Portman of Ohio mentioned that he had weighed in with Trump about who to pick for Treasury, and he shared a cell number to reach the president-elect.

Six weeks earlier I had demanded an end to Trump's political career. Now I was going to call him up and ask him to appoint an Alaskan to the cabinet. I admit it was a daunting prospect.

Normally, arranging such a call goes from Senate staff through the transition committee, but I thought this phone number would bypass some of that, getting me to Trump's assistant or a voicemail account. I woke at six A.M. in Hawaii (eleven A.M. in Washington) to get the ball rolling on setting up the call, still in my pajamas and without my first cup of coffee, and dialed the number I had gotten from Rob. A man's voice answered, and I introduced myself and said I was calling to speak to President-elect Trump.

The voice said, "I'm so glad to hear from you."

I said, "And to whom am I speaking?"

He said, "Donald Trump."

I was almost speechless. "Wow! You're kidding me," I said. "I'm just surprised it's you answering the phone."

"I give this number out to good people," he said.

We chitchatted a bit, I congratulated him on his victory, and I mentioned the Alaskan names I hoped he would consider for Interior.

"I love Alaska," he said. "I like you. I have great respect for you. Send me these résumés. We'll get along better in the future."

With a gulp, I decided to go right toward the conflict, not to skirt the obvious.

"I didn't endorse you," I said.

"Oh, I know," he responded.

"I think you will find I'm very direct," I continued. "I didn't support you, but I pledged to work with you. You won and I won. You're going to do good things for the United States, and I am going to continue to do good things for Alaska."

The call lasted fifteen minutes and ended amicably. I went to the patio, where Dorothy was starting her morning. She said I looked like I had seen a ghost. We laughed when I told her that I had called the president-elect in my pajamas. As surprised as I was that he had answered the phone himself, I was even more surprised that the call had gone so well. Certainly, I had started my relationship with Donald Trump with the right tone, showing respect for his election but no apology for my position and making no concessions to win his approval. In fact, he seemed more concerned about winning *my* approval.

Soon after Trump moved into the White House, Dan Sullivan and I decided to ask for a meeting to put our Alaska priorities before him. We needed help with tough issues that were critical to Alaska but largely unfamiliar to most people outside the state.

Some of Alaska's legacy issues had dragged on for a generation as outside environmentalists fought our congressional delegation to a stalemate. The delegation had been trying since the Clinton administration to lift a ban on new roads in the Tongass National Forest, the vast majority of Southeast Alaska, where the roadless rule stymied community projects, including transmission lines for renewable energy. Carter was president when the fight began for oil exploration in ANWR; ditto for the efforts to build a road for the village of King Cove to get access to emergency medical care through the nearby airport at Cold Bay, far out on the Alaska Peninsula in the North Pacific. On the day I was sworn into office, in 2002, my mother had asked me not to forget the people of King Cove, and I worked hard through all my years in office for that twelve-mile, one-lane gravel road. We had been foiled, over and over again, by outsiders who placed the purity of a small part of the huge Izembek National Wildlife Refuge above the lives of the village's Alaska Native people. In each case—in the Tongass and in Izembek—people were cut off by a federal designation without their knowledge or consent. Alaska has a great deal of wilderness, but we Alaskans live in much of it, and we simply want our access and livelihoods respected by our government.

We had Republican majorities in Congress, but we also needed Trump on our side if we wanted to finally win. I didn't want to alienate him any further. But before we could meet, I already found myself in that position again, with his nomination of Betsy DeVos to be secretary of education. And in the process, I learned, for the first time, how I would feel at the center of the swirling political madness that was afflicting our country.

DeVos was a wealthy Republican donor from Michigan who had worked on charter schools and vouchers for private schools but seemed to have no experience with public schools, which would be her responsibility. My friend Susan Collins and I served on the Committee on Health, Education, Labor, and Pensions, known as HELP, where DeVos would testify, and I hoped she could prove her critics wrong. But DeVos made some shockingly uninformed statements. She seemed to know less about public schools than many an active PTA parent. And some of her written answers appeared to be cut-and-paste jobs from someone else's work, without attribution—unacceptable from any student. When I met with DeVos privately, I was not reassured. She demonstrated no desire to address public school problems or fix inequities in the system. Her main interest seemed to be in vouchers to give public money to private schools.

I accord great deference to the president on cabinet nominations—for either party—but I also take seriously my responsibility to judge the qualifications of those we put into these high positions. Not every cabinet secretary must be a technical expert. I give credit for life experience. For example, Trump had nominated Ryan Zinke for Interior (not one of my names, but that was fine, and I did get Steve Wackowski into a senior position with him). Zinke had represented Montana in Congress for only one term and lacked expertise in natural resource management, but he had lived in the West, had used the public lands, and understood that culture. He called himself a Theodore Roosevelt conservationist. That was good enough for me, and I came to really like Zinke and worked well with him.

With DeVos, I couldn't even give her credit for life experience. No one in her family had attended public school. Her qualifications were too thin.

Susan and I came to the same conclusion: that we could not vote for confirmation but we would help vote the nomination out of committee, while expressing our reservations publicly. This approach would end up angering both sides. I frankly did not appreciate the intensity of feelings about these votes. The nomination was important, but the Senate deals with thousands of confirmations as officials come and go in Washington. Controversies about them are usually brief and confined to the Beltway. In the Trump era, however, it was different.

I had been at the center of national attention before, during the 2010 write-in campaign, but never like this on a nominee. Progressive groups mounted a campaign to block DeVos's confirmation, and Republicans countered them. Outrage already gripped the country. Protests had broken out in various cities on Inauguration Day, with burned vehicles in the streets of Washington. The Women's March, the day after, brought out millions of people all over the world, many in knitted "pussy" hats, with cat ears, that referenced the *Access Hollywood* tape. The DeVos confirmation would be among the first issues to reach the Senate in that atmosphere. Along with it dawned the public's awareness that the Republican leadership could afford to lose no more than two votes on any party-line vote, and that Susan and I could count for numbers one and two.

Our office phone system broke under the weight. My staff normally fielded a couple of hundred calls a day. If the lines were full, calls went into voicemail, which had a capacity of more than five hundred messages. Suddenly the voicemail was filling up in a matter of minutes. We received as many as fifteen thousand calls a day. The vast majority were angry calls generated by national groups. There was no way to do business on the phones, or even to find the messages of Alaskan constituents who might be trying to reach us for help. My new chief of staff at the time, Mike Pawlowski, who we called Fish, tried to gain control of the phones with a new system, innovative at the time, that translated voice messages into emails. That allowed staffers to roughly triage calls coming from Alaska's 907 area code, although, of course, there was no way to review all the national calls, or to absorb all the anger and fear many of them expressed.

These storms of the Trump years changed life in our friendly, cheerful suite in the Hart Senate Office Building, where the noisiest events used to be visiting school groups from Alaska looking at our totem pole and other Alaskan art. Fish recalls that his top priority was to keep our people from quitting. He sent them for protester training, teaching our young receptionists and other front-office workers how to deal with rageful people screaming at them from inches away or beating deafening drums next to their ears, always filming with their phones. Fish shared smoked salmon with the Capitol police officers at the building entrances, reminding them to call if they saw protesters heading our way. Veteran staff member Nathan Bergerbest proved to be skilled at de-escalation, and we often sent him out to lower the temperature, inviting the protesters in to talk about their concerns—or as many as fit in the office.

While the staff took the worst of it, I also had to find my way through mobs of reporters crushing against me, most often when I was getting off the Senate subway leading from the office to the Capitol. With so many senators voting the party line, my unpredictable vote would become important over and over again. Reporters would push in with outstretched phones recording sound, shouting questions, inches away while I continued to walk. I tried delivering the political "No comment" line, but that didn't seem to deter the next reporter from asking a question. I wanted to answer legitimate questions when they were asked. I just wished it weren't in the middle of a mob surging around me.

We would have to get used to this crazy workplace. The DeVos confirmation would be only the first, and far from the worst spike of intensity around a vote I would have to take. Collins and I opposed the confirmation on the floor, creating a fifty-fifty tie, and then Vice President Pence cast his tiebreaking vote in favor, the first time in American history that had ever happened for a confirmation. And then the news cycle moved on to something else. But the national mood didn't move on. It only grew darker and angrier.

A month later, near the end of a lovely spring day, Dan Sullivan and I went to the White House to meet the president to discuss our Alaska issues. Staff was not invited, but Zinke would attend, having been confirmed one week earlier. Dan and I had prepared with a long list of issues, including his focus on defense and stationing fighter squadrons in Alaska and my focus on the Arctic, the need for new icebreakers, ANWR, and our legacy issues. We had heard about difficult meetings with Trump from other senators, who struggled with his impatience and his inability to concentrate, and who could not get sustained engagement or firm conclusions. I brought along colorful maps and graphics as visual aids to keep the president's attention.

As it turned out, we did keep his attention, but not as we expected. Indeed, this would be one of the strangest meetings I ever attended. Productive, but strange.

In the Oval Office, Trump stayed at his desk, with three chairs set in front for me, Dan, and Zinke. Oddly, in addition to two senior White House legislative advisers, sitting on sofas near the fireplace were Melania Trump and a friend of hers, who was introduced as the female small business entrepreneur of the year, and a couple of other people whose identities I don't recall.

The president welcomed us warmly and enthused about Alaska, telling us about his grandfather who had made his fortune running a pair of hotels during the Klondike Gold Rush of 1898. In fact, the hotels were well known as brothels, but when I teased him about that he gave me a scowl and I dropped it, instead listening to his monologue about Alaska. He was like a kid, going on about the lure of the gold rush, his son's hunting, Alaska's wildlife, and bears. He said, "Tell me about the bears. How big are they, really?" I wasn't sure if we would get to policy, so I went along. Every lifelong Alaskan has bear stories—about Kodiak brown bears, polar bears, and grizzlies, and the danger of working around bears. He was fascinated and asked about moose and if we really eat whales. I enjoyed it greatly—it was like talking to an excited tourist—but I finally managed to steer us back to our agenda by showing him a map and pointing out the huge area in the Arctic where America needed new icebreakers to patrol and establish our presence.

The problem, I said, was that the ships would cost $850 million each.

Trump said, "Oh, I can get you a better deal than that. You just get me a memo and I can negotiate that down."

The theme of the meeting became how easy it would be for him to solve Alaska's problems. When I explained the need for the King Cove road, which had been blocked by environmental lawsuits and politics for decades, Trump told Zinke to have it built in two weeks. He asked for two months.

I was having fun. Trump seemed to think of himself like a president in the movies, making snap decisions based on a few words of explanation and expecting immediate results. I brought up the Law of the Sea treaty. It had been waiting for ratification since the Reagan administration, preventing the United States from defending territorial claims on our outer continental shelf. I showed him the vast underwater territory we could claim off Arctic Alaska, with untold riches in subsea minerals and petroleum—I knew that would excite him.

"This whole area of outer continental shelf," I said, pointing to a swath on the map twice the size of California, "we could get this if we claimed it under the treaty. But we can't defend our claim from the Russians or Canadians unless we are part of the Law of the Sea."

"Let's get that done," Trump said. "Why haven't we done it?"

I pointed out that Republicans had blocked ratification of the treaty. In fact, the treaty had languished in the Senate since 1984 and had become a Republican bugaboo. Trump turned to his advisers and said, "I want this done." They all looked down at their hands. Dan didn't say a word. I was having the best time.

We went through a few more issues—ANWR, offshore oil,

Obamacare repeal, climate change. He had no interest in talking about fighter squadrons. And then we were back discussing walruses and the size of halibut. He was funny, and I joined in with fishing stories. When he got onto the topic of Hillary Clinton and how bad she was, he launched into a seemingly endless monologue, which continued until he thought to ask us about decisions President Obama had made that he could reverse. His idea was to change the name of North America's tallest mountain from Denali back to Mount McKinley.

"What do you think about that?" Trump asked.

"Mmm," I said slowly. "Well, it was actually my legislation that had first moved to change it."

Dan added, "Sir, my wife is Athabascan. She's from that region. And if I were to go home and tell her that I had agreed that we would change the name back to McKinley, I think she would leave me. I would ask you to leave it alone."

"Okay, we won't touch that," Trump said. "We won't touch Denali."

The meeting had lasted ninety minutes—we had blocked out half an hour, and I don't know how long the White House had expected it to be. The staff was clearly itching to bring it to an end. We began to wrap up.

That was when the president turned to me and said, "You have nice hair."

I didn't know how to respond. After ninety minutes of Alaska stories and policy he sums it up by commenting on my hair?

"Melania, don't you think she has great hair?" he asked.

Melania looked up from her phone and said, "She does have nice hair."

The female entrepreneur of the year concurred with an "Uh-huh."

The president turned to Dan, with his close-cropped marine cut, and said, "It's not like you have bad hair, but I mean, she's got great hair."

And so the meeting ended.

I've been teased forever since by the GGs, who like to tell me, "The Donald would approve of your hair today."

What else came out of the meeting? Zinke and his Interior Department team put great efforts into a land exchange to build a road for King Cove. That seemingly simple, tangible project had caught Trump's interest in a way that more complex, abstract issues could not. Rather than the government building the road in two weeks or two months, however, getting a land agreement took a year, and then that was tied up in court by environmentalists, until the Biden administration came into office and reversed the decision. At this writing, eight years later, the road is as far from reality as it has ever been. But I have not given up and will not. It is a matter of environmental justice to the good people of King Cove, who are asking for nothing but safe access to a transportation lifeline.

I learned valuable insights about the president that day. He never mentioned my vote on DeVos—indeed, he seemed eager to engage and work with me, even with his weird comment about my hair. He knew he would need my vote to repeal the Affordable Care Act, still known then as Obamacare, which was the top Republican goal. I had not committed to repeal without a workable replacement.

Trump was a perfect populist politician in part because he understood popular culture as an avid consumer of it. He knew well the many reality TV shows about Alaska. Alaskans roll our eyes at mentions of these shows, because they're largely hyped drama full of stereotypes and exaggeration—viewers don't learn about the real Alaska. That kind of TV generally is mental candy. It feeds the sweet tooth of short attention spans, engaged by quick, flashy, superficial images, but without digging into substance. Populist political ideas are similar: empty calories. That's one reason why, as populists have gained power, they haven't succeeded at governing. We see that every day in the House of Representatives, as Freedom Caucus populists make showy demands but fail to pass legislation. They are unsuccessful because their reality TV–style proposals are all show. They have slogans, but slogans are not solutions.

That emptiness became especially evident in the first summer of Trump's presidency, when the Republican Party tried to fulfill its promise to repeal the ACA.

———

In the summer in Anchorage, I often connect with people at a Saturday farmers' market where my son Matt sells his fresh pasta. Friends, acquaintances, and total strangers stop to talk as I help at the booth. It's a great time to take the pulse of the community in a nonpolitical environment. I am often reminded during these conversations that most Alaskans pay no attention to the daily drama in Washington, and that what seems important in the capital often doesn't matter outside it. But the Affordable Care Act was one thing that did matter. I heard from people who said their lives were saved by the access to healthcare it provided. A close friend without insurance was diagnosed with ovarian cancer but was able to get coverage through the ACA. In the ski-resort town of Girdwood, where we have a cabin, one of our neighbors was seriously injured on the mountain when he was nailed by a snowboarder. Thanks to the ACA, he was able to get coverage and care.

In the eight years since the original Obamacare debate, Republicans had won many elections by calling for repeal of the ACA, but by 2016, the party's rhetoric had changed to "repeal and replace," because people liked many aspects of the law. In my own campaign that year, I had quietly gone down another notch. I was saying "reform" rather than "repeal and replace." In 2015, Alaska governor Bill Walker had accepted Medicaid expansion, which helped our state deal with a raging opioid-addiction crisis and provided coverage, for the first time, to 6 percent of our population. So many people were covered by Medicaid—24 percent of Alaskans—that proposed cuts could cost many thousands of healthcare jobs. Federal health spending was a major slice of our economy, with 17 percent of Alaskans on Veterans Affairs or military TRICARE coverage, 17 percent on the Indian Health Service, and 11 percent on Medicare (for those over sixty-five). With the federal government covering that combined two-thirds of Alaskans, the private market was small and extremely expensive. Only 9 percent had individual coverage. It wasn't enough to mouth the slogan "Repeal and replace." We could not repeal without a strong replacement that would address these important benefits, reduce costs, and protect our state.

Big legislation usually passes only near the beginning of a presidential term, so we had to get to work quickly on this, the Republican Party's top goal. But we didn't have a coherent plan ready for the "replace" part of that equation, just a grab bag of disconnected ideas that had been thrown out for discussion. In the spring, the Freedom Caucus in the House shot down a bill it considered too similar to Obamacare. When the House finally arrived at a compromise they could vote for, it barely passed, because many moderates were unable to accept the large number of their constituents who would lose health coverage. It became clear that the Senate would have to produce our own bill. Conference lunches discussing the options dragged on into the summer.

Alaska's unique problems and very high healthcare costs necessitated a different policy approach under the bill, which would be the only way for the leadership to get my vote. Our costs were off the charts compared to the rest of the country—literally off the charts, as the agencies handled Alaska's extremes by excluding our state from the material they produced and showing only the other forty-nine states. Alaska's individual market was so tiny, we even discussed putting this small group on federal-employee healthcare. Speculation abounded that Leader McConnell was bidding to buy my support with special carve-outs for Alaska, but I was simply holding firm to keep my constituents whole. Nothing the leadership devised worked for Alaska. I studied all the plans and realized that the status quo, while politically unacceptable, would be better for my state than the proposals on the table.

Vice President Pence came to one of our conference lunches. We were running out of time, and although what we would vote on remained unclear, he spoke to remind us that, whatever it finally looked like, we had to support it, because Republicans had run so many times on "repeal and replace." For me, that wasn't a good enough reason. I stood up and said, "I don't want it to be a surprise for anyone, but I can't support something that doesn't help Alaska." I heard groans around the room.

At that point, I thought I would be casting the only negative Republican vote, which meant the bill could still pass with one vote to spare. But as the summer wore on, our conference struggled to find a formula that could get enough votes to pass, as each new iteration lost support either on the right or with the center. Headlines covered this muddled process day by day. Healthcare affected every American. As the pressure built weekly, my staff discovered that the DeVos vote had been a mere rehearsal for a new level of attention on us. And this time, the interest came from back home, too, with Alaskans anxiously watching to see what would happen with their own care and with one of our biggest industries. We answered the phones and responded to protesters, even as some became verbally abusive with my staff. I kept quiet about my position and continued listening. Being "in play" placed me in the center of the storm, but it also allowed me to take part in shaping the bill.

Our high school interns arrive in the summer, young people who have just graduated—much like me at eighteen, when I sorted mail in Ted Stevens's office and rode the bus from Trinity College. Working with them brings fresh energy to my job. They are eager, bright, lively, and inquisitive. Their enthusiasm delights me, as they explore the Capitol, agog at the artwork, and wearing business attire for the first time. In 2017, during the ACA debate, with the swarms of reporters growing to unprecedented size, the two interns shadowing me, different each day, would act like my "bodyguards," helping break my path through the crush. "Just stay close and keep moving," I would instruct them. Some would be visibly nervous as we rode the subway, then fall in ahead of me as a group of reporters surged around us. We pushed ahead together on our one-minute walk to the sanctuary of the elevator. In the elevator we exchanged high fives, having successfully run the gauntlet.

Those light moments kept the pressure from the media from being totally suffocating, but the attention never let up. On one occasion, as I was climbing the stairs from the subway, reporters pressed so close that someone stepped on the back of my shoe and I tripped forward. Those behind stumbled into me and we began to topple, and for a split second I thought I would be at the bottom of a dogpile of bodies falling like dominoes. I halted and spoke firmly: "Everybody stop. Somebody is going to get hurt here. You've got to back away and give space."

With the legislative activity in the Senate reaching a messy crescendo, John McCain went home to Arizona for medical attention. The entire shaky effort seemed to be falling apart. McConnell knew he would not have votes to spare for any option, so he decided to wait for McCain's return. Then came the shocking and tragic news that John had an aggressive and incurable form of brain cancer. When he came back a week later, with a scar on his face, he was responding to our leadership's call to help the Republican repeal bill. That irony brought bitter criticism, since the repeal would take away from Americans the kind of coverage he was receiving. But while supporting the party, John also spoke strongly of his disappointment with the process and the decline of the Senate as a deliberative body.

On July 25, Susan Collins and I cast our votes against the motion to proceed to debate on the bill the House had passed. With McCain voting in favor, the Senate tied fifty to fifty, and Pence's tie-breaking vote kept the bill alive. The president attacked Susan and me, saying, "We had two Republicans that went against us, which is very sad, I think. It's very, very sad for them." The next day, I voted with six other Republicans to kill the president's bill to repeal the law without a replacement. Trump sprayed reelection threats over Twitter. He tweeted that I had let the country down. When the reporters in a Capitol hallway asked me about that, I answered, "Every day shouldn't be about winning elections. How about just doing a little bit of governing around here? That's what I'm here for."

That day, Trump called Secretary Zinke to pressure me. Steve Wackowski later recounted what happened in Zinke's office. Trump ordered Zinke to threaten our Alaska priorities at Interior—the ones we had talked about in the Oval Office, along with any others I might care about. Wacko advised the secretary, "Sir, do not use vinegar, use honey. If you use the vinegar, it's going to have the opposite effect. She's a U.S. senator, and you cannot bully her." Zinke was already becoming a friend. He seemed to know that Trump's approach with me would backfire, but he was also a former naval officer and would not disregard the president's direct order. He made the call, but he kept it cordial. I wasn't unduly concerned, nor did I change my mind. I understood they wanted to put the squeeze on me politically—that wasn't new. And I understood Trump and the spot in which he had placed Zinke.

But when my colleague Dan Sullivan got a similar call from Zinke, he had a very different reaction. He quickly went to the media, saying he had received a clear threat that positive policies for Alaska would stop if I, Lisa, didn't vote to repeal the ACA. For Trump, this was a fiasco. I had already made up my mind, but if I had been in doubt, I certainly would have been locked into my position by such a clumsy threat. The story had the playground elements to take off in the media, and it exploded nationally. Democrats called for an investigation. Alaskans were incensed and came strongly to my defense. None of this mattered much. A week later, Ryan Zinke and I posed for a selfie drinking an Alaskan beer together, demonstrating that all was forgiven. During a productive dinner, he told me, "I know you don't like Trump, but he respects you."

Me in 1961

A family photo used by my father's campaign
for Congress in 1970

In 1975 I served as a summer intern for Senator Ted Stevens. I am seated at far right.

The Murkowski sisters
in the late 1980s:
Carol, Eileen, Lisa,
and Mary

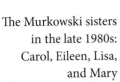

In 1993, when I posed for this photo
with my sons, Nic and Matt, I had
no notion of entering politics.

Fishing has always been a big part
of our family. Shown with Verne
and the boys and silver salmon
from Ship Creek in Anchorage.

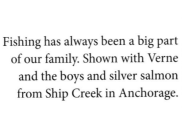

In December 2002, our whole family gathered in Juneau for my dad's swearing-in as governor of Alaska. Later that month, he would appoint me to his vacated seat in the Senate.

On my first Senate election campaign, in 2004, we took a multiday boat trip up the Kuskokwim River. Here we're visiting a village, with son Matt at left, Nic at my side, and my mother-in-law, Dorothy McCoy, in yellow.

Senator Ted Stevens and I shared an impromptu dance at the Kenai River Classic fishing event, July 2007. (Photo courtesy of Fitzgerald Photography.)

Election night 2010, when we won the historic write-in, at the Anchorage Election Central gathering with Nic and Matt

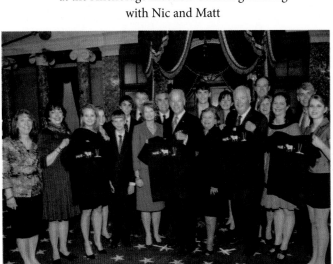

For the 2010 write-in campaign, we distributed rubber wristbands with the instructions "Fill it in, Write it in, Lisa Murkowski." Since then, I have worn a gold replica given to me by my husband, Verne.

Vice President Joe Biden posed at my swearing-in, with friends and family, after the 2010 write-in. We're all holding campaign T-shirts designed to help voters remember how to spell "Murkowski."

The salmon tender *Brenna A,* owned by my cousin Jenny Dwyer and her late husband, Pat, employed our sons for many summers in Bristol Bay. The family is shown here in Naknek, Alaska, in 2014.

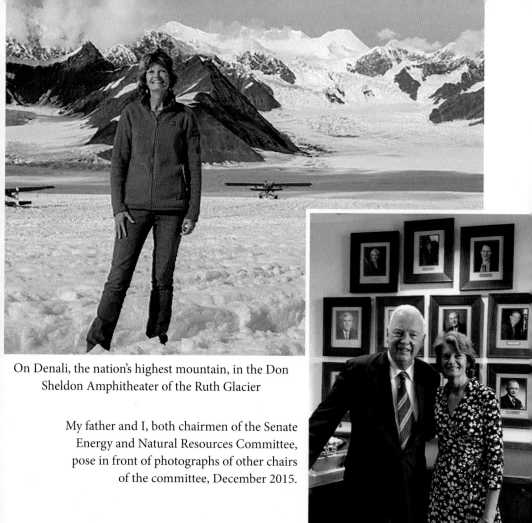

On Denali, the nation's highest mountain, in the Don Sheldon Amphitheater of the Ruth Glacier

My father and I, both chairmen of the Senate Energy and Natural Resources Committee, pose in front of photographs of other chairs of the committee, December 2015.

The GGs (Gore Girls) are the "center of my onion," and our annual gatherings are a special part of my life. Here we're shown with my mom in Palm Desert, April 2016.

Verne and I heading out to go camping on our anniversary, Eagle River Valley, 2016.

Our annual anniversary camping trip with longtime friends Bruce and Moore and Branch and Sherry Haymans, Seward 2019. There are always multiple dogs.

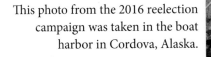

This photo from the 2016 reelection campaign was taken in the boat harbor in Cordova, Alaska.

Visiting with elders at a Yukon River fish camp near the village of St. Mary's, during my 2016 reelection campaign

Rural Alaska villages often have boardwalks instead of roads over the boggy tundra. With my son Nic in July 2016.

On the sea ice outside Utqiagvik with Iñupiaq whaling captain Arnold Brower Jr. after a successful hunt, April 2017, with slabs of maktak, the skin and outer fat of a bowhead whale

Picking berries with local government officials after a site visit in Nome

Duck hunting, Healy Lake, Alaska,
September 2016

Salmon fishing in Prince William
Sound, July 2017

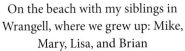

On the beach with my siblings in
Wrangell, where we grew up: Mike,
Mary, Lisa, and Brian

The Girdwood Forest Fair had rules
I could readily agree to.

With Verne at my side on the night of my primary election victory, August 2016

Alaska representative Don Young and I celebrated our reelections at the start of the new Congress, January 2017.

After the signing of the 2017 Tax Cuts and Jobs Act, I led a group of North Slope leaders to the Oval Office, where President Trump and Vice President Pence posed for a picture with them.

Cutting the ribbon on a new bridge with local officials and the U.S. Forest Service in Haines, Alaska, June 2018

ATVs, called four-wheelers in Alaska, are the most common transportation in rural Alaska villages.

At the ceremonial start of the Iditarod Trail Sled Dog Race, in Anchorage, March 2019

In 2019 I led a congressional delegation to the Arctic and visited Thule Air Base in Greenland.

Alaska representative Don Young and I shared a laugh on his eighty-seventh birthday, June 9, 2020.

I took this photo of damage to a Capitol office near my hideaway within days of January 6.

At the White House with the group of ten (G10) senators working on the Bipartisan Infrastructure Law, June 25, 2021

New York senator Kirsten Gillibrand took this selfie at a dinner for women senators at Vice President Kamala Harris's official residence, June 15, 2021. (Photo courtesy of Kirsten Gillibrand.)

With Senator Joe Manchin at a bipartisan panel discussion, February 2022

With my son Matt as he sells pasta at an Anchorage farmers' market—and I engage in "retail politics"

Senior staff of the Senate Energy Committee celebrated passage of the energy bill in February 2022 with Senator Joe Manchin and me.

Healy Lake, hunting with my sons
Matt and Nic, 2022

Healy Lake picnic up the sloughs with family

The GGs get together at Jenny's cabin: "girls just wanna have fun."

Campaigning in the 2022 general election with family in Anchorage

Anaktuvuk Pass, in the Brooks Range of northern Alaska, January 2024

I was "thrown up" by community leaders in the village of Minto, Alaska, April 2014.

In October 2024, when the U.S. Navy formally apologized to the village of Angoon for a tragic bombardment in 1882, I received a ceremonial canoe paddle from a student.

Verne and I trek across the Ruth Glacier on Denali.

Photo courtesy of Craig Hudson for *The Washington Post*

In Denali National Park

That came days after the night of the big vote on the ACA. Susan Collins and I had voted against the motion to proceed, so our position was known. The leadership would need every other Republican vote plus the vice-presidential tiebreaker for the repeal to take place. It was past midnight. Mike Pence was roaming the Senate floor to make sure the Republican votes would hold. The only person still partly in play was John McCain. Susan and I walked over to him, where he was sitting alone. If the bill passed, Medicaid expansion would be reversed, and many millions would lose their coverage. But, in truth, we did not seek to lobby John to our point of view. He looked worn down, and we stood by him to offer support as friends. John suddenly pointed at us and said, "You two are right." Then the president called, and John retreated off the floor to take his call. When he returned, the roll-call vote had progressed alphabetically beyond the letter *M*—Susan and I had already voted. John walked down to the well, reached out his hand for the clerk's attention, and made his famous thumbs-down vote. The ACA repeal was dead.

It was a dramatic moment, part of John's iconic legacy, which I don't begrudge him. He died one year later. But Susan and I did smile wryly about the laurels he received for that one vote—which came only after the two of us had already taken the heat for many days for standing up against the party on our own.

———

At the time of the ACA vote in July, we were already six months into a quiet political plan to open the Arctic National Wildlife Refuge to oil exploration. ANWR was among the issues that Trump had wanted Zinke to use as leverage against me on the ACA. As I've already explained, I am not transactional—I don't trade my vote for unconnected issues—and I was never tempted to vote to repeal the ACA in exchange for ANWR. Besides, I was pretty sure I didn't need to. Trump badly wanted to be the one president who could open ANWR.

My strategy for dealing with the president had worked. At our ninety-minute March meeting—the one where he complimented my hair—I had planted a seed. Trump was a true believer in energy dominance and saw increased American oil production, particularly in ANWR, as a home-run opportunity. In our White House meeting, we told him that many presidents had tried to open it up but that all of them had failed. Perhaps, we wondered, Donald Trump could do what no other president had been able to accomplish. He grabbed that idea and didn't let go.

By ignoring his threats, I may have improved my hand. Trump responds to strength. He bluffs and bullies for what he wants, but if he doesn't get it, he moves on and bluffs and bullies someone else. During that first year of his term, I learned that I didn't have to pay attention to his tweets and threats. After a remark I made in an interview with Katie Couric, my sister Carol gave me a necklace engraved with my quote "I cannot live in fear of a tweet." That mindset was freeing.

Ted Stevens and my father spent their long careers trying to get access to the rich resources in ANWR for Alaskans. This became the Holy Grail of Alaska politics. Not long after Trump was elected in 2016, I met with McConnell in his office in the Capitol. We sat cozily next to a blazing fire. I had already been working with my energy team to draft an ANWR bill that our unified Republican government could finally pass. Mitch suggested we use the reconciliation process. This special parliamentary rule bars the filibuster from certain budgetary bills. It would be used for the party's priority tax-cut bill, which could include ANWR—relevant because of the revenue an oil lease sale would produce. I enthusiastically agreed. I was excited that one of the greatest political minds of the Senate shared our ANWR strategy.

I asked Mitch that we keep the plan quiet for now. Having seen our ANWR legislation fail over so many years, I had decided to approach it differently this time. In the past, our side had mobilized a major public engagement and lobbying group called Arctic Power

to make our case. But the national environmental organizations always outgunned us. They also had an easier message to convey,
talking about protecting wildlife, while often using misleading
emotional imagery. Our points were about the small footprint of
development, the minimal environmental impact, and the neces-
sity of continued domestic energy production. My plan was to skip
the hoopla of an Arctic Power campaign. We would go through the
full public process and would not hide anything, but neither would
we intentionally attract attention. Making noise would only wake
the sleeping bear.

The Tax Cuts and Jobs Act of 2017, the major accomplishment
of the Trump administration, moved quickly under the reconciliation process late in the year. It ran 503 pages and had two titles.
Title I was 498 pages long and dealt with taxes and Title II was five
pages and opened ANWR's coastal plain to oil leasing, with half
the proceeds going to the Treasury and the other half to the state
of Alaska. Our strategy became evident and our chances of success promising, but publicity remained muted compared to earlier
ANWR attempts—the tax bill occupied Washington, along with sex
scandals, amid the spreading Me Too movement.

When a conference committee convened to work out the differences between the House and Senate versions of the tax bill, I
was given a seat, as the only senator who wasn't on the Finance
Committee, for the sole purpose of shepherding ANWR's Title II
through the process. Alaska's Don Young had the same role from
the House side. He deserved huge credit for getting ANWR through
the House many times over the years. And this time we won. The
bill passed just before Christmas, and we celebrated with an almost
unreal feeling that this legislative accomplishment had finally been
achieved. After so many decades, it was incomprehensible. Governor Walker declared, "This has been an Alaskan pursuit for half a
century, and today, Congress has finally unlocked the promise of
utilizing these resources."

At the White House signing ceremony, the success was all about

Trump. He told a story in various settings about how he had never heard of ANWR, but once he found out that other presidents had not been able to open it, he decided he would be the one. In his official remarks he said, "We're opening up ANWR for drilling. They've tried to get that for forty years. They've tried to get that even during the Reagan administration. They could never get it."

Clearly, I had paid no price for voting my conscience on the ACA. All that was required was letting Trump take credit.

A large portion of the Republicans in Congress attended the signing on the steps outside the White House. I stood next to the president on a dais, surrounded by poinsettias. About a dozen of my guests were in the front row. These Alaska Native leaders included some from Utqiagvik who I mentioned in the last chapter: Oliver Leavitt, who now was in a wheelchair with gout, Richard Glenn, and Crawford Patkotak. I wore a wool coat, but they, amusingly, complained of being too hot in the D.C. winter—they were Iñupiaq Eskimos, after all. (Lest anyone think that term is offensive, it is what these men called themselves.) Someone in the group asked if they could meet the president, and I said I would give it a try.

When Trump had finished speaking, I leaned over and spoke into his ear. "Hey, see that front row of people over there?" I asked. "Those are all Eskimos. Eskimos from Alaska. They came all the way to see you sign this bill. They're so happy."

Trump was delighted.

I asked if the group could take a picture with him.

"Absolutely," he responded. "Bring them over."

I pointed out that Oliver couldn't climb the steps in his wheelchair, and Trump said, "Meet me in the Oval Office."

Leaving the president behind on the dais, I charged ahead, although I had no authority other than his comment. I gathered up the guests and led them purposefully through a side door, bringing the group through White House corridors as if I owned the place. A marine guard challenged us, but I said, "We're meeting the president in the Oval Office," and he waved us through.

And then there we were, waiting alone in the heart of the White House. My guests were as excited as kids, walking around and looking at everything, trying out the different chairs. Crawford sat down in the president's chair behind the Resolute Desk. I said I wasn't sure that we should be doing that, but several more of the guests had to give it a try and get their pictures taken. Finally, Trump came in and we got our group picture with the president. He couldn't have been more friendly.

A year had passed since I met with McConnell in front of the fire, and now our bill was law. And my relationship with Trump was better than ever, despite my having voted against some of his priorities.

This had been an extraordinary legislative accomplishment, one of which I am very proud. It also helped me gain the skills to pass bigger national legislation later. But the outcome for Alaska's economy did not fulfill the promise many had hoped for. When bids for the first lease sale were finally opened, three years later, major companies with the wherewithal to develop the oil did not participate. The law requires another lease sale, and at this writing the outcome remains to be seen, after long delays due to litigation and resistance from the Biden administration. But our fight to provide Alaskans with access to Alaska resources continues. It turned out that Donald Trump was a strong ally in that work, once we approached him with the right strategy. Even in the Biden administration we were able to win the go-ahead for drilling in Willow. My job representing Alaska in the Senate will always be to work with whoever is in the White House for the benefit of my state.

CHAPTER 7

"No More Silence"

O<small>N</small> O<small>CTOBER</small> 5, 2017, *The New York Times* ignited the Me Too movement with its exposé about sexual harassment by movie producer Harvey Weinstein. On the same day, Democratic senator Heidi Heitkamp of North Dakota introduced Savanna's Act in the Senate, with my support, to begin to focus on the problem of murdered and missing Indigenous women. Who knows why cultural shifts happen when they do? We had been waiting a long time.

Savanna's Act was intended to address something far worse than the deplorable behavior alleged in most Me Too cases: Indigenous women disappearing without sufficient response from law enforcement or society at large. That summer, in Heitkamp's state, kayakers on the Red River had found the mutilated body of Savanna LaFontaine-Greywind, a member of the Spirit Lake Sioux tribe, wrapped in plastic and tape, more than a week after she had disappeared from her home. Savanna had been eight months pregnant. It turned out a neighbor had attacked her, cut open her womb to take her baby, then killed her and disposed of her body. (The baby lived.) As in many other cases involving Native American women, the police had reacted slowly to the report that Savanna was missing.

The terrible shock of Savanna's case helped open Americans' eyes to the horrifying crisis of missing and murdered Indigenous women. We didn't know how bad it was, because law enforcement agencies hadn't tracked the numbers of women involved. Over and over, we heard stories of police discounting the urgency when Native women were reported missing, assuming stereotypes of irresponsible behavior, until those cases went cold—while a White woman's disappearance in similar circumstances would produce a vigorous investigation. Activists with the Urban Indian Health Institute, based in Seattle, counted and named 506 Indigenous missing and murdered women from cities around the country, using old newspaper reports and public records requests. Silence was the ally of those responsible for these crimes. Savanna's Act was intended to break the silence by documenting these cases and the extent of the problem, and by tracking law enforcement's responsiveness, so they could be held accountable for ignoring or slow-rolling reports from Indigenous people. I was the lead co-sponsor of the bill and later also introduced the Not Invisible Act with Democratic senator Catherine Cortez Masto, of Nevada, to increase agency and tribal coordination in these cases.

I had long known about the epidemic of domestic violence and sexual assault in rural Alaska. Statistics speak to Alaska's astronomical rates of these crimes, much worse than the other states'—rape is three times higher than the national average. But the statistics don't capture the fear and hopelessness of women in some villages. Imagine yourself in a remote part of Alaska where your people have always subsisted and are profoundly at home. Newcomers are rare except by birth, because the village barely has an economy and the only way to get there is an expensive ride on a small plane, and then only when the weather allows. A woman being abused perhaps grew up seeing her mother being hit, and nothing ever being said about it. Who would she tell? And where would she go?

In conversations around the state, women have told me that rape was something that happened and was not talked about. Domestic violence, often sparked by alcohol or drugs, feels inescapable to these women. They sometimes confide in me privately, as happened when I took a trip to the tiny island community of Little Diomede about ten years ago. The Iñupiaq community, with fewer than one hundred people at the time, perches on this vertical, rocky island in the Bering Strait, two miles from Russia, and is reachable only by helicopter. I had heard from law enforcement that the community had been flooded with drugs coming through the mail and we decided to investigate. Arriving on a weekday morning, we found the place eerily deserted. Our Coast Guard helicopter was the first to make it to the island in a week due to weather, and we learned the village was out of drugs—that was why it was so quiet. We met with the school's dozen students, and as we were leaving, a high school girl came to my side and asked to speak privately. "You need to help us," she whispered. "We are not always safe here." With the drugs that had seized the community, she said, the children felt safe only when they were in school.

We did stop the drugs going into that community for a time, but I know there are many other girls like that high school student who don't feel safe and don't know where they can turn.

A 2019 *Anchorage Daily News* investigation found that one-third of Alaska communities had no law enforcement at all. Seventy of these villages were large enough to have a school and a post office, but if there was a rape or a shooting, a resident would have to call the Alaska State Troopers, who would send a trooper from a regional hub by plane, weather and daylight permitting. It could take days for a trooper to arrive while victims waited, vulnerable to their attackers. Even in communities with law enforcement, the officers tended to be unarmed locals who were often related to many residents of the village. In the southwest Yup'ik village of Napaskiak, I met the two tribal officers who policed the community of four hundred, one nineteen years old and the other twenty-one. They lacked meaningful training and the more senior officer had only four months of experience. Without weapons, one of the officers said, the only tool for handling domestic violence cases was "my voice."

One of my highest priorities as a senator is to protect the most vulnerable, particularly Native women and girls. The work has been hard, and progress has taken many years. But we are making headway. The silence is breaking.

———

Early in Trump's term, White House counsel Don McGahn contacted my office with a list of potential nominees to the Supreme Court. I respected Don and I appreciated that he'd checked in, knowing that I would take seriously the responsibility of evaluating each nominee. Judge Neil Gorsuch was eminently qualified, as a respected jurist and an intellectual who had a doctorate from Oxford as well as a Harvard law degree. In addition, as a member of the Court of Appeals for the Tenth Circuit, in Denver, he was deeply familiar with Native American law, administrative law, and western resource and public land issues, a rare advantage in a Supreme Court justice, from my point of view. Staff who sit in on my meetings with prospective judges and justices know I usually ask about those matters, as well as judicial philosophy surrounding precedent and stability in the law, and understanding of the Second Amendment. These meetings may not be exciting for my staff after half a dozen Supreme Court nominations with my consistent questions, but I usually get what I need to size up the nominee. Gorsuch was exceptionally strong, and I never had a doubt about his confirmation.

After the delay of Garland, however, the Democrats probably would have fought almost any Trump nominee. They had the votes to sustain a filibuster. Mitch McConnell changed the rules so we could end a filibuster with a simple majority, using the nuclear option, which Harry Reid had previously invoked to confirm judges for courts other than the Supreme Court. We had entered a new era in which appointments to the courts, now including the highest court, could be confirmed solely by party-line votes, leaving only a few of us still adhering to the traditions of the institution in our role to advise and consent. The loss of that tradition, especially the judicial filibuster, undermined a key part of the foundations of our judiciary, which is the presumption of objectivity by judges. Not long ago, presidents had nominated judges and justices they believed would be at least acceptable to both parties, and senators had cast "no" votes only to stop nominees with serious flaws. Now a president can rarely count on confirmation votes from the opposite party, and so can nominate anyone he or she chooses with majority-party support. The judges' credibility is the casualty, as the public, understandably, now views them as creations of politics, regardless of their actual impartiality, which I believe is still substantial. We have yet to see if this system will work at all when the party opposite to the president controls the Senate. Maybe we just won't replace any judges for those years. The intransigence of both parties seems to be leading to that level of dysfunction.

All Republicans and just three Democrats voted to confirm Gorsuch. Fifteen months later, when Trump nominated Brett Kavanaugh, I met with him and asked him the same kinds of questions I had asked Gorsuch, including about Alaska Native and administrative law. He was clearly qualified on paper and based on his responses, before his confirmation hearings started.

As the confirmation process has degraded, the judicial nominees have become ever more carefully coached and insulated by their handlers at the White House. There's a reason for that. Judiciary Committee hearings have become places of partisan drama. Nominees are confronted with every bit of potential dirt, from high school writings to random tweets. Democrats used scorched-earth tactics under Trump, and Republicans did it under Biden, too. The party in opposition to the president tears up the nominee in any way possible, while senators of the president's party do everything to gloss over any weaknesses. When the parties reverse, so do the tactics. Nominees are wise to say as little as possible in this poisonous atmosphere. If the questions aren't sincere, why should the answers be?

Unfortunately, the nominees' noncommittal responses continue in our private meetings. Senators know they won't answer questions about particular decisions or about cases that might come before the court and so don't bother asking, but there are questions about judicial philosophy that legitimately reflect on important precedents. Susan Collins and I occasionally compared notes, as pro-choice Republicans concerned about the court chipping away at *Roe v. Wade* (I never imagined the extreme possibility that it could be overturned completely). In our respective private meetings, we probed the nominees about precedence and reliance, cornerstones of the court's legitimacy and of the rule of law. Simply stated, these principles say that cases that are decided set precedents for later courts, and that precedents grow stronger as they are reaffirmed, and even stronger with time as society relies on them as the stable law of the land. After fifty years and many affirmations, *Roe* met these qualifications as settled law that could not be overturned without shaking the foundation of our system. Susan and I asked the Trump nominees—Gorsuch, Kavanaugh, and Amy Coney Barrett—and they clearly agreed with the importance of these principles.

Did they lie? I don't think so. These are intelligent and highly trained lawyers, and I believe they are ethical. They would not have crossed the line with a lie. The Senate had turned the confirmation process into a political fight club, and nominees protected themselves with complex, opaque remarks. Indeed, I knew at the time that these judges were using their words extremely carefully, even as I thought I heard them say they would not overturn established law reaffirmed by precedents and relied on by Americans for generations, which I, perhaps naïvely, interpreted to mean, leave *Roe* standing! As I think back, it's possible that I heard what I wanted to believe.

I believe abortion should be legal, with reasonable limits, and available to women on an equitable basis, but I wasn't asked how I came to hold that view until I sat down to write this book. It is an obvious question for a Republican from a traditional family, raised as a Catholic, who went to a Jesuit high school and college and remains a woman of faith. This certainly hasn't been the easy route politically or, more important, for the way it has affected my family. I faced this in a wrenching way in 2004 when my entire family—even my parents—attended noon Mass on Election Day, my first election for the Senate. A woman approached us in our pew and handed out anti-abortion leaflets critical of me, pointedly giving one to each member of the family except for me. We were all offended, but Nic, then thirteen, was angry and wanted to protect me by confronting the woman after Mass. I told him to let it go. That moment robbed him of his closeness to the church, something that continues to this day. Over the years, Alaska church leaders have repeatedly stood by me and assured me that I am welcome in my faith home, but my relationship to the church has suffered as others have said I should be denied Communion. One priest actually did withhold the host.

I take my stand on abortion because of my belief in personal freedom and liberty. We Alaskans are committed to our right to live without government interference. I believe in the right to bear arms granted by the Second Amendment. I opposed the Patriot Act for its erosion of our privacy and freedom. And, like 75 percent of Alaskans, I believe that women should make their own decisions about their reproduction—again, with reasonable limits—not the government. (Alaskans legalized abortion before *Roe* and added a specific right to privacy to our state constitution in 1972, the year before the decision.) Whatever the flaws in *Roe*, or the *Casey* decision that affirmed it, our autonomy over our bodies remains fundamental to the concept of liberty, which is the foundation of the U.S. Constitution and our form of government. There are no exceptions for the gender of an American's body.

From what I knew in the summer of 2018, however, I had no basis on which to oppose Kavanaugh's confirmation. But activists trying to keep him off the court understood that Susan and I were their best hope. If we both voted no on Kavanaugh, along with every Democrat, he would not be confirmed. They mounted a pressure campaign that took the jangling intensity of the Trump years to another high, focusing primarily on just the two of us. Susan soon had protesters demonstrating in front of her house in Maine, dressed as characters from the dystopian TV series *The Handmaid's Tale*.

A lot of that kind of pressure is counterproductive, especially the rude and threatening calls. One caller told the young woman who answers my phones that they hoped she would be raped and need an abortion. But as author Ruth Marcus later documented, more sophisticated activists studied Susan and me, our psychology and decision processes, and made much smarter choices about how to influence us. Understanding my sensitivity on Alaska Native tribal rights, opponents made sure to have a Democratic member of the Judiciary Committee ask Kavanaugh detailed questions on the subject at his confirmation hearing, with an intended audience of one: me. His answers led the Alaska Federation of Natives to oppose his confirmation, which did certainly get my attention.

But we were only getting started. Although the world did not yet know it, rumors were floating around Washington that a woman had accused Kavanaugh of sexual assault. I frankly discounted that talk as more of the character assassination that seemed to be the order of the day.

———

At the end of August I returned to Savoonga, the Siberian Yup'ik village on St. Lawrence Island where I had taken Secretary of Education Rod Paige fifteen years earlier. I chaired a field hearing of the Indian Affairs Committee on rural housing in the village's gym. Although I was the only senator on the trip, we filled two fourteen-seat Cessna Caravans with committee staff and state, federal, and tribal officials for the flight over the northern Bering Sea. For me, this was an opportunity to use my position to get people to see a problem that otherwise could remain out of sight.

Seated at plastic folding tables in the echoing basketball court, we heard testimony about the shortage of housing in the region, where overcrowding was eight times more prevalent than in the nation as a whole. In that climate, where the weather can so easily kill, there are no unhoused people—those who otherwise would be are stuffed into small houses already bursting with people. For families and children in these crowded conditions, quiet and privacy are impossible.

After the formal hearing, we toured three homes. Twelve people lived in one two-bedroom house, with four bunks in one room and mattresses covering the entire floor of the other. An elder slept in a recliner that partially blocked the front door. There weren't enough beds for everyone, so the family slept in shifts. With school starting, the shifts would change. During the summer, the children had been sleeping during the day and the adults at night, and now the children would have to be awake during the day for school.

I thought about what it must be like for a child growing up in a home like this, where no one has privacy and everyone sleeps in the same rooms—all generations, extended family, in-laws, and newlyweds included. Even in a healthy family, adult activities are not always healthy for children to see. In the presence of substance abuse or domestic violence, children could not escape trauma. Negative lessons would be learned early.

The visit helped push forward legislation for housing in Native American communities, but I remember that day as well for a strange moment that happened before we departed. I hesitate to tell the story, because it sounds like a fairy tale. We had finished our tour and piled into the back of pickup trucks for the ride to the airstrip on the edge of the village. While we stood there getting ready to board our planes, a man who hadn't attended any of the gatherings zoomed up on a four-wheeler and stopped right next to me.

He took my hand and pressed into my palm a smooth, dark green rock.

He said, "Take this, you may need it."

Rural people often give me little gifts. St. Lawrence Island is famous for its fossilized whalebone carvings. But he had given me a plain rock. I said something like "Thank you—how did you know I collect rocks?" I liked the size, smoothness, and solidity.

He just smiled and said again, "One day you may need this rock," and he took off.

As odd as that moment was, the rock didn't mean much to me at first. I dropped it in my backpack, and after Labor Day it rode with me back to Washington, where it sat on my dresser with rocks I've gathered from Greenland and elsewhere around the Arctic. But the man was right. It wouldn't be long before I would need that rock.

A few days later, a sweet ten-year-old girl named Ashley Johnson-Barr disappeared from a playground in Kotzebue, an Iñupiaq hub community of about three thousand people in the northwest Arctic. The town rallied for the search, with as many as fifty volunteers coming out, knocking on doors, looking in vacant buildings, and scanning the tundra. Ashley's family was well liked, and the community pulled together, as always. But when they couldn't find her, the Alaska State Troopers sent additional searchers to town, taking over command from the local police. The Coast Guard deployed aircraft to search out on the Chukchi Sea. Concern grew across the state. The media ran photographs of this dear child with big cheeks and an oval face, a girl who loved basketball and church, and who smiled in pictures with hearts and her favorite color, purple. How could a little girl simply disappear in a small town like Kotzebue, which sits on a spit of gravel, surrounded by water, and is unconnected to the outside world by any road? As the search continued and suspicions of foul play grew, the FBI sent in seventeen agents, adding to the all-hands search carried out by state and local agencies and friends, relatives, and neighbors.

Alaskans were gripped by fear for Ashley and heartsick over the most likely explanation of what happened to her. We had just read in the *Anchorage Daily News* about a police dispatcher in Nome who was raped—someone had briefly posted a video of the crime on social media—but whose colleagues at the police department had ignored her case and didn't investigate it for a year, until she bravely stood up and told her story to state authorities and the newspaper. One week after Ashley's disappearance, as the search continued, her case began turning into a crime investigation. All over the state, people were wearing purple for her. Forty villages and towns held vigils or marches.

That same day, in Washington, the rumors were confirmed that a woman had accused Brett Kavanaugh of attempted rape when they were both in high school. Senator Dianne Feinstein disclosed that she had received a letter six weeks earlier from this unnamed constituent but had respected the wishes of the writer to keep it secret, and had referred the matter to the FBI. I didn't pay much attention, as nothing specific had been released. I didn't want to be swayed by anonymous vilification in the confirmation process.

The day after that, they found Ashley's body among tangled brush on the tundra outside Kotzebue. Location data from a cellphone had led investigators there, and made it obvious who had killed her, a forty-one-year-old man who was her relative and whom she would have recognized. We learned nothing at that point about what had happened to Ashley before she died.

Christine Blasey Ford told her story in *The Washington Post* the same weekend. As a teenager, she said, Brett Kavanaugh, while drunk at a party, had cornered her in a bedroom and forced himself on her, lying on top of her, covering her mouth, and clumsily trying to pull off the clothes she wore over a one-piece bathing suit. Kavanaugh's friend, she said, had knocked them both off the bed and ended the incident. The friend and Kavanaugh denied that it had ever happened. But Ford had told therapists about it over the years, and the newspaper had seen the therapists' notes.

I still withheld judgment. I flew to Kotzebue for Ashley's funeral and potluck.

When my plane landed, Ashley's father, Scotty Barr, was there on the runway, but not to meet us. He worked for the airline, which had flown up bottles of water and Kleenex for the service. Scotty was a truly remarkable man. I offered my condolences, but he didn't have time to talk as he loaded the water and tissues to take to the middle school gym. He knew, as we did not yet, that Ashley had been raped and her body had been dismembered before she was dumped in the bushes on the tundra east of town. How he got through that day, I cannot imagine. The gym, festooned with purple decorations and pictures of smiling Ashley, was full of people dressed in purple. Teachers remembered her goodness, and her pastor declared that she was now in heaven. Her grave marker and flowers were purple, as well as the balloons that floated over the marker.

Scotty Barr, in a quiet but deeply powerful way, became a voice for his daughter, speaking out about what this tragedy could teach Alaska. A movement began. Women whom Ashley's killer had repeatedly raped came forward. They said they had accused him, but no one had believed them. The *Anchorage Daily News* began a historic investigation, which ultimately won the Pulitzer Prize, detailing the failure of law enforcement in Alaska and profiling women from all walks of life who told their stories of sexual violence. The stories and photos became a devastating and inspiring museum exhibit, as well as a series of articles.

"Our daughter started something," Scotty Barr told the newspaper. "No more silence."

"No more silence." The unofficial slogan of the movement.

When I returned from the funeral, Washington and the entire country were fully caught up in the Blasey Ford allegations. Supreme Court confirmation controversies tend to be abstract. Here, instead, we had the kind of drama that so many could identify with, and that captured the essence of the cultural moment. Women were breaking their silence about sexual assault and demanding to be heard. But who did you believe? There had to be evidence.

Most Republicans tried to blow by all this, but Susan Collins and I, along with Republican Jeff Flake of Arizona, had not committed to supporting Kavanaugh. When we said we should take time to understand the Blasey Ford allegations, our leadership knew they couldn't stonewall. They reached an agreement with her lawyers to hold a hearing where she could testify.

The president lashed out against Blasey Ford and also leaked criticism of Kavanaugh, who, he said, had not been angry and assertive enough in his denials during a Fox News interview. Anger and counterattack had worked for Trump in the many cases when he had been accused of groping women, and worse. He wanted the same from his nominee.

I tried to remain fair and deliberative. I was not inclined to block Kavanagh's confirmation over uncorroborated allegations. But I also knew that women must be listened to and respected. "No more silence."

"We are now in a place where it's not about whether or not Judge Kavanaugh is qualified," I told reporters in the Capitol. "It is about whether or not a woman who has been a victim at some point in her life is to be believed."

So much weight had fallen on my shoulders. Not only was I one of only a few undeclared senators, I had contradicted the president and my party by speaking up for women at this moment. Women and girls were counting on us to listen, as the entire nation was finally being forced to deal with this issue under the television lights. But I needed to be true to my principles about how I come to decisions on votes. I would have to make this decision alone. Restless nights returned, and eating fell off my priority list.

As I prepared for work one day, I saw the rock on the top of my dresser that the man in Savoonga had given me. I took it in my hand and felt the cool firmness, which was oddly calming. When I waded into the mobs of reporters that morning, I had it tightly palmed in my hand. He had said that one day I might need the rock, and I learned this day that holding it was reassuring.

People back home were watching me in this national moment, many with sympathy. For my rural constituents, Liz Ruskin was the primary messenger. Liz had covered me on Alaska public radio off and on since my first days in the Senate. Her reports on *Alaska News Nightly* reached every corner of the state. Now she started nightly dialogues with the show's host, Casey Grove, describing the crazy circus surrounding me in Washington—Liz had been caught up in a protest led by a chanting Joan Baez in my office building—as she checked up on me and reported back to Alaskans.

The exchanges between Liz and Casey are still available online. Listening to the conversation they recorded the day before Blasey Ford was set to testify, I'm struck by how genuine they seem in their concern about me.

Casey asks Liz, "How is she handling the pressure?"

"She seems to be in good spirits, mostly," Liz says. "There was one moment where she had just, you know, had it."

She plays a recording of when reporters packed in around me on the subway from the Capitol to my office. A very direct question about *Roe* struck me the wrong way. After a long period of silence, I said, "And you know what? I think I'm done answering the questions for right now. Is that okay?"

The reporter said, "Sure," in a sheepish voice.

Back in the studio, Casey asks, "Liz, was she mad?"

"No, it was more like a sudden loss of cabin pressure. But the reporters switched to just chatting with her, and she rallied for a few more questions."

"So what's her answer about whether this Me Too moment puts us at a turning point in history?" Casey asks.

I had said this was still about Kavanaugh's qualifications, but Liz plays another clip of me: "It's now a greater dialogue, a national conversation, about women who've become victims and their ability to tell their story."

Casey asks, "Have you got much sense of how she's feeling about this vote or feeling about all of this?"

"Not really," Liz says. "But I did ask her a personal question."

More tape. Liz speaking to me alone as I get on an elevator.

"A lot of American women are saying that they've had Me Too moments, and I'm wondering if you have," she asks on the recording.

My voice is small and clipped, but I say, "Yes," without a pause. And then I say no more.

I had never told anyone. More than fifty years had passed, and I had never told anyone about what happened to me when I was in second grade. (Even now, I've still told very few.) But when my parents heard my quick "Yes," on the radio, they called and asked. I said I would tell them one day, but I didn't want to talk about it. That made them even more anxious, which I understood. So, finally, I wrote them a letter. In it, I told them that when I was a little girl, walking alone on a trail in Wrangell, a man lured me into the woods and exposed himself to me and forced me to touch him. He was the relative of one of our neighbors and in the military. I was terrified. He said if I ever told anyone what happened, I would get in horrible trouble for being bad. I believed him. I never told anyone, not even my sisters. I was ashamed as well as afraid. That place still haunts me, all these years later, a dark spot in the woods, hidden in my mind.

But when Liz asked me with her microphone, I didn't hesitate. I said, "Yes."

No more silence. And I held tight to the rock from Savoonga.

―――――――

In anticipation of the hearing with Blasey Ford and Kavanaugh that Thursday, I canceled my own committee meetings. Six networks canceled their days of programming to broadcast the hearings, which had as many viewers as the Academy Awards or the NFL playoffs—but only four of us had a say in the matter, those four senators still undeclared on the confirmation vote: Collins, Flake, West Virginia Democrat Joe Manchin, and me. I settled in to watch that day's hearing on TV with an open mind. Christine Blasey Ford's testimony impressed me. She was not theatrical. She was tense and serious. She was a substantial person with significant accomplishments, but she also sounded like a woman talking about one of the darkest moments of her life, with a quavering voice. She began by saying, "I am not here because I want to be. I am terrified. I am here because I believe it is my civic duty."

Blasey Ford was 100 percent sure her story was true. I believed her—she was certain. But it was also possible that she was wrong. Recalling an event from so many years earlier, unable to remember key details, from a night when teens were drinking, she could possibly accuse the wrong person.

Trump apparently thought Blasey Ford was credible. After her testimony he thought Kavanaugh's confirmation was in trouble, according to news accounts. Trump was ready to go along with a demand to give the FBI a week to investigate the charges, but McGahn and others convinced him to stay quiet until Kavanaugh had a chance to testify.

Kavanaugh raged in his testimony, in a performance that was widely replayed and parodied. To me, it was disturbing. Rather than soberly denying the charges, he adopted the overheated rhetoric of a political campaign. He quickly denounced the Democratic senators on the committee, charged that the whole case against him had somehow been produced by the Clintons for revenge over Trump's election, and ominously threatened, "What goes around comes around." Within minutes, he had destroyed the sense that he could be fair or disinterested on the court—he sounded like a man whose anger and resentment would bias him as a justice against those he disagreed with politically.

Some of the attacks by the Democrats were over the top, but many questions were fair. Amy Klobuchar tried to get to the root of the opposite recollections of the two witnesses by probing Kavanaugh's drinking, with the implication he might have been so drunk during the incident that he lost control and was unable to remember what had happened. I like and admire Amy—she's smart but funny and a great storyteller, and she doesn't let her intellect overshadow her humanity. Kavanaugh attacked her most aggressively of all—a woman—as he evaded her questions. I understand speaking strongly to defend his honor, but Kavanaugh's response was outrageous when he turned the tables to ask about the senator's own drinking. "You're asking about blackout. I don't know. Have you?" he said.

I was aghast. Much of the country was. But President Trump was impressed with his performance, and the Republican leadership considered it a win. They planned to push to a confirmation vote right away.

Instead, the four uncommitted senators met that night to talk about our concerns. Susan and I felt strongly that the allegations needed investigation. Blasey Ford and all women deserved that. We reached no conclusions together, and none of us committed our vote.

As a member of the Judiciary Committee, Jeff Flake faced a decision the next morning, when the committee would vote on whether to advance the nomination. Reportedly he was up all night. In the morning, one minute before the committee was to convene, his office released a statement saying he would vote yes. Moments later, on his way to the committee room, Jeff was stopped in a Capitol elevator by two rape victims, who confronted him over his decision. As he stood in the corner, next to the bank of buttons, they held the elevator door open for four and a half minutes while their voices rose to shouts. CNN was broadcasting the whole thing live. Jeff nervously looked at the floor.

"Nobody believed me," said one of the women, through tears.

"You're telling all women that they don't matter. That they should just stay quiet, because if they tell you what happened to them, you're going to ignore them. That's what happened to me, and that's what you're telling all women in America."

Jeff appeared shaken. The exchange was hard to watch on the screen. It must have been so much harder to endure. With that terrible moment on his mind, Jeff listened for three hours to senators' statements in the committee room, as the vote approached. Finally, he pulled a friend aside, Democrat Chris Coons of Delaware, to discuss the idea of a one-week FBI investigation. Senators gathered around them, arguing both sides, until Jeff and Chris retreated to a phone booth, where they conferenced Susan and me on a cellphone to confirm that we would back up the demand for an investigation. With we three Republicans on the same side, the leadership had no choice, and Jeff negotiated for the investigation to go forward, while also casting his vote to advance the nomination out of committee.

Christine Blasey Ford's brave testimony, like Ashley Johnson-Barr's murder in Alaska, released a flow of women's stories. My office was besieged by meeting requests from Alaskan women who wanted to tell me about their own assaults. As I've already said, I try to meet with every Alaskan who makes the effort to travel to Washington. But now so many women came that I had to group them—and even then I couldn't meet everyone. The wrenching emotions these women carried to us overwhelmed the entire office. At the time, and until recently, I believed they had all come and paid their way individually, but I've learned that the Alaska Civil Liberties Union organized them, after the national ACLU took the unusual position of opposing Kavanaugh's confirmation and offering the state affiliate $100,000 for the women's travel expenses. When that amount was quickly used up, with many more women wanting to visit, the ACLU doubled the budget.

Whoever paid for the trips, no one could doubt the authenticity of these women's raw feelings. We would group them around a conference table, about a dozen at a time, and sometimes squeezing in more. The women took turns, going around the room. Typically, each would talk about her own story, often with great difficulty, some speaking of added trauma because they had not been believed. Christine Blasey Ford was telling the same story, and they expressed their sense of injustice that, like them, she was not believed. Listening to these stories was emotionally draining. Doing it en masse was unbearable. We got to the point we were scheduling four, or even six, of these group meetings a day. If I attended them all, that would be all I could do, so Garrett Boyle, my young legislative director (today my chief of staff), attended many of the meetings on my behalf. He recalls those weeks as the worst of his life. Day after day he listened to these harrowing, tearful stories of rape, expressed what sympathy he could, ended the meeting, then greeted another group and started again. He didn't know how to help these women. As he said, he had never been trained as a sexual assault counselor.

All this attention was directed at me because I was "in play," to use the language of Washington—meaning I had not predetermined my vote but intended to gather all the relevant evidence and decide on the merits. With only four undeclared senators left, it was almost as if no one else mattered.

At this crazy level of media attention, an insignificant gesture could be blown up into something absurd. Around this time, I saw Dianne Feinstein in a Capitol hallway and greeted her in mutual support, as I knew the Judiciary Committee hearings had been hard on her. Dianne was tired and leaned her hand against the wall behind me as we visited, but a photo of this friendly moment made it look like she had cornered me, and that "bullying" image went viral.

The insane pressure included threats. There were too many incidents to remember, but one stuck with me and wouldn't leave my head. Someone sent in a threat against my sons—that if I didn't vote to confirm Kavanaugh, this person would contrive a false sexual allegation against one of them and ruin his reputation. Of course, anyone can send an anonymous threat, and I try to ignore them if they are not criminal (we have recently had one such person go to prison). This threat against my sons hit home, however, because I could imagine just how easy it would be to carry out. And that knowledge added another layer of doubt to the choice I had to make.

On Thursday, October 4, the FBI report was completed and made available for senators to read in a secure room. I read it carefully. The report turned up nothing new. Jeff Flake announced his affirmative vote after reading it. That left it to Susan Collins or me to give Kavanaugh the last vote he needed (if Joe Manchin, a Democrat, voted for Kavanaugh, that also would be enough to assure the confirmation). On Friday morning, we would vote on closing debate (cloture), and on Saturday on the confirmation itself.

I spent much of Thursday afternoon in my last two meetings with the women from Alaska. We crammed eighteen into each gathering. In one, which lasted over an hour, the women talked about their own sexual assaults and pleaded with me not to vote for Kavanaugh's confirmation. I was shaken by what I heard. I said, "I feel six inches shorter than when I walked in here. I'm so humbled by your stories."

In every meeting, I tried to honor these women's courage and their right to speak to me. But I could not let the emotion of these sessions overwhelm my reason. The horror and destructiveness of sexual abuse in general is a different issue from whether a particular incident actually occurred, and I was not yet convinced that Kavanaugh had committed the assault he was accused of. There was no corroborating evidence. As I listened to these women, I thought, "Yes, I know your story is real. But that doesn't mean hers is real."

On the other hand, Kavanaugh's angry testimony had undermined my confidence in his temperament as a judge. On the Supreme Court, he would serve all Americans, Democrats as well as Republicans, and that would be hard after his angry statement that "what goes around comes around." That day the Senate received a letter signed by more than twenty-four hundred law professors arguing that Kavanaugh's conduct at the hearing had disqualified him. Published in *The New York Times,* it stated, "Instead of trying to sort out with reason and care the allegations that were raised, Judge Kavanaugh responded in an intemperate, inflammatory and partial manner, as he interrupted and, at times, was discourteous to senators. . . . He did not display the impartiality and judicial temperament requisite to sit on the highest court of our land."

Political bias was only one blind side to consider. I also believed that Kavanaugh should show that he understood the perspective of women who had been assaulted. He would judge cases affecting them all. Underneath the bluster and combativeness, did he grasp what this was all about? I had discussed how to weigh this with my senior team, as I always do with tough votes. Some of my staff thought the evidence against Kavanaugh was too weak—they had more than a reasonable doubt—but I countered that we were not trying him as a criminal defendant, we were deciding if he should be elevated to a lifetime office of the highest honor and responsibility. The right standard wasn't reasonable doubt, it was his fitness for this role. If he could not understand women's perspectives in this extraordinary moment, perhaps he was not fit for the court.

The other group of eighteen that day were all women lawyers from Alaska. They'd brought exactly this number of people after researching how many would fit into my largest conference room. I had met some of them professionally, but none were more than acquaintances of mine. The tone of the meeting was calm and professional. They had come primarily as attorneys, not victims. A young lawyer from Anchorage who'd organized the group gave me a copy of Rule 1.2 from the American Bar Association's Model Code of Judicial Conduct: "A judge shall act at all times in a manner that promotes public confidence in the independence, integrity, and impartiality of the judiciary." These women pointed out that Kavanaugh had failed that test. Moreover, they said his failure would undermine women's confidence that their testimonies of sexual abuse would be respected and believed.

Earlier, I had requested another meeting with Kavanaugh, one-on-one—this time with no staff present. I wanted to know if he had gained any insight about how his confirmation hearings had elevated the national discussion about sexual assault. I didn't expect him to admit anything, but I hoped he could perceive the wound that had been opened, and his responsibility as a jurist to weigh the perspective of everyone coming before the court—including women making accusations of sexual assault.

White House counsel Don McGahn had made sure to leave me alone, presumably understanding that pressure for my vote could backfire. But he had repeatedly offered help, information, or whatever I needed. The White House believed, and my staff agreed, that a second meeting with Kavanaugh had to be completely secret, or it would turn into a media circus. Indeed, there would be no way to get Kavanaugh to the Capitol or my office without generating a spike of coverage. That day, Thursday, we received word from the White House that Kavanaugh could meet me, if I could come to his chambers in the courthouse a few blocks down Constitution Avenue, just past the Capitol, in ninety minutes—one-fifteen P.M.

I had walked to work that day, and Verne had our only car. I needed a ride. My executive assistant, Kristen Daimler-Nothdurft, offered to drive me in her little car, with the tall legislative director, Garrett, folded up in the back seat, along with my communications director, Karina Borger (then Petersen). We pulled away from the Senate steps in front of the Capitol building and turned onto Constitution Avenue, and we were immediately surrounded by crowds. A large protest march opposing the Kavanaugh confirmation had overflowed the sidewalks, and protesters were spread from curb to curb. I joked that this must be what it's like to get in the middle of a caribou migration on the tundra, because moving bodies were all around the car. But the joke covered a panicky feeling. What if they recognized me? This was a huge crowd of angry people. I pulled down the car's visor, but it was tiny, and I felt totally exposed. I said, "Kristen, you need a bigger car." She said, "I'd get one if you paid me more," which was fair.

Guards were ready for us at the courthouse. We drove into an underground garage, passing into a cool, calm space that was a complete contrast to the scene in the street. Over the past week, my Savoonga rock had become my comfort rock, and I was gripping it, but Kristen wisely advised me to leave it behind, and I dropped it in the cup holder. Garrett and I were escorted upstairs, and I went into Kavanaugh's office alone.

I was direct. I said I had listened to him and wanted to believe him, but I had also listened to Blasey Ford and I believed her, too. I said his outburst at the hearing had concerned me greatly, because it did not reflect judicial temperament suitable for the court. In response, he didn't get angry, but he did become very defensive, talking about the impact of the publicity on his daughters and the unfairness of what he had endured. I understood why he would be defensive, but sometimes public life doesn't treat us fairly, and none of us, especially a judge, can afford to lose control of our emotions.

I changed the subject to the most important reason I had come. I said his nomination had brought the country into this post–Me Too moment for women who had been traumatized by assault and had been discounted or disbelieved. I asked him if he understood the emotions his confirmation process had reawakened for many victims. He really didn't. He kept saying, "But I didn't do it," and bringing the conversation back to himself rather than showing comprehension of how other women had been retraumatized because of all this. That was all I was waiting for him to express, and he couldn't do it.

I suggested that one way to help heal the national trauma would be to write an op-ed for a major newspaper, acknowledging the anger and frustration felt by women. I didn't expect, or ask, for any admission or apology, but I wanted him to show some awareness, some comprehension, so that women could feel heard and believe that he would listen to them as a justice. He agreed to do that, and the meeting ended.

I told my staff in the car, "He has no self-awareness. He doesn't realize this isn't only about him."

The Wall Street Journal posted Kavanaugh's op-ed on its website less than six hours later, that evening. It repeated his defenses while admitting only that, at the hearing, "I said a few things I should not have said." The essay didn't mention trying to understand the perspectives of women. It may have been that the White House wouldn't allow that, as it seemed to be in total control of the process. We had heard in our conference that Trump had been unimpressed by Kavanaugh's early hearing testimony and had wanted him to be angrier, and that this direction had produced his aggressive responses. If that's true, it would fit that the president also didn't want him to show any sign of empathy, which could be interpreted as weakness, in an op-ed.

With my decision due in the morning, a few key staff members stayed with me—Garrett, Karina, and Fish—and we talked the issues back and forth past midnight. This vote wasn't like the ACA, where there were policy matters to be weighed and balanced and complexities to be understood. This vote would be a deep, personal statement that could resonate throughout the country in a moment of profound reckoning—and, of course, it would affect the court and Kavanaugh himself. Rather than persuade, my staff gave me things to think about. Garrett said, "You have to wake up and like the person you see in the mirror every day when you brush your teeth. That's how you should make this decision."

He drove me home at two A.M. I stayed up writing lists of pros and cons on a yellow legal pad. After getting a little sleep, I woke up Friday morning still undecided. I texted Susan Collins that this was one of the hardest decisions I'd ever had to make. She responded that she agreed, and that she had decided to vote to confirm Kavanaugh. I just said, "OK."

At various times, commentators had predicted that my vote

would follow Susan's or that Susan's would follow mine. Pairing up would avoid either of us going it alone politically, and would make sense, given how much we have in common, as two pro-choice Republican women from rural northern states. But we also have something bigger in common: we do our own homework and make our own decisions. Susan is smart and serious and works harder than anyone I know. In 2012, Susan married Tom Daffron, who had been my chief of staff. Tom and Verne also established a link, as two senatorial husbands. But for Susan and me, work has always been the center of our relationship. We worked through issues together, but as independent minds.

Susan was a Republican representing a blue state, and this positive vote would make her reelection in two years substantially harder. For me, the situation was reversed. A vote to confirm Kavanaugh would be politically easier. But I don't think either of us weighed that in our decisions, and neither would end up voting in line with our own advantage. The Supreme Court mattered too much for that.

With the ten-thirty A.M. cloture vote approaching, I went to be alone in my office in the Capitol, a place we call the hideaway, a relatively small room overlooking the National Mall, where I could think. Only minutes remained before I would have to say yes or no on the Senate floor, and I was sincerely undecided. Sitting alone, I tried saying yes or no aloud to see how I would feel after my vote. I reviewed my yellow pad again, with the list of pros and cons. I kept coming back to Kavanaugh's performance at the hearing. I pondered what it would mean for this potential Supreme Court justice to lack the confidence of so many women. I looked up at a picture of Ted Stevens, taken with me right after I entered the Senate, and thought about how deeply he had trusted the justice system. Even after he was falsely convicted, he'd had faith that the error would be corrected. What happens if you don't believe in the system? What if you lose faith that your voice will even be heard?

And then, standing in front of that picture, I had a "What would Ted do?" moment. And I determined that I would vote no.

Ted would have agreed with me that judges must be people not only of even temperament and free from bias but with the empathy to understand the citizens coming before them. Kavanaugh had failed on those grounds, even when I had explicitly invited him to express some self-awareness about how women felt at this moment in time. He did not understand. And the Supreme Court needed justices with that awareness, because it needed to be trusted.

I took a breath and got up, ready to vote. The Senate chamber was nearly full when I walked in, with most senators already in their seats. My desk was near the front on the right-hand side of the aisle, next to Susan Collins. I touched her arm and said, "I can't vote for him."

"I'm so glad," she said. "I admit, I'm relieved."

"No, Susan, you didn't hear me," I said. "I'm voting no."

Her expression crumpled. I think both of us had expected that we would vote in alignment, offering some political cover. But we had no time to talk. Coming near the beginning of the alphabet, she had to vote early in the roll call. Jeff Flake then cast a yes vote. Joe Manchin voted yes, too, the only Democrat to break ranks with his party. His vote would give Kavanaugh one more than he needed. And I would be on my own. The roll call came to "Murkowski," and I stood and voted no in a quiet voice. I heard gasps around me. Cloture passed without the vice president having to break a tie. With the vote complete, senators got up to leave.

I wondered if my Republican colleagues would be angry with me, but Mitch McConnell was the first to come to my side. "You have to do what you feel is right," he said. "You're still on our team." Most of my colleagues awkwardly avoided me. I knew I would have to face the crush of media who would be waiting for me when I left the floor.

Without my knowing, John Barrasso of Wyoming found my

communications director, Karina, off the floor and escorted her to me. Karina and I spent something like thirty minutes talking about the decision on my vote. I told her that the threat against my sons had reared up in my mind, as I worried I had put them at risk. But I pushed my anxiety back and gathered my thoughts, because whatever I said now to the waiting media would go out far and wide, and be remembered, while a speech for the final vote the next day would be relatively ignored.

I emerged to a wall of people. In a photograph taken by one of the journalists, dozens of reporters can be seeing surrounding me at the doorway. I look small. My rock was warm in my hand. But I had no difficulty explaining myself.

I said Brett Kavanaugh was a good man, but he was not the right man for the court now.

"This [process] hasn't been fair to the judge, but I also recognize that we need to have institutions that are viewed as fair, and if people who are victims . . . feel that there is no fairness in our system of government, particularly in our courts, then you've gone down a path that is not good and right for this country. And so I have been wrestling with whether or not this was about qualifications of a good man or is this bigger than the nomination. And I believe we're dealing with issues right now that are bigger than the nominee."

I finished by saying, "I think we're at a place where we need to begin thinking about the credibility and integrity of our institutions."

———

Reporters speculated that my no vote would put pressure on Collins, Flake, and Manchin for the final vote on Saturday, but I didn't expect any change and I was correct. My no vote was recorded as "present." My friend Senator Steve Daines of Montana was scheduled to walk his daughter down the aisle in her wedding at that exact time on Saturday, so I agreed to a rarely used procedure to pair his yes vote with my no vote by voting present, allowing him to be absent from the floor without affecting the outcome. This senatorial courtesy seemed only to confuse people. My vote was definitely no.

The final vote brought out deep emotions. Women screaming in anger were dragged by security officers from the Senate gallery. I told reporters, "I don't know what you were doing when those voices were shouting . . . but I was closing my eyes and praying, praying for them and praying for us and praying for the country. We need prayers. We need healing."

That fall Heidi Heitkamp lost her election but spent the lame-duck session pleading for passage of Savanna's Act. When it didn't pass, I reintroduced it at the beginning of the next session. In Alaska, momentum continued for addressing violence against women. In May 2019, the *Anchorage Daily News* began running its Pulitzer-winning series on justice in rural Alaska, and two weeks later Attorney General Bill Barr went to my state and met with tribal leaders and heard their harrowing stories. He declared a first-ever public safety emergency with $10 million for officers and facilities. Savanna's Act and the Not Invisible Act finally passed, near the end of that Congress, in 2020.

I kept the rock. When my sister Carol was diagnosed with breast cancer, I sent her the rock to help her get through chemotherapy. I gave it to my sister Eileen when her husband, Leon, was dying. When my son Nic was taking the bar exam, I gave him the rock. He took it reluctantly, but later he admitted it helped him focus. It would help me again, too, and soon.

CHAPTER 8

In the Center of
the Impeachment Storm

IN EARLY NOVEMBER 2019, I wasn't paying particularly close attention to the impeachment inquiry in the House. I was certainly aware of President Trump's July phone call to Ukrainian president Volodymyr Zelenskyy, in which he asked for the "favor" of an investigation of Joe Biden, while he withheld military aid that Congress had appropriated. But if the Senate was to hear an impeachment trial, the House would first have to pass articles of impeachment and it was not clear what the hearings would produce, if anything. Besides, I had plenty to attend to in my own job without getting caught up in what the House was doing.

Even if I wasn't paying close attention, however, others were paying attention to me. According to Fox News, Mitch McConnell had advised Trump to refrain from insulting Republican senators, particularly me, and had recommended that he talk about supporting my energy bill rather than bringing up Ukraine. I didn't know about that at the time, but I did hear about Trump's comments the same day to an audience at a Republican fundraiser, held at his Washington hotel. He called out to the room, asking if I was in attendance, then said, "She hates me. I kind of like her but she really doesn't like me. We do so much for Alaska you'd think we'd get her vote for something one of these days."

Trump was right on one thing: I had paid little price for my votes of conscience contrary to his wishes. After the Kavanaugh confirmation, he told an interviewer that my negative vote was "unforgivable" and that Alaska voters "will never forget," but he didn't attack me personally, and when the same reporter brought up a Twitter threat from Sarah Palin to run against me in 2022, he didn't engage. Besides the disagreements I've already mentioned, I had denounced his separation of immigrant children from their families at the border, and I had voted to reverse his illegal diversion of military funds for the border wall. Yet Alaska did extraordinarily well during the Trump administration. We were making progress—or had won—on many of our major priorities. To give credit where it is due, these were big-ticket items: ANWR, the long-stymied road to King Cove, and the Tongass National Forest roadless rule.

When I heard that Trump thought I hated him, I decided to call him to say that wasn't so. I don't hate anyone, even if I disagree with them. I called him but didn't get through before boarding a flight to Alaska, and as soon as I landed my voicemail had several missed calls from the White House. When I returned the call, Trump came on the line immediately. He was gracious and thanked me for reaching out. The call reminded me of our first conversation, when he was still president-elect and I phoned him from Maui—but then, I have never had a negative interaction with him one-on-one.

For many months, Speaker of the House Nancy Pelosi had held back the members on the left of her caucus who were clamoring for an impeachment. Many Alaskans loathed Pelosi, but I respected her for her political sense and ability to lead, even while I disagreed with her politics. My respect grew as she resisted starting a process that had no chance of success, would be bad for the country, and would likely embolden President Trump after he was acquitted, as in the end it did. The House could impeach with a majority vote, which was within the Democrats' control, but in the Senate we Republicans had increased our majority to fifty-three seats, and a conviction would require two-thirds of the body, or sixty-seven votes. In American history no senator had ever voted to impeach a president of his or her own party. Removal could happen only with conduct so egregious that the public overwhelmingly demanded it. That was not the case.

In September, Pelosi had stopped resisting the Democratic tide for impeachment, when we learned from a whistleblower that Trump had withheld aid to get Zelenskyy to investigate Biden. But she apparently sought to limit the damage by moving it forward rapidly, pushing for the House inquiry to be complete by Christmas. That was a mistake. The Democrats' work was rushed and secretive, with constant political leaks. Trump stonewalled, ordering various officials to refuse to testify and to defy subpoenas, including the most important witness: former national security adviser John Bolton. Bolton had left the job early that same month and presumably was already working on the book that would come out the next summer confirming the most important parts of the Democrats' case (and would earn him millions of dollars). But he refused to testify until a court ruled on a subpoena issued to one of his subordinates, Charles Kupperman. House leaders could have fought for the subpoena in court—a judge expedited the case and promised a ruling by the end of the year—and that would have given them Bolton's testimony before they voted on impeachment. But they would have missed the self-imposed Christmas deadline for their predetermined outcome. Instead, they withdrew the Kupperman subpoena to stop the court's consideration.

For someone who simply wanted to see Trump impeached by whatever means to send a political message, and have it done before the 2020 presidential primaries, perhaps that was good enough. But if, like me, you believe that the impeachment clause of the Constitution must be taken seriously and used sparingly, the process should not be short-circuited. Impeachment should go forward based only on the content of sound, proven articles alleging treason, bribery, or other high crimes and misdemeanors. I knew I could not impeach the president for any reason that was not specified in the articles of impeachment submitted to the Senate. The House had to do its job.

How could this process have been different? I was already thinking, after my "I don't hate you" call with Trump, that a move to censure the president had a reasonable chance of passing the Senate and would be a more effective sanction than a failed impeachment. I wish I had acted on those instincts sooner. Censure could have had a chance if it had been a parallel option at the start. Instead, each side committed early to a strategy designed for the political benefit of its own party rather than trying to find a solution that would serve the nation. Late in the process, when I finally sat down with Joe Manchin to discuss a censure resolution, we realized that any language that would satisfy Democrats would be too strong for the Republican majority, and any language moderate enough for Republicans would be too weak for the Democrats. The parties' positions were as predictable as if they came from a preordained script.

I planned my holiday reading list to study the Constitution and the history of impeachments. Impeachment proceedings for a sitting president would be new territory for me, and I wanted to be well informed in the process. But my colleagues seemed to be treating this responsibility as just another day in the Senate. Leader McConnell told our Tuesday conference lunch that while he believed the Constitution required us to have a trial, we could get it over with quickly, without hearing witnesses before voting to acquit. He went on Sean Hannity's Fox News show and declared total certainty that the president would be acquitted in the Senate. "We have no choice but to take it up, but we'll be working through this process hopefully in a fairly short period of time, in total coordination with the White House counsel's office and the people who are representing the president," he said. "I'm going to take my cues from the president's lawyers."

A few days later, Minority Leader Chuck Schumer wrote a letter to McConnell calling for a trial with four witnesses, including Bolton and White House Chief of Staff Mick Mulvaney. The Democrats thought the Senate should hear this testimony even though the House had not taken the time for it. But they also wanted the trial limited. Several Democratic senators were hoping the trial would end quickly so they could get out on the campaign trail for the presidential primaries. The Iowa caucuses were six weeks away. Some Republicans were threatening to drag it out for the same reason. But Schumer made no serious attempt to negotiate the trial plan—otherwise, he wouldn't have proposed it in a public letter. He met with McConnell for only twenty minutes and then began talking to the media about the process.

I was frustrated. On Christmas Eve, a local television news reporter in Anchorage asked me about the impeachment process, and I answered his question directly. I criticized the House process, and then I said I was disturbed by McConnell's comments that Senate Republicans would work hand in glove with the White House to squelch the impeachment. I believed we needed a real trial, with a process that the American people would feel was fair.

I had come with no intention of making national news at Channel 2, seated in front of a bedraggled potted palm. I merely wanted to talk about appropriations for Alaska before my Christmas break. But I've never been skilled at ducking reasonable questions, and my comment that I would respect the Constitution filled the next news cycle for a nation on edge about the looming impeachment trial. *The New York Times* published a complimentary editorial, "She takes her public duty more seriously than party loyalty, and she can be pushed too far. If only more of her colleagues felt the same."

The next day, I received a text message from Senator Mitt Romney (a first), saying he had been thinking the same way. Soon we were putting together a group of four Republican senators to steer the impeachment process in a new direction.

The impeachment was bigger than other issues. More was on the line than Alaska's priorities or even my conscience. The institutions of our constitutional government were at stake. When I made my Christmas Eve comments to Channel 2, I was thinking of the integrity of the Senate's constitutional role. Regardless of the outcome, I would work to protect that.

Back in Washington after the Senate's winter break, Mitt and I met with Susan Collins in her Capitol hideaway office. Susan had also spoken publicly about the need for a credible impeachment trial. We believed we had the support of Senator Lamar Alexander as well. He sent staff to our meeting but could not attend because family matters kept him home in Tennessee. With our party's three-seat advantage in the Senate, we four Republicans had the leverage to change our leader's plan. But we would have to determine what it was we wanted. And we were on our own. Many Republicans had announced their votes before knowing the charges or the evidence. Some were simply afraid of Trump and his ability to end Republican political careers. The Democrats, aware that they could not win a conviction, hoped to inflict as much political damage as possible on vulnerable Republican senators. They would be playing to the cameras. Neither side was sufficiently serious, in my opinion, about the sobering responsibility of upholding our constitutional obligations.

Collins, who had been through the impeachment of President Clinton, told us what to expect from the proceedings, and led our group as we crafted our revisions to the rules with the Senate parliamentarian. We wanted a mechanism to call witnesses and obtain evidence, creating a forum like the trial courts that Americans would recognize from their own experience—although the Senate's impeachment proceeding is not, in fact, a trial. (In a court, every senator presumably would be thrown off the jury for lacking impartiality.) We met with other Republican moderates and even went to Democrat Joe Manchin's houseboat, where he lived while in Washington, and discussed the issues over spaghetti. But the core group actively working to improve the trial remained at the original four. We needed exactly four to steer the process.

The pressure from our colleagues was intense. Mitch McConnell had warned me, cordially—our interactions are always cordial—that a vote on witnesses would be more difficult and complicated than a vote on impeachment. I didn't understand that at the time, but he turned out to be correct, as he almost always would be when assessing a political situation. Our fellow Republicans also remained polite, but they held out the threat that if the trial included any witnesses against the president, they would call many more, including Joe Biden's son Hunter, and keep the process going all summer. I was ready to accept that possibility. The four of us could have insisted on a predetermined witness list from the beginning, naming only the key witnesses the Democrats had failed to subpoena during the House inquiry, the most important of whom was Bolton, who had by now dropped his resistance to testifying. I said no to making a list, because my priority was not to win certain concessions but to have an authentic process. Until I'd listened to the opening arguments from the two sides, I wouldn't know which witnesses we would need to hear from. Instead of naming witnesses, our group demanded a vote on whether to call witnesses at all. This vote would come after completion of the opening statements and the question-and-answer period, with a privileged motion that could not be brushed aside by parliamentary maneuvering.

By the time the trial started, on January 16, we had an understanding with McConnell to include our language in the organizing resolution, which had otherwise been modeled on the Clinton impeachment. But no one else had seen the document yet. The final wording would come out after we convened the impeachment proceedings. The eyes of the country were on the Senate as we received the articles of impeachment. The Senate floor felt a lot as it always does—it is our routine workplace from day to day, where we chat with colleagues and make speeches for the camera to rows of empty chairs. After years of service, the chamber doesn't hold the awe for me that it did when I first arrived. But when Chief Justice John Roberts entered in his robes, the mood changed. We rose to our feet. His presence was unique and historic. It even briefly silenced the conservative men seated behind me, whose critical, under-the-breath comments I could hear throughout the proceeding. We took a special oath, mandated by the Constitution and written in 1798, read by Roberts: "Do you solemnly swear that in all things appertaining to the trial of the impeachment of Donald John Trump, president of the United States, now pending, you will do impartial justice according to the Constitution and laws, so help you God?" After saying "I do," we came forward in groups of four to sign our names to the oath in a book. It became fully evident that something historic was happening here. I hoped the sheer weight of the moment would motivate senators to hold the institution above their partisan strategies and to abide by their oaths.

I traveled home that long weekend of Martin Luther King Jr. Day. I was on my own, as Verne had long since decided these flip-turn weekends were too crazy for him. That weekend, I arrived at our townhouse in Anchorage to find the heat had gone out and the pipes had frozen, so I went to my cousin Anne's house and we had a sleepover, wrapped up in blankets and talking about our kids— GGs going back to the center of the onion. I saw my friend Rachel Kallander and her new baby, and I had dinner at my son Matt's new house. I brought a U-Haul box of treasures from Tutu, his grandmother in Hawaii. All the things a mom with a big network of family and old friends does on a weekend in Alaska.

The national media had spun into a frenzy with the impeachment, but in Alaska hardly anyone mentioned it except to express sympathy that I had a difficult job and to share their worries about our country. I had been hearing about these worries for some time, from strangers at the airport or the grocery store: Alaskans who had never felt so doubtful about how America could hold together, saying, "I sure hope you can do the right thing. I'm so anxious about where we are right now." Doing the right thing, as I understood that comment, didn't mean voting a certain way, it meant trying to pull us back together as a nation, with our traditions of civility, integrity, and compromise.

At home in Alaska, I often heard from people who disagreed with me but still supported me because they trusted me and how I approached my job. And when they disagreed, they usually did it respectfully and at appropriate times, quite unlike the shrill and confrontational tone on the national level. That weekend, I attended a black-tie gala at a downtown Anchorage hotel raising money for Covenant House, a shelter for homeless youths. No one brought up impeachment until I was leaving, when a woman said, "Vote your conscience. But you do that all the time anyway."

If I could talk to that woman now, I would thank her for trusting in me and I would assure her that very few reasons could cause me to do otherwise than vote my conscience. But there was one reason. I would vote against my own preferences and beliefs to protect the institutions of government. President Trump deserved some kind of congressional sanction, and a poll showed that most Alaskans who supported me also wanted him removed from office, but neither public opinion nor party loyalty should come before our duty to the Constitution. The most important outcome would be Americans' belief in their government.

I took time to be alone in the cold city, painted by the golden light of winter. I drove an hour south along Turnagain Arm to our cabin in Girdwood, picked up my cross-country skis, and drove straight back along the highway, which winds between rocky cliffs and the frozen ocean. I've driven that road most of my life, but it still silences me with awe. Back in Anchorage, hoarfrost clung to the black branches of the birch trees. I skied alone under that white tracery in the still air, following a narrow trail around a frozen lake. I smelled the winter, the clean non-smell of cold air and snow. The next day, I would be back in Washington, back in the Senate chambers, in the poisonous atmosphere of the impeachment court, but I would try to hold this peace inside me. I would never be of that other place. I would always yearn to return home to Alaska, to the clean cold and the calm, where I belonged.

———

In Washington, our Republican conference met for lunch as Mitch McConnell told us about the organizing resolution he was about to put on the floor, with all our votes assumed to be in support. Without giving us a copy of the document, he rapidly ran through its provisions, checking off changes from the Clinton organizing resolution. Two changes jerked me to attention. Mitch said that instead of allowing twenty-four hours of presentations by impeachment managers over four days, he had reduced the span to two days. And instead of automatically introducing the evidence from the House, the Senate would vote on whether to allow any evidence into the proceedings. We had previously heard nothing about speeding up the trial or starting it without evidence. I assumed these changes must have come from the White House.

When Mitch asked for questions, I held my tongue, hoping other Republican senators would speak up, but I was silently fuming. Only a trivial question was asked, about when we could go home for break. Susan Collins and I then put up our hands simultaneously. She challenged the shortened time and the lack of evidence. When I spoke, next, I didn't hide my irritation, arguing that if the Senate carried out a rushed, slipshod process, we would be no better than the House, which Republicans had been so strongly criticizing. The new schedule would have us in our seats until four A.M. and returning the same morning to start again, exhausting everyone, including the public, and showing that we weren't serious.

Our comments seemed to wake up the room. Senators who already felt vulnerable over their plan to acquit the president quickly objected to holding a trial that looked like a sham. They didn't want to be seen refusing evidence or staying up late at night to meet an artificial deadline. Mitch agreed to reverse the provisions.

Mitch had already told the Republican conference that the Democrats would use the impeachment process not as a search for truth but as a way to inflict political damage on individual senators they hoped to defeat in 2020. (He was correct.) Part of Mitch's brilliance as a leader was his ability to understand the motivations of each senator and precisely turn those knobs. After many years of working with me, he knew I would not respond well to arm-twisting, outside pressure, or the offer of a deal, and he refrained from inducements to get me in line with the team. Instead, he talked about what I cared about most: the process and the protection of our institutions, which he said Democrats were abusing by using impeachment as a political bludgeon.

When the organizing resolution came to the floor, the Democrats created ample evidence for his accusation against them. Although the resolution closely copied the rules used during the Clinton impeachment, which had been approved unanimously in 1999, the Democrats turned debate over the document into a marathon. Schumer's strategy was clear: to create a spectacle while forcing Republicans with tough races to go on record with votes that could be used against them during their campaigns. Debate on the eleven futile floor votes took thirteen hours. After the clock passed midnight on Wednesday morning, House impeachment manager Jerrold Nadler accused us, the Republican senators, of treachery and a cover-up for opposing an amendment to the resolution to issue a subpoena to Bolton. "History will judge and so will the electorate," he said. Republicans groaned out loud and the president's counsel shot back at Nadler, who then called one of the attorneys a liar. Chief Justice Roberts admonished both sides, calling the Senate "the world's greatest deliberative body" and saying, "Those addressing the Senate should remember where they are." That moment was all most of the public heard reported in the news that morning. The Senate again sank in their esteem. Mitch seemed to be right about the Democrats' true aims and what they were willing to risk to attain them.

The House managers' presentation, however, impressed me. I watched from just a few feet away from the lectern, listening carefully, taking extensive notes in a bound journal, and concentrating as the hours passed by, despite the fatigue in my rear end from sitting in an antique chair made for looks, not comfort. The managers connected emotionally, presenting their speeches well for the television audience. Each had a well-defined voice in the presentation, with a well-written script that nicely threaded together their points, and which they kept to admirably. Representative Adam Schiff capped the production with his strong oratory, without notes—as I could see from close range—appealing passionately to patriotism and righteousness. Quoting Alexander Hamilton, he reminded the Senate of our role: "It is up to you to be the tribunal that Hamilton envisioned. It is up to you to show the American people and yourselves that his confidence and that of the other founders was rightly placed."

I listened, even as the presentation dragged on and became repetitive, but many senators sat passively through the time. Certain senators within my earshot made light of the proceedings—keeping score, for example, of how many times the impeachment managers replayed certain clips, such as House testimony about Bolton calling Trump's approach to Zelenskyy a "drug deal."

The president's defenders got off to a weak start. Over and over again, they said that the impeachment charges were "ridiculous" without really saying why. Susan and I communicated throughout the trial with notes and looks; we were both surprised that their presentation wasn't stronger, and I think other Republican senators felt the same way. The lawyers must have received that message, because the next day the defense generally improved. An astonishing moment came, however, when Alan Dershowitz launched his bizarre theory that since a president running for reelection believes his election is in the public interest, nothing he could do to help himself would be wrong. At that point, even the conservative men behind me were aghast, and I heard one say, "God, he's got to stop!" And after that day, for whatever reason, Dershowitz did not return.

Evaluating what we heard from either side forced us to consider the speakers' motivations, as the politics of the situation came first for so many. Hypocrisy ruled the day. Those who had been involved in the Clinton impeachment took the opposite side of the same points with Trump. As I listened, I worked to disentangle the relevant arguments from the posturing. This was an impeachment, not a referendum on Trump's chaotic presidency.

On balance, I learned what I needed to know about the case from the six days of presentations. Well before the proceeding began, I had established my view of how to evaluate whether President Trump's actions met the standard for impeachment in the Constitution with the kind of proof that I would require. My research began before the Christmas break, as I reread *The Federalist Papers* (the commentary on the Constitution by its key drafters) and examined a set of articles from law reviews about the meaning of the phrase "high crimes and misdemeanors." I studied a scholarly and even-handed forty-six-page impeachment guide written by a bipartisan pair of retired senators, Russ Feingold and Chuck Hagel, who were veterans of the Clinton impeachment.

The Senate is not a court of law—the senators are not disinterested jurors, the defendant does not have the due-process protections of a criminal defendant, and the body itself controls the proceedings, not a judge or a presiding officer—but neither can impeachment be purely political. If impeachment were decided by politics alone, our president would become like the British prime minister, subject to removal whenever his or her party lost seats in Congress. To make our system work, senators deciding impeachment must try to be impartial. Feingold repeatedly voted against his party in the Clinton impeachment to uphold the constitutional obligations of his office. In the document he and Hagel wrote, I found guidance on the standard of proof: whether to use preponderance of evidence, clear and convincing evidence, or the highest level, beyond a reasonable doubt. They said that each senator must pick his or her own standard to use, and they reviewed how individual senators had made that choice in the past. I decided before the trial that I would require the highest standard, proof beyond a reasonable doubt. Conviction would bring a political death sentence, removing the president from office and potentially barring him from future election. And it would nullify the choice of millions of voters, including those who had already begun casting early ballots in the 2020 election process.

Reaching the "reasonable doubt" standard would not be easy because of the way the House had charged Trump in the main article of impeachment. Rather than accuse Trump of a specifically defined crime, the article instead cited him for an "abuse of power." An offense need not be criminal to warrant impeachment, but to apply a standard of proof we need a clear sense of what must be proved in order to convict. What is abuse of power, exactly? Depending how the term is defined, one could say it happens all the time in Washington. Many presidents have abused their power in one way or another, but the system has ways to check these abuses. Executive branch officials can resist directives. Leakers and whistleblowers can tell the media. Congress can investigate, legislate, appropriate, and censure. The voters can choose someone else in the next election. Impeachment should be the last resort for the most egregious and dangerous conduct. An abuse of power might not rise to that level, or it might. Without a definition, it would be hard to avoid having a reasonable doubt about Trump's guilt.

The evidence also was flawed. As soon as the news broke in September that Trump tried to induce the Ukrainian president to investigate Biden, I thought, "Yes, of course that is something he would do." But a political instinct about what's true doesn't come close to proof beyond a reasonable doubt. When the House impeachment managers presented their case, I didn't hear that level of proof. They accused Trump of extorting his favor from Zelenskyy to benefit his reelection, while the defense maintained that the president wanted Biden investigated to stop corruption. It was a matter of the president's intent. As improbable as it might seem that Trump had just been focused on Ukrainian corruption or had another legitimate motive, the House inquiry had failed to rule out that argument. Its leaders had forfeited that opportunity when they'd passed articles of impeachment without taking testimony from witnesses with direct knowledge of Trump's intent, Bolton and Mulvaney.

After skipping that critical step in making its case, the House then dumped the responsibility on the Senate to call the witnesses. I didn't like that. The House had done more than pass the buck procedurally. By putting the Senate in the position of both investigating and adjudicating, it had put the constitutional process at risk. The media and many in the public never understood this threat. President Trump had ordered his people not to testify, citing executive privilege. The privilege is a limited, court-recognized right of the president to keep communication with close advisers confidential, especially when disclosure could affect national security. For some witnesses, such as those who never spoke directly to the president, the privilege clearly did not apply. But for top advisers such as Bolton or Mulvaney, there was a real argument to be made. Bolton's willingness to testify voluntarily did not change that. The privilege protects the president, and it would be up to him, not Bolton, to waive it. Certainly, the courts could have reviewed the information to be disclosed and ruled if the privilege applied, and that could have put the testimony before the House. But House leaders hadn't wanted to wait for a court ruling. By withdrawing the subpoena, they had dropped the lawsuit that would have clarified the situation, but then they wrongly demanded that the Senate call the same witnesses, with the crucial legal question unanswered. That was a key point in my considerations.

With Chief Justice Roberts sitting as the presiding officer, Representative Schiff, the head impeachment manager, argued that Roberts could quickly rule on executive privilege during the trial, allowing Bolton to testify. But that would put the chief justice in a terrible position, forcing him to make a profound constitutional decision in a political arena, and without the kind of rigorous process that the courts use to make impartial, reasoned decisions. We would be shredding the Constitution's separation of powers. I had already made a tough vote to defend the court's impartiality when I'd opposed confirming Kavanaugh. Chief Justice Roberts had repeatedly sought to defend the courts' reputation as well, as when he had issued a statement scolding President Trump for calling a judge with whom he disagreed an "Obama judge." The politics of party over country had already dragged Congress and the presidency into the mud. We needed to keep the judiciary out of that pit.

At one point in the Senate trial, the threat to the court leapt forward in a very tangible form. On the second evening of the question-and-answer period, Senator Elizabeth Warren sent forward a question for the chief justice to read aloud. From my position just a few feet away, I saw the dismay pass over Roberts's face when he read it. My side of the room gasped at the question. It asked how a trial without witnesses would "contribute to the loss of legitimacy of the chief justice." To me, the message was clear. Just as Democrats had used the impeachment trial to force Republican senators to take votes that would hurt their reelection, they were now threatening the reputation of Chief Justice Roberts and the Supreme Court if he did not side with them. Warren's implied threat stuck in my mind and would carry considerable weight in my thinking over the coming days.

Despite my concerns about the process, the second week of the trial began with near certainty on my part that I would vote to call witnesses. That Sunday, January 26, *The New York Times* reported on the content of Bolton's book manuscript. The draft said that President Trump had told Bolton directly about his intention to release military aid to Ukraine only if President Zelenskyy announced an investigation into Biden. Monday morning before work, at our house on Capitol Hill, I received a text from Susan Collins saying she had spoken to Senator Lindsey Graham, among the president's most unquestioning supporters, who'd said Bolton's bombshell would force us to call him as a witness. I called Lindsey and he told me he would soon release a statement saying Bolton should be called. I agreed and told him I thought we would all agree. I felt it was obvious that the Senate trial would be considered fair and legitimate only with testimony from such a critical witness, and that senators would be unable to resist that fact.

In hindsight, I recognize that morning as the key political moment when I should have acted. If I had made a statement immediately, it might have started a snowball of senators calling for Bolton to testify, giving greater legitimacy to the impeachment process. I walked to my office and met my staff, who I hadn't seen much of in a couple of weeks, and I thanked them for keeping up with fisheries, defense, constituent issues, and all our other day-to-day work. And I apologized in advance for the hit we would soon take from Republicans as I called for witnesses to testify in the Senate. I went downstairs and rode the Senate subway to the Capitol. When I arrived, I found Lindsey Graham telling reporters the exact opposite of what he had told me that morning. Now he said we didn't need to hear from Bolton. I regret that I didn't follow through and make my statement in favor of witnesses anyway.

The pressure only grew. Leader McConnell had predicted that the vote on witnesses, expected at the end of that week, would be the real turning point of the impeachment. Now I knew he was right. Romney had already telegraphed his intention to vote for witnesses. Three more votes, so far undeclared, could tip the balance: Alexander's, Collins's, and mine. Without our votes in hand, Mitch announced publicly that he didn't have the votes to block witnesses. But he was working on it.

Mitch is a gifted politician. For good or ill, he knows how to handle me. I didn't receive a single call from the White House, as he knew that would be counterproductive, but he kept pushing the message that the real purpose behind the Democrats' efforts was to take the

Senate. Republican colleagues facing tough races kept approaching me to talk, presumably at Mitch's suggestion. Senator Cory Gardner of Colorado, who I particularly like, was among the most vulnerable. I might not be an obedient party soldier in my Republican conference, but these people are my co-workers and friends. Besides, I held the chair of Energy and Natural Resources only by virtue of my membership on this team. Four Republican members of my committee were up for reelection, and I would need their help to pass my energy bill, which I had been working on for four years now. It was worth some sacrifice to keep these senators' support.

McConnell called a closed meeting in one of the Senate caucus rooms to discuss this issue. He called Cory up to speak, as well as each of the other vulnerable senators. They explained how they would be affected by an impeachment with witnesses that dragged on for months, into the spring. Their concerns were real. The political downdraft of the moment would likely pull strong new opponents into some of the races. Senator Schumer's strategy to gain power would be effective. The speakers didn't have to look at me for me to get the message. I know when I'm being spoken to. Their words weighed on me. I felt the weight of the room, of my party, and of my friends.

But I was also disappointed in my colleagues. Our conference found time for meetings about the political fallout from the impeachment, but we never talked about whether the president's actions had been right or wrong. We didn't sift the evidence, analyze the arguments, or talk about what decision would be best for the nation. Instead, we listened to concerns that the impeachment trial would take too much time away from campaigning. That especially frustrated me. We needed to do our job.

The full gravity of my responsibility hit fully on Thursday, January 30, the second and final day for senators' questions. It was a very long day. Before it began, I took my smooth green rock from Savoonga from the top of my dresser to keep with me. Garrett joked that my grip was probably grinding it into sand.

Susan Collins had told me, leaning over from her seat, that she would vote to call witnesses. Lamar Alexander approached me on the floor of the Senate. He said he had reached a decision on witnesses and would like to talk to me during our dinner break. That evening, the Republican whip's staff laid out a buffet of cheap franchise Mexican food in a room off the floor. Tension had taken my appetite—I had felt sick all day—and I hadn't eaten much, but I knew I needed calories, so I got in line. Lamar approached as I grabbed some chips and a glob of guacamole. We headed up to his hideaway office on the third floor, hoping for privacy, but a couple dozen people on a Capitol tour recognized us in the corridor and next came a crowd of reporters. The nation was waiting to hear how the Senate's swing votes would decide. News that Lamar and I were meeting went out across the country.

Lamar had decided that no purpose would be served by calling witnesses, because the president's actions and intent were obvious. As he said later, we didn't need any more evidence to be convinced that Trump had withheld aid for his inappropriate purpose. But Lamar also did not believe that Trump's inappropriate actions called for impeachment ten months before an election. As he later told a reporter, "It would just pour gasoline on cultural fires that are burning out there." Lamar shared a draft press release with me but said he hadn't told anyone else about his decision, not even McConnell. He asked if I needed any help. He knew the terrible position his decision would place me in.

With all the other senators' votes decided, I now had the sole responsibility of either defeating the motion for witnesses or causing a tie, which would force Chief Justice Roberts to decide as the tiebreaker. His yes vote would bring witnesses or his no vote would defeat the motion. Even if he abstained, that decision would be seen as a political vote, favoring the president. The cultural fires Lamar worried about would then consume the court, too. Lamar didn't ask for my decision. I hadn't made it yet.

Returning to the floor, I continued to struggle. The question-and-answer period was still going on, and I decided to send forward a question card of my own. My seatmate, Susan Collins, raised her eyebrows as if to ask if I was sure I wanted to send it up. Simply, I asked the president's counsel why Bolton shouldn't be called to testify, given what we already knew about his book. Bolton was saying Trump had clearly linked the political favor he requested from Zelenskyy to releasing the aid, while other House witnesses had said otherwise. Roberts read it out: "This dispute about material facts weighs in favor of calling additional witnesses with direct knowledge. Why should this body not call Ambassador Bolton?" The answer was a fair one—that the House had failed to call Bolton, and we should not create a precedent of accepting and trying to fix a half-baked impeachment—but I still found myself leaning in favor of the witness vote, which would occur the next day, even though I knew I would only cause a tie.

Walking into the cloakroom during a break, I took a deep breath and tried not to feel overwhelmed. How had I gotten myself into this situation? Taking a bottle of water from the refrigerator, I had a disturbing epiphany. Perhaps my feelings were melodramatic, but in that moment, I felt that the legitimacy of all three branches of government had somehow come to ride on this one vote that I would be called upon to cast the next day. For the presidency, the ability to expose the president's misconduct. For Congress, the ability to perform our constitutional duty as the check on the president. And for the judiciary, which so far had avoided the disrepute already attached to the president and Congress, the reputation of Chief Justice Roberts with one half of the country or the other, depending on the unavoidable choice he would have to make.

Late that night, in a puddle of light amid the darkness of my large corner office, I sat with the same three staff members who had helped talk me through the Kavanaugh vote: Fish, Karina, and Garrett. We had been through a lot together in the three years of the

Trump administration, and they understood how I consider decisions. Garrett recorded the meeting on his phone, which allowed me to go back to that conversation and all the uncertainty we felt.

Fish proposed that we try to prioritize the different arguments that were fighting it out in my mind. "The thing that's tough is the American people pay us to give you good advice," he said, "and I wish I had a better capability to do that."

"We are ripping them off," Garrett added, and we all laughed.

Fish suggested that the answer had to come from my innermost sense of what was right. Garrett said I should decide which way to vote by thinking about how the precedent would be seen in twenty or thirty years, when the next impeachment might come around. (Good advice except for the time estimate.) Karina pointed out that no vote I could cast would make my supporters happy.

"There are lots of people on both sides that hate your decisions but believe in your judgment, and they have a lot of faith that you will come to the decision you come to honestly and with intention," Fish said.

"Those are the ones that I care about," I responded.

After one A.M., before heading home, we played a quick game of Ping-Pong to release tension. At Christmas, I had replaced our conference table with a Ping-Pong table to create a social release for my hardworking staff. I did it for myself, too, as I love Ping-Pong, especially when the job is frustrating (which is when I play best).

Before we parted, they shared some of the jokes going around the Capitol. With Groundhog Day now just two days away, Fish passed on the line "Senator Murkowski stepped out of the chamber and saw her shadow, so we're going to have impeachment for another six weeks." Karina suggested I catch the exotic new disease called coronavirus so I wouldn't have to vote (the name Covid wouldn't be invented for another two weeks). And, not joking, she and the others implored me to tell them how I would vote before I went to the floor the next day, so we wouldn't repeat the craziness of the Kavanaugh vote.

At home, sleep was impossible. I kept flipping on the light to jot down thoughts in my journal. Verne gave up and went to sleep in one of the boys' bedrooms. I sat up to write out everything I was thinking, breaking the considerations into tiers, from least important to most important.

At the lowest tier: the political impact on me. Polling showed that my supporters wanted witnesses. I had established a reputation for defending the process, even at political cost. If I voted with my party against a complete process, these people would feel I had betrayed my principles.

The next tier of my considerations was for my colleagues. If I voted yes, creating a tie, each Republican facing a tough race would be at greater risk. All of them could be attacked for not being the fifty-first vote.

The Senate itself was on the third tier. On one hand, holding a trial without witnesses would expose the process as a sham. On the other hand, calling for witnesses would walk us into a trap set by the House, requiring us to strip the president of his executive privilege, which was not our role under the Constitution. Either choice was awful.

Above those considerations, I weighed the threat to the judicial branch, thinking of the question Senator Warren had given Chief Justice Roberts to read, threatening his legitimacy.

"I've always known Elizabeth Warren to be very partisan but this to me was over the top," I wrote in my journal. "She expected a tie vote and this would be the pressure on him to vote in the affirmative and allow witnesses and thus preserve the legitimacy of the court. Awful. We put political pressure on one another in the legislative and executive branches, but we've always acknowledged (and respected) that the judiciary should be apolitical. Maybe that too is a dinosaur."

Finally, at the top tier of my concerns, I cared about Alaskans' needs. Nothing about the impeachment should affect my work to provide fishermen with docks or science to safeguard the ocean, or to pass legislation protecting Indigenous women from violence. Those were the issues folks back home came to talk to me about every day.

"It does matter that their view of a fair trial—which includes witnesses and cross-examination—is upheld," I wrote. "Alaskans want a fair process, they want me to do my job and be effective for them, and they want me to be thoughtful and honest."

At four A.M. I made a decision and wrote a statement announcing that I would vote for witnesses. I prepared to send the statement to my three key staffers, but I lay down to sleep without doing so. When I next woke, I hit Send on the message. But at the same moment, I received a message from Fish with a statement he had drafted, saying the opposite. Fish pointed out that a vote for witnesses, with all its costs for the Supreme Court, wouldn't actually accomplish anything.

I had also received many other voice messages, emails, and texts, including a note from my office to call Mitch McConnell. I ignored them all. Instead I got ready for work, taking the rock from the top of my dresser.

I knew I would need the rock that day, and I also wanted company for my walk to work. I sent a text to my son Nic, joking that I needed him to be my emotional support animal. At the house, I showed Nic the statement I had written and the contrary one sent to me by Fish. Then, as we walked to the Hart building, I went over the concerns and considerations that had pulled me back and forth the night before.

"I don't know if I have the strength to do the right thing," I said.

Nic replied, "Whatever you do will be the right thing."

As a mother, I felt his words go right to my heart. They were almost exactly the words his brother, Matt, had used, a decade before, when I was struggling with my decision about whether to run a write-in campaign during the 2010 election. Matt's words, which I had ultimately interpreted to mean that I had the right answer in my heart, had helped bring calm and clarity to my decision to run. Now I thought about using Nic's words the same way.

I could be the Lisa that people expected and vote for witnesses. That decision felt right and would surprise no one, while a no vote to protect Roberts from voting would probably be misunderstood. At the office we talked more about the implications of each choice. I finally called Mitch McConnell back. He noted that I had a tough decision to make and that I already knew where he stood, but he said he wanted me to see a video that was circulating. The video, from a left-wing legal advocacy group, showed the C-SPAN feed of the chief justice presiding over the Senate, but with his image doctored to make it look like he was wearing one of Trump's red MAGA hats. I was disgusted and disappointed. It seemed we had fallen to a new low, and I didn't know how to fix it.

With only twenty minutes left before the floor session, I asked everyone to leave my inner office so I could just think. Anger overcame me. I had always thought that when the gravity of impeachment settled on the Senate, we would begin to take our responsibility seriously. I had tried to work with my colleagues to keep a path open to a credible proceeding. But we had failed. The institution had failed because the people responsible for protecting it were thinking only of their own short-term political benefit. I was seething. But then I stopped and questioned my own anger. I realized I had failed, too. I was doing the same thing as the others, putting my interests first by planning to vote for witnesses to protect my brand, my personal preference, when I knew intellectually that the better choice for my state and our country would be to vote no and protect the chief justice, the court, and my ability to work for Alaska's priorities.

I was still angry, but now I knew what to do. I called the team back into the office and told them my decision. Voting to protect my brand as a principled institutionalist, while hurting the institution of the Supreme Court, would make me like the hypocrites who vote against appropriations and then celebrate the money coming home to their states. I had clarity. We quickly knocked out a statement I could take to the floor, Karina making edits while Garrett, Fish, and I called out changes and alternative words. The Senate subway would be an impossible crush, with everyone focused on me and my decision, so we decided to drive the few steps to the Capitol—again, as during the Kavanaugh confirmation, in Kristen's little car. We laughed again about how she needed a raise to get a bigger one. Only minutes were left.

On the Senate floor, I read the statement, letting the world know what I decided.

Given the partisan nature of this impeachment from the very beginning and throughout, I have come to the conclusion that there will be no fair trial in the Senate. I don't believe the continuation of this process will change anything. It is sad for me to admit that, as an institution, the Congress has failed.

It has also become clear some of my colleagues intend to further politicize this process, and drag the Supreme Court into the fray, while attacking the Chief Justice. I will not stand for nor support that effort. We have already degraded this institution for partisan political benefit, and I will not enable those who wish to pull down another.

We are sadly at a low point of division in this country.

With my no vote, the motion to call witnesses failed, forty-nine to fifty-one.

The New York Times carried a photo of me leaving the Senate chamber with my head bowed, the rock just visible, held tightly in my left hand.

———

The talk of the Capitol was all about what I had gotten in exchange for my vote. After fighting for a trial with witnesses, I had cast the vote that prevented witnesses from being called—so I must have made a deal. A colleague brought that up with me directly after the vote, saying, "I sure hope you got something for this." I was steaming over that comment when John Thune, the majority whip, approached me. I said, "John, I want you to know what I want out of this. I want this Senate to start standing up for itself. We kowtow to the president because we need him for our elections. We're afraid to work with our colleagues on the other side of the aisle because they're all running for something. And in the meantime, we are not doing what we need to be doing as a legislative body."

A rumor developed that I had traded my vote for passage of my energy bill, a story that traveled far and wide. It was a fantasy that said more about Washington than about me, as the fate of the bill would soon demonstrate.

The next week, President Trump was acquitted. Although I had weighed voting to convict, after reviewing the evidence again I could not support removing him from office on the basis of the flawed articles the House had given us. I again spoke, this time to an empty chamber, of my anger and disappointment, the president's shameful and wrong behavior, the hypocrisy of my colleagues, and the rock-bottom point we had reached. Forty-eight voted to convict, with Mitt Romney the only senator to cross party lines.

My feelings didn't improve. Trump held a bizarre victory celebration in the White House and began firing those who had testified truthfully about his misconduct. Many commentators blamed me for hoping he would behave any better and attacked me for my votes. It became clear to me that my two speeches had not made sufficiently clear why I voted to end the trial—people did not understand the need to protect the chief justice from being forced to break the tie. I added that to my pile of regrets. When I had drafted and delivered my remarks, in the powerful emotion of the moment, I had conveyed too much of how I felt and not enough of the thinking behind my decision. Voting against my own wishes had made me angry, but I should have expressed less of the anger and more of the reasoning.

For the first time in almost twenty years in the Senate, I didn't want to go home, feeling my true supporters would be disappointed with me. I stayed in Washington over another weekend, adding to an unusually long stretch for me to be away from Alaska. Feeling a bit sorry for myself, I wondered why I even remained in the Senate, if I was unable to influence such a dreadful outcome. I walked from my house to the Capitol through the rain in my Xtratuf rubber boots, dressed like an Alaskan but feeling anything but extra-tough, and wishing I had handled the past weeks differently. And yet I knew that, in the end, I had done what was right for the country.

Another text message arrived from Mitt Romney that day. I had reached out to support him after his historic vote of conscience to impeach the president, which I respected. Mitt wrote back, "Thanks much, Lisa. You taking the bullet on the witness vote was impressive, and the fact that almost no one will ever understand that makes it even more so. With admiration, Mitt."

The first day back at work in the office started getting my head right. During the weeks of the impeachment trial, I hadn't been able to keep up with meeting every visiting constituent, but now I did. We sat down to talk about high energy costs and rural health. I remembered why I was in the Senate. Alaskans were counting on me.

In the third week of February, I traveled through Southeast Alaska for five days. The trip was rejuvenating. The rains and storms of February bring the hardworking people of these island communities indoors to talk and listen, pondering issues and reconnecting. They welcomed me with classic Alaskan warmth. Folks wanted to talk about timber, fishing, and transportation—the Alaska Marine Highway ferry system was not running because of state budget cuts. Our Alaskan concerns and how we access our own opportunities were so basic.

A high school senior in Ketchikan politely asked me to explain my thought process during the impeachment trial, and I spoke for ten minutes to an auditorium full of teens, giving the most in-depth public explanation yet of my vote. I met no protests. An old friend said she thought I'd made the wrong call on witnesses but added that she couldn't believe how difficult my job was. No hard feelings. I knew I was back where I belonged.

CHAPTER 9

The Crises of 2020

A T THE END OF February 2020, all my attention was on the energy bill, which looked like it might finally pass. Of course, the big news was the virus that was sweeping through China and into Europe, and was breaking out here and there in the United States, but I thought our country would be largely immune, with our amazing medical advancements and technologies. Epidemics were a thing of the past in America. Alaskans collectively remembered the flu pandemic of 1918, which had been devastating to Alaska Natives, wiping out entire villages. But our early Senate briefings never suggested to me that we could be facing anything of that magnitude.

The energy bill had been through various incarnations since I'd launched it with Maria Cantwell in 2015. With the new Congress in 2019, she had given up her position as ranking member on Energy and Natural Resources to be ranking on the Commerce Committee. The Democrats replaced her with Joe Manchin of West Virginia. Environmental organizations complained bitterly about having two senators from fossil fuels states—West Virginia coal and Alaska oil—taking the helm of a committee with a big role in addressing climate change. But Joe and I both knew that in order to address climate change, our outdated energy policies needed to be revamped. Our "all of the above" energy bill, if we could get it to pass, was the only game in town for significant action on climate.

Joe and I had much else in common. We were both Catholics from conservative states trying to follow our own paths. Our voting patterns put us closer to the center than any other senators (indeed, I was sometimes to Joe's left). We both had special relationships with our voters at home, allowing us to serve states that the political professionals would not have expected to elect us. And we both knew what it was like to represent a state facing the decline of the export that employed our people—coal or oil—and that much of society had newly decided made us villains rather than providers of a universally needed resource. We visited each other's states together and developed a great working relationship, as did our staffs. Everyone likes Joe. He is a regular guy who enjoys telling stories and spending time with friends, often inviting colleagues to his houseboat on the waterfront for dinner.

The American Energy and Innovation Act combined fifty-three stalled bills at that point, and its potential to pass many senators' priorities made it popular with a wide range of colleagues. I was pushing hard for its passage, and by March I thought we had the pieces to get a positive vote. Under our party's seniority rules, I was nearing the end of my term as chair of the committee, and this year would be my last chance. But our apparent likely success proved to be a hazard. When a major bill seems close to becoming law, it becomes an attractive vehicle for carrying other bills to passage. A dispute about the details of one of those last-minute add-ons tripped us up. We could not untangle that problem in time for our cloture vote, which we lost. I was heartbroken that we had stalled again after so many years of work, but we committed to keep at it.

Two days later, Wednesday, March 11, the World Health Organization declared a pandemic and President Trump made an Oval Office speech to the nation announcing a ban on flights from Europe, along with other measures. That evening the NBA suspended its season in the middle of a game when players tested positive for the virus. Colleges and universities were already sending students home, and schools in some communities were closing.

On Friday, I flew to Anchorage with Secretary of the Air Force Barbara Barrett aboard a military passenger jet. I was happy to be going home and looking forward to our planned visits to Air Force facilities, all the way up to a radar station on the Arctic coast, returning on Monday. Saturday dawned crisply in Anchorage, with a bright winter sky, snow on the ground, and delicious, cold, clear air, a perfect day for flying. But when we gathered at Joint Base Elmendorf-Richardson, it was apparent that something was wrong. Secretary Barrett had just spoken to the Pentagon. The Department of Defense had canceled all discretionary travel as of Monday, and she needed to return to Washington immediately. She offered to take me, or I could stay in Anchorage.

The magnitude of what was happening began to hit me. Much of the federal government was essentially shutting down. We were facing a national emergency unlike anything in my experience. I needed to be where I could do the most good, knowing that wherever I chose to go, I might not be able to leave for some time. I boarded the plane back to Washington.

Senators began working mostly remotely, with some members staying home in their states. I set up an office at my dining room table in Washington, with racks of file folders on the kitchen counter behind me. Without in-person constituent or committee meetings, my days were spent endlessly on Zoom. For weeks, the Senate conducted no business. Later, we would dash onto the floor individually to cast our votes. It was hard to communicate without the casual encounters that usually happen there, especially with members of the other party.

Amy Klobuchar's husband was hospitalized with Covid—the first person I knew who had it. Within two weeks we were seeing images of refrigerated trucks parked outside New York hospitals to hold all the bodies.

The number of cases remained low in Alaska. Our state seemed relatively safe from infection, with limited points of entry at airports that could be monitored and the steady leadership of Dr. Anne Zink, the state's chief medical officer. With the cultural memory of 1918, Native villages set up systems to keep the virus out and protect elders, including complete lockdowns allowing no one to enter the communities. They would allow planes to land with mail and supplies, but pilots and passengers could not come into the village. When a fire broke out in the Southwest Alaska village of Kasigluk, outsiders were not allowed in to help. Covid was a greater fear than fire.

The systems put in place during that first year of the pandemic largely worked. But the threat to the economy was extreme in every part of the state, and people were scared. Oil prices crashed. Fish processors didn't know if they would be able to operate in their crowded plants and bunkhouses. And the tourism industry, one of Alaska's largest employers, appeared headed for a complete collapse. Most coastal communities in Alaska make their money during the summer, some from cruise ships, others from fish, and some from both. Their small economies rely on those reserves through the winter, and by spring they're coasting on financial fumes while waiting for the ships and fish to return. In March 2020, it became obvious the ships weren't coming. The number of cruise ship visitors would drop from 1.9 million in 2019 to twenty-six in 2020. Those twenty-six came in on a single small-vessel cruise that had to be canceled halfway through when Covid was found on board. I could skim the chamber of commerce membership directories from these little towns and mentally cross off the names of businesses that had no chance of survival without major federal help. The towns would be hollowed out.

The CARES Act passed quickly, appropriating $2.2 trillion for relief, and we at least had a chance to help save these towns. That spring I worked as hard as I ever have, sitting by myself in my home office, collaborating by Zoom and phone with my colleague Dan

Sullivan, helping manage the process of getting money from the federal government through local banks to small businesses and communities. For many Alaskans, personal relationships were their economic lifeline during Covid. Some called their banker and some called their senator. I worked individual problems, and as a senator with seniority and a seat on the Appropriations Committee, I also made it my job to send as much federal money to Alaska as I could. Our economy would be among the worst hit and the slowest to recover from the pandemic, and federal spending became its chief savior over the next few years. I made no apologies for my efforts. After we restored the practice of individual senators inserting funding earmarks into appropriation bills in January 2021, I proudly used that process for congressionally directed spending for Alaska. The Constitution prescribes that the legislative branch has authority over spending, but in recent years we have ceded much of that to federal agencies, which may not understand a state's needs. Earmarks don't add to overall spending, but instead allow us to direct agency funds that have already been budgeted. In 2023, I delivered more earmarks to my small state than any of the other forty-nine received.

We never thought at the time that we would look back on the early months of the pandemic with any fondness. For many it was a time of anxiety and hardship. But many families reconnected, and neighbors formed "Covid bubbles" to get one another through. I enjoyed the D.C. springtime, taking long walks for fresh air, during which I would photograph flowers and my neighbors' front doors, sending the pictures to my cousin Anne, in Anchorage, to help her choose the new color scheme for her house. Although I was alone in the house—I had wanted Verne to stay in Alaska, where it was so much safer at the time—my nieces Kimberly and Grace were living nearby, and they often came to cook dinner and play games through the evening. The country had pulled together in the crisis. People put encouraging signs in their yards and front windows—THANK YOU HEALTHCARE HEROES and the like. And the lockdown did slow the virus.

But for reasons I never understood, President Trump didn't focus on that success or the many remarkable accomplishments of his team, including the rapid economic relief and amazing medical advances, including developing vaccines. Instead, he divisively questioned public health measures from his own administration and criticized stay-at-home orders. By the summer, he had helped split America into two camps, with Democrats tending to be more cautious with the virus and Republicans more likely to be skeptical of its severity, resistant to public health measures, and suspicious of vaccines. The debate over vaccines split friends and divided families, including my own. Research at Utah State University showed that by the second year of the pandemic, counties where voters heavily favored Trump had a Covid death rate three times higher than strongly Democratic counties.

Tragically, that trend would affect my state, too. After Alaska effectively blocked Covid in 2020, the virus became politicized in 2021. In Anchorage, resistance to public health measures degenerated into ugly conflict, making international news in the fall when protesters wore the Star of David to compare mask rules to the Holocaust. Amid that conflict, which felt so foreign to my home, infections and deaths spiked as hospitals became overwhelmed and were forced to ration care. With their limited capacity to treat Covid patients, Alaska hospitals often went to "divert" status, meaning that a patient from Fairbanks could be diverted to Anchorage, or even outside Alaska, for care.

Populist anger and division had made us weaker when we most needed to work together.

————

At the end of May 2020, I had a welcome respite from a year that already seemed like it would never end. At home in Anchorage, still unable to hold public engagements, I enjoyed days of tired muscles while working in the garden. Anne and I divided raspberry starts out of a patch in her yard and moved some of them to plant in

Carol's and Matt's yards. In the spring sunshine, I let myself disengage from the news, at least emotionally, at a time when the country was going through a new stage of trauma.

On Memorial Day in Minneapolis, police officers killed George Floyd. Protests erupted, beginning there and quickly sweeping across the country. These events felt far away. I had grown up respecting the police and law enforcement in general, and I think most Alaskans feel the same way. I assumed the officers who killed George Floyd were bad apples. I made the same assumption about the looters whose violence undermined the message of the huge nonviolent protests.

Over a Sunday dinner at Anne's house, family members expressed worries about my going back to D.C., as I planned to do the next day. There had been looting in downtown Washington. Demonstrators had fought police in Lafayette Square, in front of the White House. The Secret Service had locked down the building, and agents had rushed the president and the first family into an underground bunker. Trump then lashed out against demonstrators on Twitter, further heating up the tensions.

I slept poorly that night, but not just because of what was happening in Washington. I felt the nation was going through a historic reckoning. Hundreds of protests were springing up every day, all over the country, with millions of people participating, including in Alaska. But I hadn't made a statement. A young man who had been an intern for me ten years earlier sent me a text. It simply said, "I'm so disappointed by your silence."

Of course, I knew that inequality remained a deep problem in our country. I had seen prejudice firsthand. But for someone like me and for many of my colleagues, who are not regularly confronted by discrimination, it is easy to let these issues fall from the top of a list of daily priorities. Our Republican leadership asked Senator Tim Scott of South Carolina, the only African American member of our conference, to find a legislative approach to the policing issue that our side could support. Tim had a personal perspective that he shared—about being taught by his mother, as a teen, that if he was stopped by the police he should not look the officer in the eye, should not talk back, and that bad things could happen. And he shared his own stories of being targeted by police, including when he was on the way to Senate votes. His stories surprised us all.

I accepted that the policing problem was real, but I felt this moment was about more than the police. We were talking too much about the details, about chokeholds or body cameras, while a large part of society demanded change to the systemic issues that perpetuate inequality in many aspects of life. Those concerns had merit, and the ways in which the movement later went off track should not make us forget that. As I listened, however, I still didn't know what to do or say.

On Monday, I flew to Washington. On a conference call with governors that day, Trump had demanded that they dominate protesters with force. That evening, speaking in the Rose Garden, he said he would deploy the military to suppress protests in states where governors didn't crack down, and he announced that he had ordered units into Washington. Just before the speech started, officers from several federal agencies confronted protesters in Lafayette Square, in front of the White House, charging into them with shields and firing rubber bullets. Trump emerged to walk across the cleared square to St. John's Church with members of his administration, including Secretary of Defense Mark Esper and Chairman of the Joint Chiefs of Staff Mark Milley. He held aloft a Bible and posed for pictures.

The next morning, Verne decided to walk me to work for my safety. At the Capitol, we came upon a cordon of police guarding the plaza, an officer stationed about every ten feet. These were my friends, people I greeted every day, and it was strange to see them ready for combat.

After a routine vote, our conference gathered for our weekly lunch meeting. It began with a short video reel of senators' appearances on Fox News, responding to the protests, and then we moved on to other business. I was incredulous that we wouldn't have more discussion about the events that were convulsing the nation.

I received another text from a young man who had supported me, working for my campaign as a teenager in 2016. He said he would no longer support me because I had not used my independence to speak out on racism.

Receiving criticism is part of my job. It is often harsh and personal, but after so many years, that doesn't bother me. These text messages affected me differently. These young men had believed in me for the right reasons, and I had disappointed them with my silence. And I knew they were right. My unique position demanded that I say something more than the party-approved pablum I had been releasing. My silence even seemed to acquiesce to Trump's call for violent suppression of the protests. But I still didn't know what to say.

I felt so lost that after lunch, I impulsively sent a message to the Senate chaplain, Admiral Barry Black, asking to meet. I knew him, but not well. He had grown up in a Baltimore housing project and attended a historically Black college, before serving twenty-five years in the Navy, so he understood the weight of power and the challenge of making wise decisions. Every morning, he opened the Senate's proceedings with words that always seemed right for that moment. I thought he could give me insight. We agreed to meet the next morning.

That evening I contacted an old friend, who advised me to pray and sent me a statement President Bush had released that day. They were words worthy of a president during a crisis. "This tragedy—in a long series of similar tragedies—raises a long overdue question: How do we end systemic racism in our society?" Bush wrote. "The only way to see ourselves in a true light is to listen to the voices of so many who are hurting and grieving. Those who set out to silence those voices do not understand the meaning of America—or how it becomes a better place."

Again, I could not sleep. Holding my rock gave only slight comfort. In the morning, I went to meet Chaplain Black, without telling anyone, not even Verne. He turned to the Bible, reading the story of Esther as well as the story of David and Goliath. He reminded me that David came to the fight as he was. There was no armor that fit him and no weapon that was his. But he was not afraid, because he believed in the cause. "You will know the words to say," he finally said. "God will give you the words."

His words gave me comfort I had not felt in some time.

I spent that day on my usual business, including preparing for a long-planned floor speech the next day, marking the centennial of women's suffrage and urging passage of the Equal Rights Amendment. The speech my staff had drafted was not up to the moment. I knew I couldn't just repeat platitudes about women pioneers. I would have to write something from the heart, taking into account the racial issues shaking the country.

That evening, I read a statement released by former secretary of defense Jim Mattis, defending the protesters and challenging any militarization of the response as unconstitutional, unwise, and morally dangerous. And he went straight to the source of that decision. "Donald Trump is the first president in my lifetime who does not try to unite the American people—does not even pretend to try," Mattis wrote. "We are witnessing the consequences of three years of this deliberate effort. We are witnessing the consequences of three years without mature leadership." I shared the statement with Verne and said I thought it would make a difference, because Mattis was so respected. Esper that day declared that troops should not be used against protesters, and Milley would soon apologize for his presence at Trump's Lafayette Square photo op.

I spent the night awake, thinking about what was happening and how I would respond. As I walked to work the next day, I passed a yard sign with a quote attributed to Martin Luther King Jr. that I had seen many times before. Today I took it in: "Our lives begin to end the day we become silent about things that matter." It was time to speak.

About midday, I was walking from a committee vote to my hideaway office, where I would work sequestered from interruption until my speech later that afternoon. Paul Kane of *The Washington Post* caught up with me at the elevator. I respected his work and didn't mind taking his question. He asked what I thought of Mattis's statement. He held up his recorder. I frankly told him, "I thought General Mattis's words were true and honest and necessary and overdue." I told him how I had been struggling to find the right words but thought that Mattis's comments might make many of us more open about our true convictions.

As I spoke, I could see Paul's eyes widening above his mask. He had not expected this; no other Senate Republican had challenged Trump in this way. Paul asked if I could still support the president. A smart politician would have deflected that question, but now I was bent on honesty, and my words flowed. "I am struggling with it," I said. "I have struggled with it for a long time." I pointed out that I had not supported Trump in 2016 but that I had tried to work with him for the benefit of Alaska.

The media blew up with my remarks while I was alone in my hideaway getting ready for my floor speech. My poor staff had nothing to give them. Unfortunately, much of the coverage that day concentrated on my comments about supporting the president—which I didn't consider to be news, since I never had endorsed him—while I would have preferred for it to have reflected the comments on our racial reckoning that I made later that day on the floor.

As it happened, the Senate floor was occupied before my allotted time with the Emmett Till Anti-Lynching Bill. The bill had passed the Senate unanimously the previous year. Now it had come back from the House, where it passed with only four members voting in opposition, and was ready to become law. Both sides were hoping this legislation could pass on this day, by unanimous consent, as the nation observed George Floyd's memorial in Minneapolis. We could demonstrate that Congress had heard the American people and did care.

Senator Rand Paul of Kentucky, who had supported the bill previously, now rose to offer an amendment to weaken it—one the sponsors could not accept, and that would make passage impossible on that important day. Even without his amendment passing, he would prevent unanimous consent, which alone would stop us. Kamala Harris of California spoke first in response, her feelings driving powerful oratory in her clipped, precise style. Next Cory Booker of New Jersey rose to speak, his voice full of emotion, addressing Rand Paul directly, accepting Paul's sincerity and calling him a friend, while pleading with him to allow this one moment of historic justice, this acknowledgment of the brutality of America's racist past.

Rand Paul coolly refused and quickly left the floor.

My time came immediately after the drama of their words. I took the lectern. "Before my colleagues exit the chamber," I said to the African American senators, "I want to acknowledge your words. I want to thank you. The passion, the emotion, the true rawness in your words are words that I think all of us as members of the Senate should hear, reflect, and respect."

Then I talked about the protesters, their just cause, and the gaping wounds of racism that had never been allowed to heal. Our system did not work fairly for everyone. And we had a duty to acknowledge the failures and to vow to address them.

"I have been chastised by some very close friends who have said, 'You're silent, Lisa. Why are you silent?'" I admitted. "I have struggled with the right words. As a White woman born and raised in Alaska with a family that was privileged, I can't feel that openness and rawness that I just heard expressed by my friends Cory and Kamala. I haven't lived their life. But I can listen and I can educate myself and I can try to be a healer at a time when we need to be healed. And that's my commitment and my pledge."

Back at the office, I apologized to my shell-shocked staff, who certainly hadn't expected media attention that day, since the last they had heard I planned only a short speech on women's suffrage.

They had been besieged by reporters seeking to confirm my comments to the *Post* and to get more. But they assured me that this was good—they thanked me for speaking from the heart.

We waited for the president's tweet responding to my Mattis statement, which we knew would be coming. I wasn't worried for myself as much as for Verne and my boys. They sometimes get testy messages about me. To Verne from a friend: "What's wrong with your wife?" And to Matt, at the farmers' market: "Why can't your mom support the president?" I've told my family, all with their own views, that they don't have to defend me. But they do defend me anyway.

At about six P.M. we got a warning from the White House that a tweet was coming, and it went out an hour later. When I read it, I wasn't bothered. He didn't give me a demeaning nickname, and what he said was essentially true: I had voted against him on Kavanaugh and the ACA, and he had done good for Alaska. "Few people know where they'll be in two years from now, but I do, in the Great State of Alaska (which I love) campaigning against Senator Lisa Murkowski," Trump wrote. "Get any candidate ready, good or bad, I don't care, I'm endorsing. If you have a pulse, I'm with you."

"Good," I thought, "that's how democracy works. Bring it on."

We could call my opponent "Pulse."

Plenty of people wrote messages and newspaper columns of support, but the message I got that night from Reverend Black is one I will always save.

"Senator, no one knows where he or she will be two years from now, for we borrow our heartbeats from the sovereign God of the universe," he wrote. "You have come to the kingdom for such a time as this. History will record your courage. I am proud of you. Barry."

––––––––––

Late summer can be a frantic but energetic time in Alaska. The stars start coming back in August as the long summer days grow shorter. Rainy days and cooler nights set in long before Labor Day allows us to speak of autumn. Normally, this is the home stretch for many Alaskans' earning seasons. In another month or two, many businesses will shut down until spring, while others will send their summer staffs back to school and shrink to just the essentials.

But in 2020, this familiar time of year felt totally different. Like a terrifying void. Alaskans were panicked and needed help. The off-season had lasted all summer.

The national economy crashed with the shutdowns in March and April, but after Congress responded with unprecedented speed and scale, the fall abated. By May, some hiring started again. A few industries came roaring back. While some federal appropriations may have been poorly targeted, we did the best we could in a crisis, and the overall result was surprisingly good: the U.S. economy avoided a recession after that first shock. In a year the enormous job losses would transform into a worker shortage.

In Alaska, as well as some other rural and resource states, the story was much worse. Early in the pandemic, Americans' vacations had been postponed to late summer. Now they were canceled altogether. By late July it became obvious that we would lose a year's worth of economic activity. Streets were deserted. Flights were scratched and even whole small-town airports shut down. Many Americans faced the end of benefits without an income or a safety net. The initial federal money was drying up. Congress had waited to see what would be needed, and now we seemed incapable of passing a follow-up.

I was as discouraged as I had ever been in office. All focus in Washington was on the election, but at home people were focused on economic survival. Mitch McConnell unveiled a Covid bill that everyone knew was not intended to advance. I couldn't engage with constituents as I normally did—at the airport, the farmers' market, or a Costco aisle—and I couldn't talk to most of my Democratic colleagues, whom I rarely saw. Covid had made us disorganized and seemingly powerless.

In September, a public radio interviewer randomly asked me

what I would do if a Supreme Court vacancy opened up before the election. I said we should follow the pattern we had set when Justice Scalia died, of holding the seat open until after the election—which was only two months away, not eight months away, as when Merrick Garland was nominated. The next day, Ruth Bader Ginsberg died. I held to my stand, but my Republican colleagues planned to rush through a nominee while Trump was still president, twisting logic past the breaking point with self-serving explanations of why this would be okay when Garland's nomination had not been.

I met with Amy Coney Barrett and questioned her as closely as I could. Nothing disqualified her; she was eminently qualified. That had been my standard for many years, and I knew I must stick to my own rules. That meant I would support her nomination if it came to the floor. But I opposed letting it come to the floor, to be consistent with how the Garland nomination had been handled. I voted against cloture, the motion to bring Barrett's confirmation to final vote, as I had pledged to do. But with only fifty-one votes needed, cloture was invoked and the confirmation came before us. I voted to approve the confirmation itself, which also represented my principled stand on how we should judge nominees who were objectively qualified. I had honored my commitment to process by opposing bringing up the vote, but when I lost that issue, the question in front of me was whether she was qualified. I felt she was.

To say these votes were misunderstood would be an understatement. My two votes appeared to be a flip-flop to some voters. Conservatives were angry that I opposed holding the confirmation vote. Many pro-choice women felt betrayed that I voted to confirm Barrett. Some told me this confirmation was the time to abandon my commitment to process because the underlying issue was so important. I reject that reasoning. That slippery slope had already slid us down into the ditch we found ourselves in, with our institutions degraded. Those who respect the rules only so long as they help advance their issues don't really care about the rules at all.

With the election nearing and Covid relief still unsettled, I took my chance to pass the energy bill before the 116th Congress and my chairmanship ended. I worked one-on-one with any senator who was interested to iron out innumerable other details. Building toward passage felt like setting up an intricate line of dominoes designed to fall in sequence, each an issue valued by one of the seventy senators who had a piece of the bill. Finally, I was ready to calendar the bill, as if delicately placing the final domino. And then one objection turned up, completely out of the blue. It was Rand Paul.

I asked other senators to talk to Paul. They said he wouldn't move. I sat down with him to ask about his concerns. He demanded an amendment that we both knew would kill the bill. He said he didn't care. I explained that many colleagues had priorities in the bill. He refused to listen to the provisions that would benefit his state of Kentucky.

"I'm from an oil state," I said. "Manchin is from a coal state. Do you think that we're going to do something that is going to hurt the interests of the people in your state?"

He said, "I don't need to sit here and listen to you lecture me."

"I'm not lecturing you," I said, using my reasonable-mother voice. "I would like to share with you what's in the bill so that I can gain your support or at least so that you're not in opposition."

He closed me off. He kept saying, over and over, "I don't need to sit here and listen to you lecture me."

I finally lost my cool.

"It's clear that I'm not going to get any cooperation from you," I said. "And, you know, you are probably the number one reason that the Senate is so dysfunctional right now."

He looked me straight in the eye and said, "You are probably the number one reason that the Affordable Care Act is still law."

It was time for me to walk away. There was no way for me to get the bill back on the floor. I had tried to move major legislation through the Senate the right way, using the traditional committee process. But I wasn't going to give up and admit we could not accomplish anything. I hatched an alternate plan.

The House had passed its own energy bill, a partisan Democratic product that had no chance of passing the Senate. My staff and I went to the sponsors and suggested we put together a conference version combining the two bills—although mine had never passed the Senate—and then attempt to attach it to the year-end, must-pass appropriation package. Our staffs began working through the weeks of autumn to stitch together a version that could encompass all our partisan differences and individual state priorities. This behind-the-scenes process was not how I had imagined negotiating a conference package, but the bill had been through six years of open process already.

Election night passed with Trump's apparent defeat. I had mixed emotions. I felt relief that he would no longer be in the White House, but also concern that Alaskans would be disadvantaged by a new president whose values about resources did not align with ours. I still thought, however, that we would win the Senate, as we needed victory in only one of two runoff elections in Georgia for a majority. Those runoffs would be held January 5.

Amid the chaos of Trump's attempts to challenge and overturn the election, we had a lot of work to do in Congress. Americans—and especially Alaskans—were desperate for help. A new wave of the virus was rising, people were still out of work, businesses were failing. Scientists had created a vaccine, but distributing it would take many months. No major Covid aid had passed since the spring, while the party leaderships dug in their positions on each side. Among various disagreements, the Democrats insisted that a relief bill had to be at least $2 trillion, with direct payments to Americans, while the Republicans would agree to no more than half that amount. Neither side would budge, so nothing happened.

Susan Collins returned from her reelection in Maine disturbed by what she had heard from voters about the need for Covid relief. Several other Republican colleagues agreed. I approached Virginia senator Mark Warner on the floor and asked if senators on the Democratic side felt the same way. The answer was yes—many senators wanted to get relief out to their constituents, but the leadership remained stuck in place. We agreed we needed to put together a bipartisan group of those of us who did want to legislate a solution. We started making plans right then. I said we needed to meet in person, not on Zoom, and preferably off-campus, on neutral ground. Mark suggested dinner and offered to arrange for a restaurant. But that seemed too public, especially since Covid might force us to sit outside, so I offered my house on Capitol Hill for the meeting. My table was big enough for eight.

We invited four senators from each side. The Republicans were Collins, Romney, Bill Cassidy of Louisiana, and me. The Democrats were Warner, Manchin, Jon Tester of Montana, and Dick Durbin of Illinois, their party's whip and the only member of leadership invited. Mark ordered the food from an upscale Italian place, much better than the standard dinner-meeting pizza. Before the dinner, we got news that Chuck Grassley of Iowa, the oldest senator serving, had come down with Covid. We were rattled, worrying about Chuck, and wondering if we should still meet—many of us had recently been with him, and we might be carrying the virus, too. Mark and I decided to go ahead and see who would be comfortable enough to come. When he arrived with the food, we decided to sit spaced out in the living room rather than side by side at the table, and we opened all the windows, getting ventilation from two sides of the room and letting the chilly night air waft away any germs.

Everyone came. We talked a bit about how to get the Senate to work better, but we spent most of our time on Covid relief. The group didn't have a leader, although Manchin and Warner jousted back and forth for control. We discussed what each of us had seen in our states and where we saw the highest need for relief. Sitting in the room looking at one another, as eight caring people, leaders who wanted to do what was best for our states, our trust rapidly grew. But the hardest part was where to start. The barrier between the two parties had been built over months of disagreement on tough issues.

The crack in that wall came from Durbin. He suggested that rather than trying to pass a bill that addressed everything, we should think about bridging the support people needed until the spring, when the new administration could pass its own bill. The idea removed perhaps the largest sticking point, the size of the package. At any other time, the $900 billion Covid appropriation would be considered enormous—the 2008 TARP rescue package that spawned the Tea Party movement had been $700 billion—but it was less than half of what the Democrats had been demanding, and that got Republicans moving toward agreement. Biden reportedly liked the idea, too. Trump paid no attention, as he was fully occupied with his election contests, but Treasury Secretary Steve Mnuchin would get behind it.

That night, November 17, proved to be a turning point for cooperation in the Senate and the start of a two-year period of exceptional bipartisan accomplishment. We learned over the following weeks that our group, our gang, could write legislation that would work. We used the framework of a bill developed by a similar bipartisan group in the House, the Problem Solvers Caucus, cut it down to the size we had agreed upon, and added members from both sides of that House group to our negotiations. To tackle the thorny individual issues in the bill, we broke up into subgroups, spending hours on Zoom or convening in person, in dark offices over cold pizza, or calling in from highway rest stops. We had Zoom cocktails and laughed together, even as we dealt with tough disagreements that took hours to untangle. We didn't hand the work off to staff. This was our project, and it depended on the relationships and trust we were creating. As Susan said, this felt like what we were supposed to be doing. For me, it felt like a fog was lifting, as the power of cooperation cut through the partisan impasse that had seemed so hopeless. Joe Manchin kept us on track as we met through the Thanksgiving weekend. In two weeks, we had an agreement and held a media conference, presenting a one-hundred-page bill.

The Democrats liked it. Durbin had kept their leadership briefed. President-elect Biden wanted something in place so he wouldn't come into office with a nation in a deep economic crisis. We four Republican members of the group went to meet with Mitch McConnell. He was not particularly encouraging about our ideas at first, but within a week, he did see the promise, and he soon put a further compromise offer on the table. The four top leaders from each side of the House and Senate began meeting directly and hammering out a final bill. We had opened the door and given this a push, and now they carried it onward.

The government was in danger of shutting down that Christmas as well—what else is new?—and we needed to pass a huge omnibus measure to fund the departments for the year ahead. That would be our vehicle to solve many problems at once. The day before the omnibus would reach the Senate floor, I got my energy bill attached. Covid relief was tied in as well. And we added legislation to end surprise medical billing and a package of water bills from my committee. The legislation that landed on our desks was 5,593 pages long, the longest Congress had ever passed—so long, in fact, that printer problems delayed us from voting until the night of December 21 (the energy bill was 532 pages of that pile of paper). We received the usual complaints about the lack of time to read the bill, as if anyone ever has time to read more than five thousand pages. In fact, anyone who wanted to know what was in the energy bill could have found out in the painstaking process we had worked through over the years of my chairmanship, when we constantly updated members on changes. After the omnibus bill passed with overwhelming bipartisan majorities in both houses, President Trump unexpectedly threatened to veto it, even though his own Treasury secretary had negotiated the provisions of the Covid relief and had urged passage. Trump demanded drastic changes and then ultimately signed it anyway. Our energy bill was finally law. Our entire energy committee and staff, Republicans and Democrats, right down to the administrative assistants, celebrated at a big party in a bar on H Street.

Both industry and environmental organizations praised the en-

ergy bill. We had included funding for nuclear energy, carbon capture, and sending carbon underground to enhance oil production,
but we also supported wind and solar. Critics on the left of the green
movement said the bill didn't go far enough, as if that were a reason
to oppose it, but the Natural Resources Defense Council called the
bill "perhaps the most significant climate legislation Congress has
ever passed." Critics came from the right, as well, saying the bill
didn't do enough to advance production of more fossil energy. We
had our Goldilocks bill. It was the result of compromise on all sides,
representing the first major update of our energy laws in over a decade, with policies and big investments to advance energy storage
and transmission that would be the foundation for the future energy system.

We got much more attention for the Covid bill, with detailed stories about how it had come about, birthed in my living room, then
nurtured into existence through the many personal meetings, until
a final toast with Joe Manchin's moonshine. What had happened
gave people hope. We had shown that even in the most polarized of
times, senators could come together and solve big problems. Suddenly we moderates who had been the weird kids on the playground
became the cool kids. Several senators asked to join our gang, and
some were envious that they hadn't been asked to join the original
group.

As the final days of the Trump administration approached, I had
a new sense of possibilities. At least 2020 was ending, with vaccines,
new Senate cooperation, and federal support that folks needed back
home. But I had no idea what was coming.

————

President Trump declared on election night 2020, without evidence,
that the vote was rigged and that he had in fact won in a landslide.
He had been saying all along that if he lost it meant the election was
crooked, so I didn't take his claim very seriously. Trump simply
couldn't admit he had lost. When the Associated Press called Biden's

victory on the Saturday after the election, I quickly wrote a statement congratulating him and encouraging the peaceful transfer of power. I was still working on my statement when Don Young issued his congratulations, and I was afraid I was late. Mitt Romney also promptly acknowledged Biden's win. But then only a few other Republicans followed us. After that, silence or denial. I was astounded. I had never thought that recognizing the result of an American election would be turned into a partisan political act.

Trump's odd band of attorneys produced some theories and allegations about the election that were dubious on their face and a few others that deserved a hearing. Courts struck them all down. There was no evidence of any large-scale voter fraud. Dozens of cases were judged on the merits; in some of them, the president's lawyers were sanctioned for frivolous or false pleadings. Any election in a huge country like ours has minor flaws, but after U.S. attorneys around the country looked into the claims, Attorney General Barr announced there was no evidence of fraud that would be significant enough to change the outcome.

Most of my Republican colleagues, however, went along with Trump. That decision proved to be a critical one for the terrible events that would follow.

Republicans were afraid of offending Trump's base by disagreeing with him. And Senate leadership believed that Trump could help us hold the Senate by going to Georgia to campaign for our candidates in the runoffs. Of the many shortcuts I've seen senators take, compromising our democratic institutions for short-term political gain, this was perhaps the most damaging of all. When they repeated phony doubts about the election, their supporters naturally listened. Intelligent people adopt false beliefs when they are misinformed. At dinner one night with Verne, I mentioned my surprise that the election controversy was still going on and he said, "Yeah, but we really don't know who won." He had been watching Fox News and had seen their supposed exposés, which we later learned even the broadcasters knew were not true. So many people

I know and respect were convinced Trump had won. Why shouldn't they believe it when the president, party leaders, senators and congressmen, and their news sources all presented this information as factual? But it wasn't.

After the courts and other authorities had shown Trump's claims to be without merit, his supporters in Congress kept up the challenge on the basis that the public doubted the outcome of the election, even if misguided, and so further investigation was needed to assuage public concerns. But, of course, these members of Congress were the same people who had helped produce those concerns, for their own purposes—largely, to curry favor with Trump so he would help them win the two Senate seats in Georgia. As so often happened, however, Trump didn't follow the script. His message to Georgia voters was all about himself and his claims that elections could not be trusted, persuading Republicans not to cast ballots. He sank the Republican candidates and helped the Democrats win control of the Senate.

On New Year's Day we were on the Senate floor for the successful override of the president's veto of the National Defense Authorization Act. I had left a Christmas break with Dorothy and my family on Maui to come and vote, and I was grumbling about missing the rest of the family vacation, as I would need to be in Washington for the election certification on January 6. John Barrasso overheard my plan and said he was concerned about me being alone at home in Washington. He was a member of leadership, and they had been picking up some crazy stuff about protesters coming to D.C. on January 6. So, after the vote, I cashed in airline miles and took the twelve-hour flight back to Maui rather than staying in Washington for those few days.

On my way back to D.C., I got my first look at the people converging on the capital. Connecting on a red-eye flight at LAX on the night of January 5, I was surrounded by red MAGA hats. A guy at the gate was shirtless, with an American flag draped around his shoulders. I was glad I wasn't easily recognizable, wearing a mask and a hoodie, and with hair that looked like I had come straight from the beach. Most of the travelers slept through the night flight, but I didn't. We had already decided that Garrett would meet me with his big pickup truck, as we weren't sure of the situation on the ground in D.C.

I only had time to change my clothes before going to the Capitol. When I got there, my fatigue from the cross-country red-eye flight overcame me and I went to my hideaway in the Capitol to close my eyes for a few minutes. The certification process would begin with a joint session in the House before the Senate and Vice President Pence assembled back in our chamber. I planned to skip the joint session, monitoring it on TV. The session in the House had just broken, after one P.M., when I heard the bathroom door across from my office thrown open and a terrible retching sound. A Capitol Police officer was at the sink in the tiny bathroom, rinsing his eyes of pepper spray. He had been sprayed in the face. As I asked if he was okay, he looked up, eyes squinting and streaming, and said, "I've got to get back out there and help." Senators Tina Smith and Catherine Cortez Masto had popped out of their offices, too, and we watched the officer dash away. We couldn't see or hear what was going on outside. Our windows faced the mall, but they were covered by temporary scaffolding set up for the inauguration. We assumed the officers were dealing with a protest, something that happens frequently, although the pepper spray was clearly outside the norm.

Under the law at the time, a single senator and representative could challenge a state's electoral votes, causing each house of Congress to meet separately to debate and vote on the challenge. We convened on the Senate floor for a challenge to Arizona's votes, with the vice president presiding. Seated at my desk there, I could hear a strange background sound from outside, an undertone of white noise like the roar in a seashell. Most of us had no idea what was going on out there. Inside, Mitch McConnell spoke for the majority of Republicans, who opposed challenging the electoral votes. His points sounded like the arguments I had been making for years, in my often lonely calls to bring us back to respect for our institutions and the process that keeps our democracy whole—and which weeks of humoring Trump's election doubts had now put at risk. Mitch said, "Self-government, my colleagues, requires a shared commitment to the truth and a shared respect for the ground rules of our system. We cannot keep drifting apart into two separate tribes with a separate set of facts and separate realities, with nothing in common except our hostility towards each other and mistrust for the few national institutions that we all still share."

The debate had gone on for only about forty-five minutes when two unfamiliar men suddenly appeared on the Senate floor, one approaching the vice president and the other Senator Grassley, the president pro tempore. I heard Grassley being directed to immediately take Pence's place in the Senate president's chair. Everyone watched at the unprecedented interruption—like someone walking up to the altar in the middle of a church service—that left everyone confused. Then Pence was whisked away and Grassley quickly moved into the presiding officer's chair, where he was instructed to recess the session. I heard crowd noise outside the door. All the outer doors were quickly closed, and I could hear their heavy bolts closing. As if appearing magically, men in suits with assault rifles across their chests were in our chamber. Two men stood around McConnell. A member of the sergeant at arms office stood on the dais and announced that the Capitol had been breached and we should stay calmly in our seats. I looked up at the press gallery and those open doors, and I realized that if there was an active shooter in the chamber, we would have nowhere to hide and we could not leave. The Senate floor would be like a shooting gallery.

We were all seeking news on our phones, but the news hadn't caught up yet. Then we heard that the mob had breached the House chamber. I was incredulous. This was the United States Capitol, the center of the most powerful country in the world, with our own large police force protecting us. Senator Todd Young, a former marine, stood next to Susan Collins and me, chatting, and I appreciated it, feeling like he was standing guard to protect us. I texted my boys. I knew Verne was in the air, flying back from Maui, and wouldn't hear from me, but Nic and Matt were still in Hawaii, and I didn't want them to worry if they saw the news. And I wanted to tell them I loved them, because I wasn't sure what was going on, and I felt completely vulnerable in the fishbowl of the chamber. Matt texted, "I love you back," and added, "Are you OK?" My reply said it all: "Scared but secured." But, in truth, I sent that "I love you" text because I didn't know if I would ever see them again.

We were told we would be moved to a secure location, and senators got up and began to calmly exit, joined by the cloakroom staff, parliamentarians, and pages. One of the parliamentarians told Tony Hanagan of the cloakroom staff to take the ceremonial box containing the original ballots from the states, which we were in the process of certifying. As we walked, the voice of the person directing us rose to an elevated tone of urgency, hurrying us along. The tension in the room shot up, and people began moving quickly, squeezing together to go down the back stairway to the point where I was afraid someone would get hurt. Spotting Dan Sullivan ahead of me in the surging group, I quickly wormed my way to him and linked arms, saying, "I need a marine." Dan was still in the reserves at that time.

He said, "You're my partner."

On the first floor we passed a corridor where officers had formed a human barricade to protect our passage. We could hear the chaos and see people swarming on the far side of the officers' line of bodies, and I realized just how close we were and how out of control the situation had become. They took us down a narrow staircase to the Capitol's basement tunnels. How would the older senators and Tammy Duckworth in her wheelchair manage this? Dan and I were near the front of the group. He looked down at my shoes and asked if I could run. I said yes, and we picked up the pace. I matched his stride, jogging down the underground corridor to the Dirksen building, then on to the Hart. Almost the entire Senate was deposited in a room, the so-called undisclosed secure location, along with the staff and journalists who had been swept up in the evacuation. The majority and minority leaders had been taken somewhere else, and a few stragglers were hiding somewhere on their own.

The secure location was hardly secure, and our security team was less than reassuring. One of their plans was for all the senators to walk out and board buses. It seemed crazy that they thought we would make it through the angry rioters, and that plan went nowhere. We could get only fragmentary and disjointed information about what was going on. When they finally brought in a TV, we saw the shocking image of the guy in furs and horns sitting in the seat of the president of the Senate. Senators phoned their contacts in the White House to beg Trump to call off the attack and send a statement to his supporters to stop the violence, but he did nothing to calm them or back them off. To the contrary, he continued his Twitter attacks on the election and on Vice President Pence (who was not with us). Other senators were calling their contacts at the Pentagon, asking why the National Guard had not stepped in. I called my family and asked the boys to keep Tutu from watching the television. Kristen and Garrett were alone in my Hart building office that day. I called to check on them and learned that Garrett's huge husky, Ivan, was on guard. I called Don Young as well. He had stayed in his office on the House side. Don said he had the door locked and his hunting knife in his boot: "Let 'em come at me." And then, bizarrely, as the battle continued outside, someone decided that what we really needed was to be fed lunch—we weren't fed information, but we did get take-out salads and sandwiches.

When the mob had finally been cleared, about eight P.M., we headed back to finish certifying the election. It was eerie to walk through the building where the chaos had occurred just hours before (although we would only later see the broken windows, trashed offices, debris, and even human waste). Those who stormed the

Capitol had been intent on disrespecting and degrading our country's seat of democracy. A woman was shot and killed in the fighting, and six other deaths were linked to the event, according to a bipartisan Senate report. More than 150 officers were injured. Many of them were my friends, and I could only imagine what they had been through—we had not yet seen the video of Trump's supporters cursing them, beating them with sticks and clubs, spraying them with chemicals, battering against them in waves, and jabbing them with flagpoles. The psychological toll would be incalculable, with officer suicides to come. We had all been deeply affected. But we were determined to finish our work.

Pence brought us back to order with a simple and deeply inspiring speech. He sounded like a true president. "As we reconvene in this chamber, the world will again witness the resilience and strength of our democracy," he said. "For even in the wake of unprecedented violence and vandalism at this Capitol, the elected representatives of the people of the United States have assembled again on the very same day to support and defend the Constitution of the United States. So may God bless the lost, the injured, and the heroes forged on this day. May God bless all who serve here, and those who protect this place. And may God bless the United States of America. Let's get back to work."

We all rose in a standing ovation.

Mitch McConnell spoke next. "They tried to disrupt our democracy. They failed. They failed," he said, his voice quavering with anger. "This failed insurrection only underscores how crucial the task before us is for our republic. Our nation was founded precisely so that the free choice of the American people is what shapes our self-government and determines the destiny of our nation. Not fear, not force, but the peaceful expression of the popular will."

We went back to functioning as the Senate again, to certify the results from the states. And then I found myself disappointed almost as much as I had been proud when several of my colleagues once again raised their futile and disingenuous challenges, attempting to curry favor with the same group who had overrun the Capitol, even after everything that had just happened. It was shameful.

When the Senate was finished, after midnight, most senators went home, but about fifteen of us crossed back over to the House to deliver our certification with the vice president. It was important to show that we were not deterred from our responsibilities and that the rioters had failed. I spoke into the vice president's ear. No one had been more at risk than he was that day, with the crowd chanting for his neck and the president egging them on in tweets. "I am extraordinarily proud of the role that you have played here today, ensuring this transfer of power, and that we were able to complete this," I said. He was dry-eyed but his voice was emotional.

Susan Collins and I stayed until after the Senate delivered the certified ballots to the House (the House didn't finish certifying the election until three A.M.). I wouldn't let her go to her house, as her husband, Tom, was out of town and she would be alone. We rode to my place in a van provided by Senate security officers, who insisted that senators be escorted safely home that night. Verne had arrived back in D.C. that evening, and had seen the news after he landed. He built a fire for us, opened a good bottle of red wine, and left us alone. We talked far into the night, downloading what had happened and sharing our feelings about it. As tired as we were, we knew we could not sleep without beginning to process that long day.

————

The second impeachment was an easier decision for me. How could it not be? An American president had attempted to thwart the peaceful transition of power after losing reelection. Trump had been instrumental in inciting his supporters. He had started and endlessly repeated the lie that the election was stolen; he worked his supporters into a frenzy, pointed them at the Capitol, and then worse, refused to intervene to stop the violence and destruction while Congress was locked down. Yet only ten House Republicans voted with the majority Democrats to impeach Trump. Their political fate explains why more didn't join them. Only two remained after the next election, the others having been defeated in their primaries or having retired to avoid that fate. Representative Adam Kinzinger was even denounced by members of his own family, who said he had embarrassed their name and should be removed from office.

In the Senate, the impeachment managers' video of the insurrection silenced even those senators who, as in the previous impeachment, generally refused to pay attention and take the proceedings seriously. Partly, we were reliving the trauma. But also, the video reminded us of the destructive behavior of the insurrectionists, their disrespect and brutality toward the police, and their clear intent to stop the election certification process and harm the elected leaders responsible for it. Many Republicans who voted against impeachment hid behind the flimsy argument that the impeachment process was inoperative after the president had left office. I could see no logical reason for taking that stand, other than the desire to avoid convicting Trump out of fear of the personal political consequences. I believed that the facts, not party loyalty, should determine the judgment of guilt or innocence. I felt that Trump had failed to uphold his oath of office—to protect and defend the Constitution—which met my standard of a high crime and misdemeanor. I was among seven Republican senators who voted to convict, along with all the Democrats, but we needed seventeen Republicans to reach the two-thirds majority required. Among the seven, only I was up for reelection in the next cycle. The others had more years on their terms or already planned to retire. Several of us were censured by the Republican Party in our states.

For weeks after, the Capitol remained surrounded by metal fencing and guarded by troops—twenty-five thousand National Guard members, some of whom slept on Capitol hallway floors, early in the deployment. My independent life changed, too, as my staff discouraged my solo walks to work, and for several months I was escorted through airports by air marshals, who flew incognito aboard planes when senators traveled. The country's vulnerability had not passed. We were briefed about the domestic terrorist groups that were still operating: the Proud Boys, White nationalists, and others. The threat remained, not only because so many Americans still believed that the election had been stolen but also because of the much more deeply rooted hatred in these violent groups and their allies. A democracy can survive only by the consent of the governed, and these Americans had come to see the government as an enemy to be taken down.

In fact, I was on edge for a while, sensing threats when there were none, and troubled by paranoid thoughts. A Lime scooter left too long in front of the house looked to me like a bomb. A man in fatigues working out at my neighborhood gym unnerved me so much that I had to end my workout and go home. I was no longer comfortable in my hideaway office. The first time I went back, a couple of days after the insurrection, the space had a spooky, haunted feel. I hadn't intended to go there, but I had been delayed and couldn't get to my main office in time for a scheduled call with an Alaskan reporter. Rioters had not entered my hideaway, but the three offices immediately above mine had been trashed, with one of the windows shattered as a means to gain entry into the building. Glass, broken furniture, and papers were still scattered everywhere. I should have rescheduled the call, but instead, affected by my surroundings in the hideaway, I unloaded in discomfort and anger with that reporter, blasting Trump and demanding that he resign, which became a news story.

When I had a chance, at the start of the next Congress, I chose a new hideaway. I wanted to leave the ghosts of that day behind.

I knew I needed to take a break from the tension in D.C., and I told Verne I wanted to go to our family duck camp at Healy Lake. This was a totally unrealistic request with no planning, as the cabin is not set up for winter and just getting to the remote area would be an expedition. But I needed to be away from other people and to walk on the clean, white frozen lake and rivers. Verne suggested Chena Hot Springs, a more accessible winter spot in Alaska's interior. I rejected it—it had people. We ended up going to a Kenai River cabin without water, plumbing, or heat, a deserted spot in winter. The river ice was chaotic and jumbled, but underneath I could hear the flow of the river, continuing uninterrupted by the chaos on top, a promise of spring and hope. It was the therapy I needed.

Months later, a *New York Times* writer interviewed me about the psychological effects of January 6 and I told some of these stories. I was amazed when she said I was the only Republican senator who would speak to her about it. No one wants to appear weak or admit to feeling afraid. The Republican strategy seemed to be simply to get beyond this—so no more talking about it. But not talking about it doesn't make what happened go away, it just represses the emotion for a time. Telling these stories honestly could have made us all more human and helped others.

Eventually, I came out of my fog. I learned (from that same *New York Times* article) that hypervigilance and unwanted thoughts are normal after a traumatic event. January 6 was a terrible day and there was nothing wrong with being deeply disturbed by it, but that's over now. Unfortunately, the impact on the country didn't last much longer. The insurrection gave our nation a shock, and for a time it seemed that might be enough to end our period of toxic partisan extremism. Unfortunately, the populists set out to change this reality, just as they tried to erase Trump's election loss to Joe Biden. They accepted a fantasy world, one that now featured the repugnant denial of the harm the attackers caused—in which the rioters had been more like enthusiastic tourists, Pence had never been in danger, and those who had tried to violently overthrow the democratic system by stopping the certification of the election were actually patriots.

I'm happy to say that this nonsense didn't bother me as much as I would have expected, because I didn't spend much time thinking about it. Instead, I got to work in the new Congress with our newly empowered gang of senators who wanted to get stuff done, and we began working on legislation. I felt strong and confident. My lonely work supporting institutions and bipartisanship suddenly seemed more important to many more people. I knew Trump would try to end my Senate service, but I figured I could count on Alaskans to stand by me.

CHAPTER 10

Success and Survival
in Washington

OVER MY YEARS IN the Senate, I never gave up on my belief in good government and the still-viable institutions of American democracy, even as extreme partisanship turned to violence and critics called my lonely institutionalism naïve or outdated. Then, in the 117th Congress, during the first two years of Biden's presidency, my optimism was validated. Senators worked together and bridged differences for the most productive Congress in my memory, passing bipartisan bills that addressed problems that had vexed Americans and Alaskans for many years. My prescription to fix American politics had always been simple: we needed to roll up our sleeves and take on the real, practical needs of our constituents. We did that, and, for a time, the system really did work.

During those two years, we made our country safer and more competitive, protected vulnerable women and same-sex couples, and helped prepare the economy for the future with the largest investment in infrastructure in recent history. We safeguarded future presidential elections, addressed gun violence, and brought the American economy back from Covid. We also laid the groundwork that would later convince the president to open Willow for oil exploration and production.

With the Senate balanced fifty-fifty, Democrats could win party-line votes only with complete unanimity and Vice President Harris's tiebreaker. That put the moderates in charge. Joe Manchin and Arizona's Kyrsten Sinema, as moderate Democrats, were now in the same role Susan Collins and I had held when Republicans' narrow majority required our votes to pass legislation—and when our opposition had prevented the repeal of the Affordable Care Act. We were also energized by our success with the Covid relief bill in December, when we had shown that a committed group of lawmakers could steer the agenda toward solving problems and away from partisan gridlock.

Not all the legislation in that Congress was bipartisan. President Biden signed the oversized American Rescue Plan economic stimulus fifty days after taking office. The Democrats used reconciliation to pass their priority bill without any Republican votes, avoiding the filibuster. This $1.9 trillion in spending, coming barely two months after the previous $900 billion package, helped spin up inflation, which became Biden's biggest political liability, as it hurt the lower-to-middle-income Americans the Democrats wanted to help. Wholly partisan legislation also does nothing to promote stability in the law. One-party decisions—particularly executive orders, but also laws—can be reversed with a change in who holds power. Bipartisan law tends to stick, allowing us to move forward rather than re-fighting the same controversies at every election. Making law should be hard and require a process considering many diverse interests. The Senate's filibuster helps, too. Critics often say the filibuster is undemocratic because it allows a minority—forty senators plus one under current rules—to stop action. I say the opposite: by requiring support from members of both parties, the filibuster forces us to work together to make better, more enduring and democratic laws.

In March and April, Biden announced the rest of his enormous Build Back Better plan, of which the American Rescue Plan was only one part. This New Deal–scale proposal included a huge infrastructure plan, plus healthcare elements, pre-kindergarten and child care, climate change measures, free community college, care for elders and disabled people, housing—it was everything for everybody—with a ten-year price tag (as all congressional spending proposals are measured) of some $4 trillion. In addition, the bills would roll back much of the tax cut that had been Republicans' signature accomplishment during the previous administration. There was no way Republicans could ever swallow this and the bills stalled.

Those of us in the bipartisan group that had first met in my living room months before felt we had to do something. The American public believed Congress was broken. Our walls had been breached and we needed to restore a sense of hope that our country would be okay. We discussed what we could take on to demonstrate that, and infrastructure seemed to be the strongest option and something we could all agree on. Politicians had talked for years about the need for a major investment in America's roads and bridges, and many Republicans agreed—including former president Trump. But talk was all we got. We thought we could assemble a bill with hard infrastructure projects needed across the country that both parties could support. We would attempt to work through the committees when we could, but our group effectively wrote the bill.

Our bipartisan team of eight added Sinema and Rob Portman, the moderate Republican from Ohio. We were called the Gang of Ten, or G10. Portman could create coalitions because of the high esteem in which he was held by all his colleagues. Sinema contributed with her remarkable ability to communicate with every member and close deals. When we were struggling to find common ground on an issue, and the conversation would veer off into minutiae or philosophy, she would pull us back to the big picture and our shared goal of showing the American people we could get the work done—or, in her words, "Get shit done."

Kyrsten showed a lot of courage for working with us as closely as she did—and for standing up, with Manchin, to some of her party's

excesses. Without the restraint they imposed, the Democrats' infla-
tionary and unsustainable spending would have been much greater,
and the economic problems the country faced under Biden would
have been worse. Most important, Manchin and Sinema saved the
filibuster by denying their party the votes needed to change the
rules. They both took extraordinary heat from the left, ranging
from vitriol to ridicule. I have great respect for how Kyrsten and Joe
supported the institution over their party. It is interesting to note
that both left their party in the end to become independents.

President Biden also had to fight his own side to work with us.
Joe Biden and I had been friendly for many years. He was warm
and gregarious and dispensed encouragement freely, as he did
when I lost my primary in 2010. He had seemed to enjoy being a
senator and making deals. He was also a liberal and an adversary
against much of what I wanted to do for Alaska. As my colleague
Dan Sullivan frequently pointed out, Biden issued more executive
orders locking up Alaska's resource opportunities than any other
president. We didn't share a political outlook or life experience, and
his willingness to deny Alaskans' access to resources showed his
ignorance of our needs. But despite our differences, we could find
areas to work together, and he made sure everyone in the White
House knew it. My calls were returned quickly and my concerns
were treated seriously—an unusual and very valuable status for me
to hold as a member of the opposite party and the minority.

Liberals in Biden's party thought they could get everything he
had asked for, and more, by jamming spending through Congress
in the reconciliation process. When our group brought him a
smaller package of hard infrastructure projects, Biden reacted with
his big smile and said we could work together, using this offer as a
base to build from. But his staff was obviously uncomfortable when
he said that, and the next day he changed his tone, saying the offer
wasn't good enough and the Democrats would go their own way.
But our group of moderate senators from both parties held the ulti-

mate keys for anything being able to pass. We continued to work on our bill, with the endorsement of Mitch McConnell.

We gave ourselves a difficult assignment. Besides the size of the bill, we had to figure out how to pay for it without ballooning the national debt or breaking Biden's pledge not to increase taxes on those who earn less than $400,000 a year. Normally the gas tax pays for roads, but he considered the gas tax to disproportionately affect lower earners and, therefore, was opposed to increasing it. And Republicans would not roll back the 2017 tax cut, either. Although these were challenging constraints, we did put together a package that stayed within everyone's hard lines. By the summer, our group of ten had an agreement in principle with the president. Biden had become our ally.

"We all agree that none of us got all we wanted," he told the media. "But this reminds me of the days when we used to get an awful lot done up in the United States Congress."

We were all pleased and said positive things, although we still had plenty of work to do on the details. But after the announcement, Biden again offered a caveat, saying he would sign the infrastructure bill only if the other part of his plan—the massive social spending initiative—also made it to his desk under reconciliation. Many of us felt this was a bait and switch. It would make negotiations on the Republican side much harder.

As much as the extremes in the two parties loathed each other, they had much in common. They usually delivered the same product: rhetoric and legislative failure. The left of Biden's party, like the right of mine, wanted everything or nothing. To get the bill through Congress—and begin building roads, ports, airports, railroads, ferries, power lines, water projects, and broadband connections—we would need to find the narrow path between those on either side who would prefer to simply vote no and keep their hands clean from the hard work of compromise.

Our formula followed our successful previous collaboration.

Senators stayed directly in contact, using staff only to do the as-
signed homework. That prevented the ping-pong effect that often
happens when staff members negotiate, then return to their bosses
for authorization. We also worked with the House side, which was
unusual, adding to our team the leaders of the bipartisan Problem
Solvers Caucus. Bringing all these lawmakers together would have
been a logistical impossibility if we hadn't jointly decided that passing this bill was our priority. I would drop almost anything I was
doing to make it to a meeting. It was invigorating. We were working
on something that would affect many lives for a long time—a generational investment—and we were getting results.

The bill passed the Senate in August with sixty-nine votes in
favor. The trouble came in the House. Members on the left continued to insist the bill had to be paired with Biden's big social bill,
whose passage now looked even less likely as inflation had already
taken off. When Speaker Pelosi ended that discussion and pushed
the bill forward on its own, she lost some votes from the left of her
caucus. On the Republican side, the empty politics of populism
took hold. Trump attacked the bill. The previous year, as president,
he had called for a $2 trillion infrastructure bill, without specifying
any of its contents or funding, and had gotten nowhere. Now we
were offering a $1.2 trillion bill that was filled out with investments
for every part of the country, and fully paid for. He attacked it as a
socialistic Green New Deal, a left-wing idea that conservative media
had made into a bugaboo. Of course, the true reason for his opposition was because Biden supported the bill, as Trump and his allies
publicly said at times. As *The Washington Post* reported, "For Trump
and many Republicans, their love of infrastructure has turned to
loathing now that it bears Biden's imprimatur."

Trump threw his weight against this broadly popular legislation,
calling individual members of Congress to rally them in opposition. Don Young, who had always loved to build things and had
passed a huge transportation bill almost twenty years earlier, supported what we were doing and was very clear with Trump when he

called to denigrate our bill. Don described the conversation to me this way: after Trump yelled at him about the bill, Don said, "Mr. President, you clearly haven't read this bill, because if you had, you would see that there's so much in it for Alaska. I know my state, and this bill is good for Alaska."

Trump responded, "Well, you realize that it was that bitch Murkowski that wrote this bill."

"That's exactly why I'm going to support it," Don shot back.

Don Young was never afraid of anyone. He had been recognized as the most bipartisan member of the House, he had the most seniority—indeed, he had served longer than any other Republican in history—and he always did what he believed was right for Alaska. Even his strongest critics admitted that. But other House members weren't as secure. Trump's anger and exaggerations were picked up by his allies to demonize any House member who would vote for our bill. Threats flooded in against these Republicans, targeting them and their families. After the violence we had seen, we were all taking threats seriously. Of course, political fear was probably a more influential motivator. Trump's political allies called for House members to be stripped of committee posts if they voted for the bill.

In early November, the bill passed, with six Democrats voting against it and thirteen Republicans voting for it. We called them "the Don Young thirteen." Without those brave Republicans, including some we had worked with all summer, the bill would not have become law.

We had done something big that was good for our country. The Bipartisan Infrastructure Law was extremely popular, and its popularity only grew as news of long-needed projects and upgrades filtered out across the states. Senators and representatives realized their constituents would be thrilled when they saw these investments in their districts. It did not go unnoticed that, at the ribbon cuttings, those who had fought the bill hardest were often among those on hand to take the credit.

————

Don Young was right, I did get a lot for Alaska in the infrastructure bill. While the national economy was growing, Alaska was facing a second year with almost no tourism. Alaska really was different. Nationally, the recovery was well underway. Everyone who wanted to be vaccinated had gotten a shot, and we had all learned how to handle the virus to some extent. The economy was bouncing back, with jobs returning to pre-Covid levels by June 2022 and continuing to rise from there. That didn't happen in Alaska. Our recovery lagged behind every other state's. Alaska's overall job numbers wouldn't reach 2019 levels until 2024, and many communities and industries still have not gotten back what the pandemic took.

In early 2021, the cruise industry, which brings 65 percent of visitors, remained locked out of Alaska. Due to Covid restrictions, Canada would not allow the ships into its ports, and U.S. law required vessels to Alaska to stop in Canada if they were foreign-built hulls, as virtually all cruise ships would be. Changing the law that mandated a Canadian stop would not be easy, and most said it would be impossible. Protective legislation for the maritime industry has many defenders in Congress, but we needed an Alaska fix. I felt we had no other option to help our struggling economy, which relied so heavily on tourism. The entire delegation worked on this. We explained the dire situation to members, I wrote a bill that would grant only a narrow exemption to address the crisis, we worked every angle with the administration, and by Memorial Day we had defied the skeptics and passed a law to allow cruises to operate. That summer, Alaska had 124,000 cruise visitors—less than 10 percent of normal, but better than none. Passenger numbers wouldn't touch 2019 levels until 2023.

While I was occupied by this work, the MAGA populists were focused on the next election, a year and a half away, in November 2022. Trump had made a point of going after me. Just two weeks after his acquittal at the second impeachment, Trump began his revenge campaign in a speech to CPAC (the Conservative Political Action Conference). He listed as targets each Republican who had voted to impeach him, as well as those who had denounced the insurrection—including Mitch McConnell—or who had otherwise resisted his attempt to overturn the election. Of course, I was on the list. A week later Trump released a statement to the media recommitting to my defeat. "She represents her state badly and her country even worse," he wrote. "I will be . . . in Alaska campaigning against a disloyal and very bad Senator."

A week later, the Alaska Republican Party's central committee voted to censure me and recruit an opponent to run against me in the primary. Two weeks after that, Kelly Tshibaka declared her candidacy against me with every appearance of having been cued up by the MAGA wing of the party and these preliminaries. Tshibaka had a Harvard law degree and seventeen years of experience in Washington working for inspectors general in federal agencies, but she hadn't lived in Alaska between her high school graduation, in 1995, and 2019, when she took a job with Alaska's Trump-aligned governor, Mike Dunleavy. Trump endorsed her, and members of his team went to Alaska to work on her campaign. Trump had defeated Biden by 10 percentage points in Alaska in 2020, and his people began shopping around a poll showing he was more popular than I was in my state. I doubted that, but I had no doubt that Tshibaka would be a serious candidate. She boldly began calling my oldest and best-known supporters to introduce herself and solicit their backing. In our first debate together, I looked over and saw pages of printed scripts she was using, her hand following along with the words even though she never looked away from the audience. She had memorized the whole thing.

But it wasn't immediately clear why she was running, other than because the Republican Party of Alaska desperately wanted me out. Being a senator from Alaska is more like being a local government leader than a member of a national team. Alaskans pay attention to what their delegation does. Voters feel they know you, and a lot of them do. The issues they care most about are those closest to home, like the sewers and ferries I had been finding money for, as well as oil development, access to public lands, gun rights, and public safety. Nationally, commentators viewed my race as a showdown between me and Trump, testing his power against the only senator running who had voted for his impeachment. But I didn't view it that way, and I don't think most Alaskans did, either. I didn't expect that just being the Trump candidate would be enough for Tshibaka.

First, however, I had to decide if I even wanted to run for reelection. I had good reasons to go home and an equal number of reasons to stay in Washington. We were really helping people. My boys and their now-wives were supportive—this was about their future. And Verne agreed that my work was too important for the state for me to stop now. Their support meant everything. While I would face the headwind of Donald Trump's determination to get rid of me, that was a minor factor. I didn't really care what he thought. Besides, Alaska's new voting system would limit his influence. In a closed primary, Trump's endorsement probably would have been enough to beat me, as Joe Miller had done in that previous, polarized time, but we didn't have a closed primary anymore.

A bright and enterprising lawyer had drafted a voter initiative that changed our system, and I think what Scott Kendall did in Alaska could help empower voters all over America. Scott had defended my write-in victory in court in 2010 and had supported other mainstream Republicans. Governor Bill Walker had hired him as chief of staff late in 2016, during a period of economic decline in Alaska, as the end of state oil wealth forced huge budget cuts and a search for new revenue. Scott's two years working with the legislature on these tough issues left him frustrated. He repeatedly ran into the same excuse for inaction: fear of a party primary. Over and over, Scott said, members agreed with Walker's fiscal plans but said they couldn't vote for them because the party would not allow it. Republicans and Democrats wanted each other to fail, and some on both sides wanted Walker to fail.

After Walker lost reelection in 2018, Scott immediately got to work trying to open the primary. He read academic research on the best election systems and tested those ideas with the smartest Alaskan pols on both sides of the aisle. He also traveled the country to learn what was working or not working elsewhere. The proposition he finally wrote had three parts: an open primary in which everyone would run on the same ballot, with the top four vote getters moving on to the general election, regardless of party; a ranked-choice-voting general election in which voters could designate their first, second, and third choices; and a campaign finance disclosure law.

The initiative was complex and took a long time to explain. When I was briefed, I had doubts. The open primary and campaign finance reform elements made absolute sense to me (Alaska had open primaries prior to 2002), but the ranked-choice provision seemed unnecessarily complicated and likely to discourage voters who might otherwise support the initiative. I said as much in my feedback, but I didn't have any further involvement. I think my team insulated me from the issue to avoid the appearance that the initiative was intended mainly for my benefit.

As it turned out, my political judgment about the initiative was dead wrong. The voters easily understood ranked-choice voting. It isn't hard to understand—we rank things all the time. A child might rank her choice of Popsicles, saying, "I'll have a red, and if there aren't any reds, a purple, and if there aren't any purples, an orange." Voters do the same without much prompting, and errors or spoiled ballots are rare.

The counting process is only slightly more complex. Officials count only first choices in round one. If a candidate gets over 50 percent of those first-choice votes, that candidate is the winner. If not, the lowest vote getter is dropped and the second choices on those ballots are distributed to the three who remain. This continues until a candidate gets 50 percent. The open primary is even simpler. Just vote for your favorite among all the candidates, regardless of party.

The top-four primary and ranked-choice voting work together. With four primary winners, the general election has more points of view. Then the ranked-choice phase narrows four down to one. To win second-choice votes, smart candidates campaign on themes beyond their party platforms and avoid bashing opponents whose supporters they may need to attract. In practice, this means campaigns are more civil and more moderates make it to the general election and then win.

To put it simply, Scott's system made the process more democratic by opening it up to more people and electing candidates whose positions more accurately represented broad public opinion.

Both political parties hated the initiative because it would take away from their own power. Sixty-three percent of Alaskans were neither Republicans nor Democrats, and within the parties a minuscule number of the most dogmatic members participated in committees and conventions to make decisions. Those small groups had been running things for a long time, with disappointing results. While it is hard to say why the initiative narrowly passed in the 2020 election, I suspect the opposition of the parties was one reason. Partisanship was a major factor in the political dysfunction in Alaska. If the parties were against it, that must mean it was good.

As I looked forward to the 2022 election, the open primary gave me new confidence. Consultants had always wanted to appeal only to Republicans for the primary, then switch to a broader message for the general election, but now the whole campaign could be directed to every Alaskan from day one. That was how I had been campaigning since the 2010 write-in, and now it would be good political strategy, too.

———

The U.S. Supreme Court's *Dobbs* draft decision striking down women's right to abortion leaked before Mother's Day in 2022. I was astonished by the decision and appalled by the leak. The decision, if it became final, would strip away a freedom that women had relied on for fifty years, one that protected their most intimate decisions about their bodies. Countless lives would be changed. I understood why young women and their advocates were coming unglued. I came somewhat unglued myself.

A lot of blame was directed at me and Susan Collins, the pro-choice Republican women who had voted to confirm Trump's nominees to the court—in my case, Justices Gorsuch and Barrett, and in Susan's case, Justice Kavanaugh. Some said the decision was our fault because we should have stopped these justices from getting on the court. Commentators charged us with being naïve or hypocritical for believing the nominees' statements about their respect for precedent and the public's reliance on settled law. Besides that criticism, which I disagreed with but thought was inbounds, my office also received a surge of threats.

Susan Collins was furious. During the confirmations, she had pressed hard on precedent and reliance with the three Trump-nominated judges. We all knew the nominees danced around questions in their confirmation hearings, but we had also sat with them in private to better understand their beliefs. Susan told me, "I've got my notes. I can tell you exactly what was said."

I was angry, too. I told reporters that the judges' comments had convinced me that a full reversal of *Roe* would not happen. Besides the human impact of the decision, the leak called into question the credibility of those three justices. I said, "If it goes in the direction that this leaked copy has indicated, I will just tell you that it rocks my confidence in the court."

When the actual *Dobbs* decision came out in June, with the concurrence of six justices, Susan quickly released her meeting notes. She said Gorsuch and Kavanaugh had misled her. Indeed, in their meeting, as well as his hearings, Kavanaugh had emphasized the strength of precedent over and over, in formal and colloquial language, in a way that could hardly be interpreted any other way than as saying *Roe* should not be overturned. "*Roe* is forty-five years old, it has been reaffirmed many times, lots of people care about it a great deal, and I've tried to demonstrate I understand real-world consequences," he had told Susan. "I am a don't-rock-the-boat kind of judge. I believe in stability."

More than being angry, I was discouraged. I had believed that the court would keep Americans' trust as an institution, as we needed it to do. Now the justices appeared to many people like politicians who would say whatever was necessary to get into office so they could then follow their own will. That was partly the fault of the Senate for degrading the confirmation process, but it also went deeper. It shouldn't be possible to use elections to change our basic rights. The Supreme Court is responsible for upholding the stability and predictability in the law that contributes to our success as a nation—these reassuring, conservative values—and for safeguarding the immutable freedoms that make us American. The meaning of those rights has changed gradually through the centuries as society has changed, but not because one party or the other won an election. We had respected the court because it stayed above politics, bound by law and reason.

The dissent to *Dobbs* by Justices Stephen Breyer, Sonia Sotomayor, and Elena Kagan made this point directly: "*Stare decisis* is the Latin phrase for a foundation stone of the rule of law: that things decided should stay decided unless there is a very good reason for change. It is a doctrine of judicial modesty and humility. Those qualities are not evident in today's opinion. The majority has no good reason for the upheaval in law and society it sets off. . . . Nothing, in short, has changed. . . . The Court reverses course today for one reason and one reason only: because the composition of this Court has changed."

To be clear, I do not accept responsibility for the *Dobbs* decision. That criticism implies that I should have countered those who politicized the Supreme Court by politicizing it for my own ends instead—voting against nominees regardless of their qualifications to prevent a particular decision based on political alignment. But I didn't believe the court should be political at all. I evaluated nominees' fitness to serve, including their dedication to stability and the rule of law, their judicial temperament, and their absence of bias or partiality. I had been consistent in that policy. Everything I did was meant to uphold the court's traditional, constitutional role. Adding more politics, for whatever cause, would erode that.

The majority in the *Dobbs* decision wrote that they didn't intend to affect anything but abortion, but their reasoning was directly applicable to other freedoms of bodily integrity, family relationships, and reproduction. The dissent listed several threatened court decisions and the protections they validated: for private sexual acts, for same-sex marriage, and for use of contraceptives. The dissenting justices made the point that nothing but hypocrisy could protect those decisions from being overturned by the *Dobbs* precedent. In his concurring opinion, Justice Thomas called out those decisions as well, suggesting that they needed review under the new precedent, and that many others should also be overruled.

I had expected the fear and anger of young women after *Dobbs*, but the alarm in the LGBTQ community caught me by surprise. People quickly realized that their families were at risk: the Supreme Court could strike down their right to marry, and states could then invalidate their marriages. Based on what the court had already done, that didn't seem like an unreasonable fear. The Respect for Marriage Act passed the House that summer, codifying the right to same-sex marriage and to interracial marriage, as well, which the Supreme Court had protected in 1967. In the Senate, we had a majority for the legislation, but we were short of the sixty votes to stop a filibuster, as there were legitimate concerns about religious freedom and the right of churches not to participate in same-sex weddings against their beliefs.

The lead sponsors, Susan Collins and Democrat Tammy Baldwin of Wisconsin, needed more time to get additional Republican votes. They were sure of only four and would need at least ten, in addition to all the Democrats. But the Democrats feared that a delay that put the bill beyond the election would kill it, as Republicans would lose their motivation to support the popular measure. Fortunately, a few key members built a bridge of trust. Majority Leader Schumer seemed to accept the sincerity of the bill's sponsors and allowed the delay.

———

Trump came to Alaska in July to hold a rally for Tshibaka. This would be her big boost from the biggest Republican figure to visit our state in years. My team was worried. Intensity and turnout make a huge difference in these races, as I had learned when I'd lost to Joe Miller in the 2010 primary. In Anchorage, a small media market far away from any big city, it is rare for any A-list performer or celebrity to make an appearance, and Trump was as big as they get. Even those who didn't support him would take notice. The excitement alone could give Tshibaka the attention she needed.

But Trump's support for Tshibaka didn't seem as enthusiastic as it could be. She had held a fundraiser at Mar-a-Lago, but Trump had made her cover the cost. He was stingy with his financial war chest, as well, while McConnell invested $7 million in an independent expenditure campaign for me. Later we learned that Trump didn't even pay for his big rally in Alaska. Campaign disclosures showed that Tshibaka rented the arena and covered Trump's expenses. After all her work, Tshibaka seemed to be running on her own much more than she had probably expected.

When the rally came, it overflowed a sports arena at the University of Alaska Anchorage, drew saturation media coverage, and spawned a carnival of activity in the parking lot, including a giveaway of *Star Wars* lightsabers by Tshibaka's campaign. But in his long speech, Trump didn't say much about Tshibaka—he listed just the most superficial facts—behaving as if she really were the "anyone with a pulse" candidate he had called for. He said more about me, calling me a RINO, "very bad," and "the worst." And he threw out criticism that most voters would know was not true—suggesting, for example, that I had opposed opening ANWR. But, as always, he talked mostly about himself, in that disjointed, stream-of-consciousness style we're all used to. It was hard to watch the whole speech, but from what I saw and heard from others, the rally didn't have much impact. And I gave no statement or reaction. I pretended it hadn't happened.

Tshibaka had a problem finding issues that would stick when she attacked me, because my positions were generally popular with Alaskans. Early that summer, after the horrible school shooting in Uvalde, Texas, a bipartisan group of senators led by conservative senator John Cornyn, of Texas, had crafted a bill addressing gun safety and mental health. We passed it with sixty-five votes in the Senate. Based on that, Tshibaka said that I had voted for gun control—but the provisions of the bill were commonsense and supported by a large majority of voters. Besides, Alaskans knew from watching me work for twenty years that I strongly supported the Second Amendment. Her attack just didn't work. Likewise, when she charged that I had helped President Biden block Alaska oil development, or that I somehow was not authentically Alaskan, she simply wasn't credible. Sometimes she showed that she didn't understand Alaska politics at all. When she criticized me for infrastructure and earmark spending that she called pork, I just hoped she would keep it up, as that support from Washington was exactly what Alaskans were asking for. Funding for water and sewers, ports and harbors, broadband and airports wasn't pork for most Alaskans—it was long-overdue investment in needed infrastructure.

The most potent election issue that year worked decisively against Tshibaka: abortion. Ironically, *Roe* had protected anti-abortion Republicans for many years, allowing candidates to take strong positions in their primaries without losing too many pro-choice voters in the general election, since *Roe* would keep abortion rights safe regardless of who was elected. After *Dobbs,* abortion became salient to many state and federal races, because elected officials now had the power to take away these rights. My moderate position was a major asset. It put me in line with most Alaskans—simple math the MAGA populists didn't seem to understand.

Tshibaka tried to shade her hard-line anti-abortion stand in some settings, but with one group she stated it very directly, embracing a ban on sending abortion medication in the mail. Asked if she would apply that ban to birth control, too, she said, "I would." An independent expenditure committee supporting me put that video clip on frequent rotation on TV and in social media. Tshibaka tried to amend her words, but the ads were devastating.

As the summer progressed, I felt the new voting system might work. Often enough I had been accused of flip-flopping or I had infuriated the Right or the Left for being ideologically inconsistent in their view. But most Alaskans are independent-minded like me, and a fair system of voting should allow them to pick a senator. They had felt disenfranchised and often had not participated in the closed primaries, as they did not feel they had a political home, but the open primary would give that moderate majority a new voice and new power. Regardless of Trump's wishes, I sensed that happening.

On August 16, in the top-four primary, I finished first, 6 percentage points ahead of Tshibaka. That didn't mean I would win in November. More people would be voting in the general election, and she would have twelve weeks to catch up, but the race was definitely leaning in my direction.

———

Don Young died on an Alaska Airlines jet seated next to his wife, Anne Walton, on March 18, 2022. They were on a flight from Los Angeles to Seattle, heading home.

Don was eighty-eight years old and had been a member of Congress for forty-nine years. To say his passing marked the end of an era would be an understatement. Don was a holdover from a world that no longer existed. He had begun as a brash young conservative on Congress's far right; half a century later, he was considered moderate, although his politics had not changed—the body had changed. He was considered moderate because he was willing to work with anyone and everyone to pass legislation. He still looked and behaved like a Yukon River boatman from pioneer days, with a big laugh and salty language appropriate for holding court in a rural roadhouse. The identity Don brought to Congress wasn't an image or an act—the unvarnished, off-color, and occasionally outrageous things he said were a pure reflection of who he was and where he came from, and we loved him for it. He could be irascible and raise his voice, even with friends, but he was kind, loyal, and had a warm heart. They really don't make people like Don anymore.

The head of Alaska Airlines in Alaska, Marilyn Romano, called to tell me about Don's death within an hour after it happened. Don had died in his sleep in a first-class seat. Marilyn made arrangements for Anne to be taken to a Seattle hotel, where I reached her on the phone. She had determined that she would not leave Seattle without Don's body, and she asked that he be honored by lying in state in the Capitol. As he had been the dean of the House, that would seem appropriate.

I called Nancy Pelosi to make the request on Anne's behalf. I expected a quick, businesslike call, but Pelosi wanted to talk about Don. She was truly sorrowful about losing her colleague of thirty-five years. For almost half an hour, she shared her memories with me. Other Republicans had demonized Pelosi, but Don worked with her, because together they could get things done. She said she always knew she could turn to Don to broker a deal, knew he would keep a secret, and he never broke his word. They were political and cultural opposites, but that was okay in the old school, because the House had been a place for differences to mingle and get resolved. We also laughed about the crazy stories of this cantankerous conservative, such as the time he waved around an oosik (the penile bone of a walrus) at a committee hearing; or when he pulled a knife on Speaker John Boehner, who then became his close friend; or, at another hearing, when he thrust his arm into a bear trap.

Pelosi ordered that Don would lie in repose in Statuary Hall (having him lie in state in the rotunda was not within her authority), and we had beautiful services in Anchorage and Washington. But well before that could happen, the political scramble began among Alaskans who wanted to take his place. Perhaps that's why Don's death didn't produce the same period of mourning that Alaskans observed for Ted Stevens. The battle for his seat started, as one consultant said, thirty seconds after the news hit that Don had died.

The race would be the first election run under the new rules, creating a chaotic jump ball. We would have an open primary to pick four candidates for the special election to fill the months remaining in Don's current term, then a ranked-choice special election among those four candidates and, on the same day, another primary for the next full term. More than fifty candidates declared for the special election open primary. The list included many respected mainstream leaders and many more complete unknowns. Name recognition would be key, a factor that leaned in favor of a socialist member of the city council of the town of North Pole, who had legally changed his name to Santa Claus.

Sarah Palin was among those stampeding into this cattle call primary. Trump quickly endorsed her (and would include her in his big Anchorage rally with Tshibaka). Commentators Outside picked her as the likely winner. I wasn't so sure. The endorsement wouldn't help her much, because the people who loved Trump already loved her. Her problem—their problem—was that beyond that group of true believers, many Alaskans had strong negative opinions about Palin.

Similar situations were playing out across the country. Trump had weighed in heavily to influence the midterm elections. Normally, halfway through a Democratic president's first term, the Republican Party would gain many seats, and we had been favored to take over the House and Senate. But like the Tea Party candidates before them, the MAGA candidates tended to be extreme or just plain odd. McConnell called this the "candidate quality" problem.

Nick Begich III had already been running against Don when he died. Nick III is the nephew of Mark Begich and the grandson of Nick Begich Sr., who held the seat after beating my father in 1970 but disappeared on a campaign flight in 1972. Don first won the next year. Unlike his uncle Mark Begich and the other Democratic members of that political family, Nick III became a conservative Republican. He had co-chaired Don's 2020 reelection campaign, and Don gave him a House pass and run of his office. But then he declared as a candidate to run against Don, using what he had learned in the office against him. He criticized Don's work ethic and vigor, attacked him for requiring masks during Covid, and even questioned his support for gun rights, which was absurd. As a staffer told a reporter, all you had to do was look at the walls of Don's office to see he had shot at least one of everything that walks on four legs. Don, who rarely spoke negatively of anyone, felt deeply hurt, and he spread word of this betrayal through his network of friends and supporters. When Don died, Nick had an early advantage in fundraising and campaigning, but he had burned too many bridges to consolidate support.

I got a text message from Mary Peltola on the day of Don Young's service in Washington, asking for my advice. She was considering jumping into the race, which she described as "the most crowded clown car ever." I had known Mary when we were both in the legislature, and we were friends—she was a warm, positive, smart, and authentic Yup'ik woman. She had seven children. When we served in Juneau together, my boys had been young and Mary was a new mother trying to take care of a baby on her own away from home, and we bonded as working moms. Mary made friends with everyone, regardless of party or background, and had a good relationship with Palin, too. We stayed in touch over the years, swapping pictures of our kids and talking about fishery issues, which were her expertise, and she brought me jars of smoked salmon or occasionally hand-sewn Yup'ik summer parkas called kuspuks.

I could not endorse a candidate in that race. I had too many friends running. Mary was a Democrat, and I couldn't support the Republican front-runners, Begich or Palin—Begich because of my loyalty to Don Young, and Palin because she had already shown her lack of commitment to Alaska when she'd quit as governor. As the campaign progressed, they became harsh rivals, viciously tearing each other down. Mary, meanwhile, ran positively, with her slogan "Family, Fish, Freedom," her big smile, and the reservoir of goodwill she had earned around the state. In the top-four primary, Palin and Begich came in first and second, with Democrat Al Gross third and Mary fourth, with just 10 percent of the vote (Santa Claus got 5 percent). Gross dropped out and supported Mary, but too late for anyone to take his place, so she would be the only Democrat in the August special election, with Begich and Palin.

Surprisingly, she won that race. Mary had remained on warm, friendly terms with both of her opponents and had kept sending out her authentic smile while they trashed each other. In the first-round voting, she received 40 percent, followed by Palin at 31 percent and Begich at 28 percent. The conservative voters might normally have combined after that, but too many people disliked and distrusted Palin, and Begich's attacks had only made those feelings stronger. When the second-choice votes on his ballots were counted, Palin got only about half of them. A fifth of those voters didn't declare a second choice at all, and the balance picked Mary, enough to put her over the top.

Now she unexpectedly had two weeks to become a congressman. Although she was a Democrat and had flipped a seat my party had held for forty-nine years, I thought of her mostly as a friend and mom suddenly in the middle of the complex, high-pressure world of the House with no time to prepare. I remembered what that felt like. When Congress convened in September, I offered her my son's room to stay in and tried to make sure she got fed. She retained much of Don's staff, but I also sent some of my staff over to help her in the first few weeks. I advised her when I could, telling her she didn't have to answer every reporter's question—although I could have taken that advice myself at times.

In an email from that time, Mary said, "Hey, I really appreciate your advice. I don't know if you remember, but our first year [in the legislature], you told me I didn't have to nurse Baby Conrad until he was one or two, which is what I'd been told. And I could stop when he was four or five months. This advice saved my life. I was so overwhelmed with being new in the State House and learning how to manage being a mom, telling me that was the best thing anyone's ever told me."

By now, Baby Conrad was in his mid-twenties.

I responded, "And Conrad turned out just fine, right, Mom? The hardest thing you'll find is to give yourself a little grace to not be perfect. Apologize to your family ahead of time for not being the best mom, the best wife, and ask their permission to be the best candidate to serve a state we all love. Heart is what it takes, and you have it."

Twenty years earlier, when I came to the Senate, I had needed someone to tell me that. I thought of my lonely tears during that first year. I knew Mary would struggle, too, and I wanted to do anything I could to support her. Thanks to the ranked-choice voting system, Alaska had chosen an authentic, good-government moderate, and she would need help in the harsh climate of Washington.

Pride swept over much of Alaska when Mary was sworn in as the first Alaska Native to serve in Congress and the first woman to represent the state in the House. The media carried pictures of her raising her right hand with Pelosi to take the ceremonial oath, wearing Yup'ik mukluk boots, her husband, Buzzy, in an embroidered kuspuk, and her seven children and grandchildren gathered around, a beautiful Alaskan family. On the House floor she took the official oath and gave her first speech, talking about her ancestors and subsistence traditions, Alaska fish, bipartisanship, and the legacy and love of Don Young, whom she saluted in the Yup'ik language. The

House gave her a standing ovation, and we shared a warm hug. The national media fell in love with her, too. It hadn't seemed possible, but voters had replaced Don Young with that very rare person who was just as Alaskan as he was and had just as big a heart.

————

My brother Mike sat in on a campaign meeting as we discussed strategy to win the general election under the new ranked-choice system. How important would second-choice ballots be? My team was accustomed to the heat we got from the Left to go further left and from the Right to go further right—it did often feel like we made almost everyone mad at different times but pleased hardly anyone most of the time. If voters were going to stick to their camps, a strategy of campaigning for second-choice votes would make sense. The group talked about how to do that. I could campaign as a safe choice, a good-enough choice. I could be sold as a nice person.

That seemed like a risky strategy to me. The second-choice votes might not even be counted. The discussion was long, but finally Mike weighed in, saying, "We don't settle for second place. We need a strategy that says we are going for number one." Finally, the table agreed. We would persuade voters that they should choose me first.

The ranked-choice system did play into our thinking, however, because there would be a Democrat on the ballot whose voters were unlikely to pick Tshibaka as their second choice.

The Senate Democrats did not recruit a challenger to run against me, and many let me know they were rooting for me. Pat Chesbro got into the race late, inspired by the *Dobbs* decision, and would likely sop up many Democratic votes. She was an intelligent, gracious woman who had never held office and had no hope of winning. I would often run into voters who said they liked me but they had to vote for the Democrat—Pat—because they were disgusted with the Republicans. I wouldn't argue with them. I just asked for them to make me their second choice.

Our union supporters took the same approach. The unions had been with me since the 2010 write-in, and we had benefited from their well-run system of getting their people and allies out to the polls. Those operations normally use phone banks to identify likely supporters and then to repeatedly remind them to vote. This time around, the callers would remind Chesbro voters to turn out, too, because they would most likely rank me second.

Our strategists firmly decided against an endorsement of Mary Peltola. To openly support a Democrat in a year when the Republican Party had a chance to win the House would be a bridge too far. Mary's supporters already knew me—rural Alaska was my strongest base—but for Republicans and for Alaska's many conservative independents, an endorsement of Mary would only raise questions about why I would potentially enable a Democratic agenda that could hurt Alaska's resource economy. Indeed, Mary's biggest challenge, like that of statewide Democrats before her, was to distance herself from her party's unpopular stands and declare her support for the Second Amendment and for oil, gas, and mineral development. National observers often didn't get this, creating some double takes, as when Judy Woodruff asked Mary, on *PBS NewsHour*, if she would support an assault weapons ban. Mary said, "I do want to make sure that Alaskans understand that I am a staunch advocate for our Second Amendment rights. I myself have 176 long guns in my home. We are avid hunters. We are very, very tied to our subsistence resources and having access to wild game."

In coastal communities, yard signs had already appeared that paired Mary's name and mine as pro-fish, paid for by a political action committee in Bristol Bay. There was no need for me to make the connection myself, and I agreed with my advisers to keep my mouth shut on that subject.

As the election approached, I felt serenely confident. That annoyed our team. Polling in the ranked-choice election was difficult and untested, as pollsters subjected respondents to many more questions to tease out the various scenarios. I've learned over the years not to look at polls when I am campaigning. It is a distraction. I prefer to go into a room knowing that everyone is a potential supporter rather than having been told 30 percent don't like me or that I need to work on a specific demographic subset—White men over fifty, or something like that. My strongest asset as a campaigner is that I connect with people one-on-one. I like people. I can remember their names and the things they tell me about their families. I want to think of those I meet as potential friends, not data points. And I can judge how a campaign is going myself, based on my gut and the temperature I pick up in the community. In 2022, the vibes were positive. I knew we would win.

The trend also looked good for Mary Peltola, now running for the full term in the general election. Mary had come to represent the positive, optimistic politics that most of us hunger for. For Alaska Natives, she was a powerful symbol, and for those of us committed to equality, her election was an emotional milestone.

These feelings came out fully in late October when we appeared at the Alaska Federation of Natives convention in Anchorage. The audience stood and roared with love for Mary. My welcome the next day was extremely warm as well. I received AFN's endorsement and a standing ovation, and my comments were frequently interrupted by applause. This was the first in-person AFN meeting since Covid, and I talked about all the good things that were happening. I described the Bipartisan Infrastructure Law and how it had started in Alaska villages. "It's my travels around the state and to your communities that not only inform me but inspire me," I told the convention. "I hear your asks for housing, for water, for sewer, for broadband, for protection from climate change and the storms. And together, we did this. I partnered with you. That is now bringing unprecedented funding to your communities. It starts with infrastructure."

I left on a high, filled with optimism and good feelings about the togetherness here. As I often do at the Dena'ina Center in Anchorage, I took a shortcut through the kitchens and popped out into a quiet corridor, where I met two reporters, Zachariah Hughes of the *Anchorage Daily News* and Leigh Ann Caldwell of *The Washington Post*, who had been shadowing me. Zach noted all the positive things I'd been saying about Mary—coincidentally, I was even wearing a kuspuk she had given me the year before. He looked me in the eye and asked me directly if I would be ranking Mary first on my ballot. I didn't blurt out my answer. Leigh Ann timed my pause as a full eighteen seconds. But I knew that Zach knew the true answer, and so did everyone in that convention hall, and I felt too good about the day to go with anything other than the truth—so I said, "Yeah, I am." And then, to myself, but apparently loud enough for them to hear, I added, "I'm going to get in so much trouble."

Leigh Ann asked how I could endorse a Democrat. I teased, "You can tell she's a D.C. reporter." But then I answered, "Because in Alaska, I think it's still different."

The reporters found Mary to ask her about the apparent endorsement, and she said, "I'm voting for her, so we're even-steven."

Someone even got a picture of us together in our kuspuks, made by the same Yup'ik seamstress in Bethel.

Election night was strange. My campaign had rented an event space in downtown Anchorage called Williwaw Social. After the polls closed I went upstairs, where the numbers guys were monitoring the returns, bypassing the big bar downstairs where the party was going on. The upstairs room was silent as the team studied their screens. No one looked up. The first round of returns, showing first-choice votes, had come in favoring Tshibaka. And then the second round came in the same way. It felt way too much like the 2010 primary, and Steve Wackowski advised me to stay there, and not to go downstairs to the party yet. But I was still confident we would win, even if we had to do it with the second-choice votes, and I insisted on going to be with my supporters.

The mood was indeed growing gloomy down there, but I wasn't going to be part of that. I felt upbeat and crazily optimistic, and entered the room humming my favorite song from *The Sound of*

Music, "I Have Confidence." Shortly, my sister Carol, sister-in-law Karen, and a collection of nieces joined me in belting it out:

> *I have confidence that spring will come again*
> *Besides, which you see*
> *I have confidence in me*

That made the paper and, with it, the observation that we were right to be confident. The early numbers had come from Tshibaka's strong areas, and we steadily rose to about a tie by morning. But neither side could declare victory until the lengthy ranked-choice counting process was complete.

Verne and I went to Hawaii for our annual Thanksgiving visit with Dorothy. On the afternoon when they would announce the results, we sat on the patio in front of an iPad. Verne poured champagne. We won—by a lot—and toasted with our champagne. That was the whole celebration.

It turned out we had never needed the second-choice votes. We were ahead on the first-choice votes, and the ranked-choice tabulations just helped us win by a lot more. Mary won, too, in a rerun of the special election, but with a more decisive victory than before. She finished the first round far ahead of Palin, just shy of 50 percent—a remarkable accomplishment for any candidate in a four-way race, and unheard-of for a Democrat in red Alaska.

Trump had vowed to beat me, and he had failed. In the end, he hadn't even mattered much. Tshibaka's poll numbers had peaked after the rally in July, but that excitement was a brief sugar rush, soon gone. She ran a good campaign, with enough money to get her message across and strong support from the Right. But my coalition was larger. Contrary to the conventional wisdom, we proved that a moderate could blaze a path down the middle, never completely pleasing either side and disappointing everyone at least once, so long as people trusted her to be sincere and thoughtful, hardworking, to play by the rules, and to focus on the good of the state and the country. That's why I won. I didn't have a magic formula for bucking partisanship or a secret strategy to mobilize the middle. I didn't advance a twelve-point plan to change the system. Everything I had needed was within the system our forebears gave us. All I did was use it. Most Alaskans liked having a senator who respected democratic institutions and thought for herself. With the majority participating in the open primary, I was able to win.

The national media talked endlessly about Trump and how he had wanted to defeat me. In their narrative, I was a plucky hero fighting against the big bully. But I didn't hear much about that on the campaign trail, and I certainly didn't talk about Trump. I didn't fight the bully, I simply ignored him. I focused on Alaska. I was true to my campaign theme: Alaska first. Always.

––––––––

Trump's clumsy intervention in the midterms, with his election denial candidates, cost us a Republican Senate and limited our party to a very slim, unmanageable majority in the House. Passing bills would be difficult, and the 118th Congress would be far less productive.

But back in the lame-duck session of the 117th Congress, we stayed on a roll. We still had some important work to do. Susan Collins and Tammy Baldwin, working with Kyrsten Sinema, Rob Portman, and Republican Thom Tillis of North Carolina, reached an agreement on the bill to protect same-sex marriage, and they managed to gain support from a total of twelve Republicans. They had added protections for religious liberty and had clarified that we weren't legalizing polygamy. We had rewarded Schumer's trust in letting us wait till after the election. It was a true accomplishment: a bipartisan compromise that advanced an important right, overcame a filibuster, and became law.

We also passed the Electoral Count Reform Act. It would stop a coup like the one Trump had encouraged on January 6, by clarifying the process for certifying the presidential election and making

it much more difficult to challenge. Collins and Joe Manchin negotiated the bill, and it passed just before Christmas, near the last moment before the next election cycle would begin.

Verne stoically began another six years of traveling back and
forth between Alaska and D.C. Nic moved to Nashville to practice
law and married Morgan, while Matt and his wife, Brooke, remain
in Anchorage, where he runs the pasta company. The GGs kept ex-
changing text messages, with mutual support and jokes.

In the Senate, we were a long way from getting over the toxic
partisanship and division that had infected our country and cost
us the people's faith in their democracy and courts. But I knew
what I needed to do, and I could see that it was working, at least
in my corner of the world. Alaskans had solidly elected and reelected a moderate, bipartisan senator who wanted to be part of the
solution—me. And I had no intention of changing a thing about
how I represented them.

EPILOGUE

O N A WEEKEND IN November 2024, after the election, I was due to travel to a ceremony and celebration in Newtok, the village I described at the beginning of this book that was at risk from climate change. Almost all the residents had finally made the move to the community's new home at Mertarvik, nine miles away on higher, safer ground, with new houses, a village store in a temporary location, and classes held in a community building until the new permanent school could be completed. This work had taken more than twenty years. The land exchange that provided the Mertarvik site had been among my earliest pieces of legislation in 2003, and I had delivered significant funding from the 2021 Bipartisan Infrastructure Law. The move was happening just in time, as Newtok collapsed into the thawing permafrost and the Ninglick River. Despite the long trip to attend the afternoon event, I was looking forward to being with these friends, and out of Washington, for their big day. But weather in western Alaska can be unpredictable in the fall, and the organizers had to cancel, as it would likely be impossible to travel.

That's okay. The work is not done. We still need to finish many pieces that go into building a community. And Newtok's forced relocation is just the beginning of the disruption we are seeing in Alaska, with dozens of communities being threatened by slow-moving disasters. That's one reason, among many, why I cannot get distracted by elections or the current drama in Washington. Addressing Alaskans' challenges is more important to me than who wins elections or which party holds power, and certainly more important than what anyone thinks of me. I have to continue working with my colleagues, and to work with President Trump, as I work with whoever is president, because these people are relying on me.

My sense of responsibility drives my work and explains my purpose in writing this book. Political memoirs often seem to focus on advancing political careers or polishing legacies. I am interested in showing our obligation for service, and its rewards. I've tried to be honest about my doubts and failures, and the always unfinished kind of work I do in places such as Newtok. But I am also proud, for example, of collaborating with our group of ten senators to pass a generational infrastructure bill that helped so many people across the country, including in Newtok. I feel tremendously honored to use my office to fulfill these needs. Many more of us could share in this success, if we can stop the destructive politics. If I could offer a single message to my colleagues and our entire political system, this would be it: Do the work. Don't worry so much about keeping your job.

Doing the work also turns out to be a successful political strategy. I did my best to care for Alaskans' needs—so when the Tea Party tried to take me out in 2010, and Trump tried again in 2022, Alaskans stuck by me. This is part of the genius of our American system of democracy. It can't just be about scoring political points and playing for the cameras. We can earnestly work through the process, seek common ground with our adversaries, and pass good laws. As it turns out, that wins elections, too. The difference between the two approaches is that doing the work also helps people, strengthens our institutions, and builds a better, more stable society and nation. Rather than a legacy of individual recognition, I would prefer to leave that as my contribution: a better Alaska and a democracy that functions properly for the next public servant who takes on this work.

I have been blessed by the opportunity to serve. I've seen more of Alaska—the most beautiful place on earth—than anyone I know, and I've met more amazingly capable, warm, and mutually supportive Alaskans than I could have encountered any other way. Legislating can be hard, slow, and frustrating at times, but the successes more than make up for the effort. We passed important laws and appropriations that helped good people have better lives. I don't have to wonder why I do this work or why I make the sacrifices it costs. The evidence is all over Alaska in friendly faces and genuine hugs.

In 2003, on my very first flight home from Washington as a senator, I met Will and Jane Madison, both retired teachers, who had worked for years to get a three-mile stretch of road paved in Soldotna. Their local government hadn't helped, so they had flown to Washington on their own dime to meet Ted Stevens, who'd also shown little interest. The project was too small. On their flight home, they happened to be seated a row ahead of me, and Jane turned around in her seat to introduce herself and explained the issue. I admired their community spirit and committed to try to help. We were successful a few years later. Will and Jane, who are now dear friends, exemplify the public advocacy that prompted me to public service in the first place.

Democracy will be renewed from the ground up. Leadership matters, but the public is in charge. With my elections, we proved that a diverse center coalition can win, but I didn't make it happen on my own. I've always been conscious that the seat did not belong to my party, my family, or to me personally—it belonged to these voters, who believed in integrity and good government. They didn't demand that I do their bidding, but they would be disappointed if I didn't adhere to my own honest reasoning about what was best for Alaska and the nation.

How can my relationship with voters be replicated for other senators? I don't have a multi-part plan to fix democracy. Overcoming division is up to each of us. It starts quite simply, with civility and mutual respect. But there are changes to the system that would make it easier, too. Party insiders on both sides have built barriers to promote their own power and block centrists. Closed primaries are their most damaging tool, forcing candidates to cater to the extremes. The fear of primaries enforces party-line adherence and makes compromise harder.

The willingness to work with those with whom we disagree is essential to democracy. As much as we would like easy answers—for example, for the other side to simply give up—there is no path out of division other than respecting the legitimacy of the opposing group and trying to work with them. Granted, this is hard, and it doesn't always go as planned. Sometimes those on our own side are the least receptive. I've heard some in my own party say they would prefer to have, as a senator, a Democrat they could always oppose rather than a Republican they could count on 90 percent of the time. Purity tests affect both parties, with those on each end of the political spectrum viewing their opposites as enemies to be defeated at almost any price. But most Americans are centrists whose main political goals are to live happy, productive lives with their families and neighbors, and who get greater satisfaction from cooperation than from conflict. More of them dislike than admire the political parties. Working with that majority of people is rewarding and constructive, bringing successes that can build into a virtuous cycle: as people see what we can accomplish through compromise, we gradually move more allies away from the extremes and back to the center.

In 2024, Alaskans narrowly voted to retain our promising new voting system, with the top-four open primaries and ranked-choice general elections. Despite the divide in the Alaska electorate, I feel this is the most direct way to give power back to the majority and encourage new ideas and minority points of view. In 2022, the odds had been against me and I likely would not have won a closed Republican primary, so the new law helped me. And while I would have won in the general election that year without ranked-choice voting, the second- and third-choice ballots gave me a majority coalition. Alaska's system works well in our low-population state, where more than 60 percent of voters choose not to align themselves with either of the two major parties, but variations of our system could probably be similarly helpful in other states. The most important aspect is to empower all voters to participate at each step of the process. Unfortunately, seven other states turned down these reforms in 2024, when they voted against open primaries, ranked-choice voting, or both. Major change is hard and takes time. The two parties, deeply ingrained in every state, are threatened by these changes and have the machines to fight back. But we have few other viable options to the two-party system. Third parties have never had much impact, and even independents who are elected to Congress must choose to caucus with one party or the other to meaningfully participate. Given this two-party structure, open primaries are the best way to ensure that the majority can choose its leaders.

My other prescription to fix American politics is simpler: Get involved. School boards, town councils, PTAs, and even homeowner associations are the seedbeds of American democracy. They train citizens in participation and leadership. These community-level positions remain the realm of true service, where those elected are unlikely to be motivated by self-interest or the drive for power or prestige, since they get few of those benefits but must put in a lot of work. For the same reason, these bodies are often under the radar of the political parties. Yet from among these community volunteers come mayors, legislators, governors, and members of Congress, rising to those positions with experience solving problems among their neighbors. I caught the bug for public service on the PTA at Government Hill Elementary School, and the skills I learned there were kernels for what I do now in my third decade in the Senate. Periodically, culture warriors try to take over school boards or other local bodies, but I don't think that will succeed in the long term. Community leadership is hard, and the rewards come from the satisfaction of working together. That positive energy isn't available to those using the system for other purposes.

All these ideas come down to the commitment of ordinary Americans to our system of self-government, our duties to participate and serve, our respect for the institutions of democracy, and our willingness to follow the rule of law. The work begins with each of us. We cannot accept attacks on democracy or our institutions, but within the framework of our system we must learn to accept one another. The way back from the brink really is that simple.

Being a positive centrist isn't easy. Those seeking power by degrading the system often attack compromise as unethical and call moderates indecisive or disloyal to party. In my own life, harsh voices declared I was not a good enough version of who I am—a Catholic unworthy of Communion, a Republican in name only, and, according to Kelly Tshibaka, not even a real Alaskan. I wish I could say the criticism never affected me. I don't read online comments or follow social media because I won't let myself be dragged down by the negativity, but attacks can sometimes undermine my confidence. Perhaps I should say I've always been strong and none of this mattered, but that wouldn't be true.

Recently, on a bright spring Sunday in Anchorage, I attended a Mass with my family where my cousin Anne would be playing the flute. I found them in a pew near the front, where my cousin Mary Gore always insists on sitting; alongside her were my brother Mike and his wife, Karen, and my cousin Bryan. Mike and I sang the processional hymn loudly and off-key and congratulated each other for our joyful sounds.

As the service progressed, that familiar feeling of being judged by others surfaced again. Were those around me questioning whether I was a good enough Catholic? I kept my eyes forward and recited the liturgy, as I knew it by heart. When it got to the reflective time of the service and we sat down, I found myself asking what I was doing here. Why would I go to a place where I had to wonder if people thought I was good enough?

In that quiet moment—as, admittedly, I ignored the homily—I began to have a conversation in my head. And the answer came: "You're here because this is what your family has always done on Sunday morning, from the first time you can remember." I am Catholic because my parents baptized me in the church, and because I came to know Sunday mornings as a special time when family came together in a special space. I grew up believing and trusting in God, in the power of love and forgiveness, and in the dignity of life and the respect due to all people. No one could withhold those beliefs from me—they could not take my faith. My faith is part of who I am. It was instilled in me, not through a catechism but through a life. My parents never had to tell me, "Love thy neighbor," because that was how they lived: in the regard they held for each other as a husband and wife, and in their care for their children and neighbors. And I realized, in that moment, in Our Lady of Guadalupe, that this love and faith was inherent in me, too. Unless I gave it up myself, nobody could take that from me.

The conversation in my head shifted to my political values. Who was to say if I was a "good Republican"? I am not a Republican just to be a member of a party; I call myself a Republican because of the values I hold, such as personal responsibility, small government, a strong national defense, and the individual's right to make her own choices. These are my values because of who I am and how I was raised. I learned personal responsibility in a family in which I was free to make my own choices and my own mistakes and to live with the consequences. I learned the value of hard work by doing it, both as a responsibility to myself and to contribute to my family and others in the community. The Republican Party could censure me and call me names, but they could not take from me the values deep in my core as a person. I am a strong person in my faith, and I hold my values strongly. My parents gave me that, because they were rock-solid. And the people seated around me in that pew were a part of that gift, too. The voice in my head said, "This is who I am, and nobody can take this away from me."

I leaned over and whispered to Mike, "I just had an epiphany."

He didn't hear me at first. And then he thought I was saying I'd had an epiphany about whatever the priest was relating in his homily, which added to his confusion. I said, "No, it's an epiphany about me."

After Mass, we stood together in the pew and I shared what I had just processed in my head, bubbling with my own self-revelation.

I said, "I know why it is that I do the things that I do. Why I'm not afraid to stand out there. It's not courage—it is the strength of knowing who you are. Because no one can take from me who I am and what I believe, unless I give it up."

Labels may be a convenient way to describe people, but it's not the label that should define us. Our values define us. I'm proud to be a person of faith and principle, and connected to Alaska and our people, true to my Tlingit name, "Lady of the Land." I bear allegiance to the Constitution. I serve Alaskans as best I can with conscience as my guide. I'm not giving any of that up.

ACKNOWLEDGMENTS

I NEVER SET OUT TO write a book, but like many things in life, events happened, and it just seemed inevitable. The idea for this book goes back fifteen years, to the conclusion of my successful write-in campaign for reelection in 2010. Many of us sensed we had been through something significant and special and believed we should somehow capture the moment, including my sister Carol Sturgulewski, the family writer and historian, as well as others who made notes and saved material. But serving in the Senate doesn't leave much time to write, and we didn't make much progress.

Then, in 2019, I reconnected with a former Government Hill neighbor, Charles Wohlforth, when he visited my office in D.C. We shared stories about kids and politics, and he reinforced that I should write a book someday. I replied that I didn't have the time and didn't know how. His response was, "Well, that's what I do." This book reflects that partnership. It took us a while as events kept getting in the way: an impeachment, a pandemic, an insurrection, another impeachment, a very active legislative period, and another reelection campaign in 2022. Finally, after my return to the Senate in 2023, the story seemed to have reached if not an end, at least a reasonable pause that allowed for some reflection and a plausible stopping point. The most intense period of writing began that summer and was completed about a year later.

As this story suggests, my time is rarely my own, and representing Alaska overfills my days. Any success I achieve depends on a team that backs me up in my life, my work, and with this new endeavor, my book project. We're in it together, including my wonderful and loving family, my capable and insightful staff, and the people who helped me author this book.

First, I must thank my husband, Verne Martell, who has patiently supported me and my service through so many years and so many challenges and times of separation. As I make clear in the book, he made our family life and my service possible. Similarly, my boys, Nic and Matt, have always been my source of joy and inspiration. Nic has perhaps been my most insistent promoter of sharing my story, along with my vivacious mother-in-law, Dorothy McCoy, a woman who never fails to inspire and motivate me. Carol put considerable effort into the book over the years, and my cousins Anne Gore and Jenny Dwyer also contributed with interviews, materials, and advice. As the book describes, the GGs are the "center of my onion" when it comes to encouragement and unconditional love: Carol, Eileen, Mary, Karen, Mary G, Jenny, Anne, and the original GGs, Nancy and DD. Thank you to my brothers, Mike and Brian, who always have my back; to my strong daughters-in-law, Brooke and Morgan; and to my many nieces and nephews who fill my life with loud, rambunctious family love. And, of course, I owe my deepest debt to my parents, Frank and Nancy, who gave me my values and my sense of who I am. I have an extraordinary family because of them.

Many, many staff members, campaign workers, and volunteers have made my work possible over my decades in public service, and I wish I could mention them all. Those who particularly helped with the book include Mike "Fish" Pawlowski, Steve "Wacko" Wackowski, Karina Borger, Garrett Boyle, Kevin Sweeney, and Kristen Daimler-Nothdurft. Kristen deserves a special shoutout as, without her, I would not have the focus and organization to take on the day-to-day responsibilities of my job, as she brings order to our often chaotic surroundings. I'm also grateful for help on the book from friends I have worked with over the years, including John Tracy, Scott Kendall, and Andrew Halcro. I apologize if I've omitted anyone, but I'm blessed to have so many people who lift me up.

After Charles and I started working together in 2019, the process of gathering stories happened in real time. We did interviews right amid the events the book would cover, sometimes in Washington, at his home in New Jersey or mine in Alaska, on the phone or via Zoom, and sometimes as I dictated voice memos—we did nearly fifty of these sessions. Charles conducted many other interviews and collected extensive research separately to add dimension and color and to verify our perceptions. Finally, he wrote the first drafts that we worked on together over many hours of editing and shaping the manuscript. This was a satisfying and productive five-year partnership, and I thank Charles and his wife, Sarah Rowland, for their friendship (and good dinners). I also thank my effective literary agent, Gail Ross, for sticking with me as we developed the project, and my skilled and thoughtful editors at Forum, Matt Burdette and Derek Reed.

Finally, I must thank my constituents, the people of Alaska, for entrusting me with the responsibility of representing them—including the many who probably don't agree with me a lot of the time but who trust me to make careful decisions on behalf of our state. I hope this book makes clear how dearly I love Alaska and her people. You are the reason I serve, and your confidence in me is the greatest honor of my life.

ABOUT THE AUTHOR

LISA MURKOWSKI is a third-generation Alaskan proudly serving as the state's senior senator. Since joining the Senate in 2002, she has earned a reputation for her ability to work collaboratively and across the aisle to reach commonsense solutions. She lives in Anchorage, where she and her husband, Verne, raised two incredible sons.

ABOUT THE TYPE

This book was set in Minion, a 1990 Adobe Originals typeface by Robert Slimbach. Minion is inspired by classical, old-style typefaces of the late Renaissance, a period of elegant and beautiful type designs. Created primarily for text setting, Minion combines the aesthetic and functional qualities that make text type highly readable with the versatility of digital technology.